The Source for Learning & Memory Strategies

Regina G. Richards

LinguiSystems®

Skill Area:	Learning & Memory
Age Level:	6 through 18
Grades:	1 through 12

LinguiSystems, Inc.
3100 4th Avenue
East Moline, IL 61244-9700

800-776-4332

Fax: 800-577-4555
E-mail: service@linguisystems.com
Web: linguisystems.com

Printed in the U.S.A.

ISBN 0-7606-0480-0

Regina G. Richards, M.A., is a Director and President of Richards Educational Therapy Center, Inc. and RET Center Press. She founded and was Director of Big Springs School for 27 years. Her professional emphasis has been in developing and providing multidisciplinary programs for students with language-learning disabilities, especially dyslexia and dysgraphia. Regina began her career in bilingual education, working on curriculum development and test design. A practicing educational therapist in Riverside, California since 1975, Regina has authored a variety of journal articles and books on reading, dyslexia, dysgraphia, learning/memory and visual development. She is a member of her local branch of the International Dyslexia Association, the Inland Empire Branch, where she served as president for seven years. She presents workshops and classes at the University of California Extension programs at both the Riverside and San Diego campuses. She is an accomplished speaker and presents at numerous conferences and workshops nationally.

Regina is also the author of *The Source for Dyslexia and Dysgraphia*.

Dedication

To Dovid M. Richards,
Forever in my heart.

Table of Contents

Foreword

by Mel Levine, M.D.

Professor of Pediatrics
University of North Carolina Medical School
Director, The Center for Development and Learning
Founder and Co-chairman of the Board, All Kinds of Minds

Memories Are Made of This

"Every time I write, I lose my memory."

"I always understand stuff when she, like, explains it to us in class, but then I completely lose it on the test."

"Paul seems to have no trouble learning procedures in math, but then he can never seem to remember how and when to apply them when faced with a problem."

"We drill Myra over and over on her spelling words — it's incredible how hard it is to get new material into her head. But I will say this: once she knows something, she really knows it — forever."

"Why is it that Billy can remember what color tie Uncle Stan wore at Thanksgiving five years ago but can't remember his vocabulary words from last night?"

"Keisha knows what sounds go with what letter combinations, but when she sounds out an unfamiliar word, by the time she gets to the last sound, she's forgotten the first two, so she has trouble re-blending the word and putting it all back together in her mind."

These authentic quotations capture the agony and confusion of the many children who struggle valiantly but are overtaken and overcome by the unremitting onslaught of memory demands in school. Too often their obstructed remembering goes unrecognized by their teachers, their parents, and by the student victims themselves. To rekindle such students, we need to start with greater adult awareness of the kinds of memory processes required for academic success. Additionally, educators and clinicians must be able to identify and treat the diverse forms of memory shortfall that impede learning and academic output in otherwise competent students.

The Source for Learning & Memory Strategies will contribute substantially to our grasp of the wide-ranging memory issues that confront all learners while it will enable us to recognize and help those underachieving children and adolescents who may be much better at understanding than they are at remembering. As we absorb the pages of this volume, there are certain points that should be borne in mind (if not in memory):

✔ *School work demands far more memory agility than is required in just about any career you can identify.* Our grown-up occupations allow us to open up the same general kinds of memory files day after day for years and years. During elementary, middle, and high school, students are expected to transition with efficiency and precision from memory for math to memory for Spanish to memory for chemistry and on to memory for history. A seemingly unending succession of files must be opened and closed every 50 minutes or so, and for the most part, these files contain mainly new acquisitions. Kids with memory impairments need the justified reassurance that if they "hang in there," life will become easier, as their chosen career niches will inflict far less strenuous memory wounds than they had to contend with at school.

✔ *There are numerous forms of human memory.* No one of us possesses a uniformly good or poor memory. We always have to inquire, "Which kind of memory" and "Memory for what?"

✔ *Memory is not monogamous; it is wedded to multiple partners.* It relates intimately to attention, language, sequencing, and even motor function. Trouble with memory may masquerade as an attention deficit (i.e., why listen if you can't remember the input?), a language dysfunction (such as weak memory causing trouble with word retrieval), a sequencing weakness (trouble remembering steps in the right order), or a motor deficit (poor recall of letter formations while writing).

✔ *It is easier to remember something you understand than it is to remember that which makes little sense to you.* Education, therefore, always must calibrate the precarious balance between understanding and remembering. Imbalances lead to tenuous learning.

✔ *Some students endowed with high memory capacities may come to over-rely on rote storage and recall, receiving exemplary grades and gratifying teacher plaudits because they are so phenomenally talented at regurgitating facts and mimicking procedures on examinations.* Consequently, their understanding and their joy in learning may be underdeveloped. In fact, teachers should take care not to administer tests that are pure memory assessments (i.e., fail to tap into authentic comprehension, conceptualization, and critical thinking).

✔ *There exist intuitively endowed memorizers; they know how to operate the intricate memory circuits that support learning.* They don't need our help to remember. But other learners have to be taught to apply conscious strategies in order to retain information and skills. Fortunately, memory is one component of neurodevelopmental function that is most amenable to the application of clever cognitive tactics, the well-targeted approaches readers will encounter on the pages of this book.

Clearly, the roles of memory and the manifestations of impaired memory are complex and varied. Yet, those of us who work with students, whether we realize it or not, are forever grappling with the mysteries of memory. We must offer well-informed support to the many frustrated learners who have trouble storing and accessing skills and information. With the publication of *The Source for Learning & Memory Strategies,* clinicians, teachers, and concerned parents will have a worthy opportunity to peer into the recessed vaults of memory in order to help children and adolescents become much more effective and gratified learners.

All too often, children and adults have little awareness of how memory works and how to best work with it. This book addresses directly the practical measures that can be so highly effective in priming and maximizing memory capacity without sacrificing memory's learning co-star, insight. In a clear and totally sensible manner, Regina Richards describes the various pathways for retaining knowledge and skill while providing readily applicable methods for assuring optimal storage and retrieval. Hopefully, readers will use this volume as a springboard, custom-fitting the author's suggestions to students whom they know, while generating additional techniques of their own.

The Source for Learning & Memory Strategies should serve as one of the vital road maps for exemplary schools of the future, guiding them along a well-lit thoroughfare upon which the informed education of students derives from a keen understanding of learning processes, along with a compassionate view of the widespread differences in learning that beckon us to value and nurture all kinds of minds.

iii

Preface

In presenting workshops on learning strategies, teachers frequently ask questions about their students whom they describe as "seeming to have no memory." That, of course, is a fallacy. What they mean is that some students struggle much more than others to hang on to and retrieve school-specific information.

These questions, combined with my own curiosity, led to me to explore memory and learning issues. As I began to investigate these areas, it seemed as if memory materials were everywhere: technical and strategy chapters in books, whole books devoted to the topic, and articles in popular magazines. In one issue, I ran across the following recommendations for improving memory:

1. relax
2. concentrate
3. focus
4. slow down
5. organize
6. repeat the information
7. visualize the information

These general strategies can help many students of differing ages in either traditional or special educational classrooms. What is interesting is that these strategies are also applicable for adults. The strategies were printed in an issue of *AARP*, a newsletter for retired persons.

The moral of this story is that we can all benefit from knowing more about memory and using memory strategies throughout various life stages. It is my hope that this book will add in a positive way to this goal.

The strategies in this book were developed because of my work with students over several decades. Many techniques resulted from brainstorming sessions with other professionals in workshops, classes, and school environments. It is difficult to directly identify the sources of all the activities I have used. Even those that I feel are original may actually have a root in a suggestion presented by another professional. Schacter calls this phenomenon by the wonderful name *cryptomnesia*, which he defines as a situation wherein people misattribute novelty to something that comes from another source (Schacter 2001, p. 108).

I want to express my appreciation to all those professionals and students with whom I have interacted in various capacities, and from whom the roots of many of these ideas may have generated. The specific acknowledgments detailed on the following page are warranted for some special people who have had direct interaction with this manuscript and the ideas contained within.

- **Jeff Bleszinski**, Educational Therapist: Thank you for reading portions of the manuscript and for contributing the Bleszinski Method in Chapter 6, on pages 142-143.

- **Jim Hite**, Ph.D., School Psychologist: Thank you for your many comments and suggestions that greatly helped clarify my explanations and descriptions. Our brainstorming sessions were immensely valuable.

- **Paul Johnson**, Editor, LinguiSystems: Thank you for your creativity, suggestions, and skill in formatting this manuscript.

- **Benjamin Kohn**, O.D., Developmental Optometrist: Thank you for your assistance in creating the graphics in Figures 2.1 and 2.2 (pages 17-18).

- **Alan Kwasman**, M.D., Pediatrician: Thank you for your comments and suggestions on several chapters, especially those pertaining to medical and physical aspects.

- **Melvin D. Levine**, M.D.: Thank you for sharing your philosophies and ideas on the importance of observing and analyzing students' work and processing. I have greatly benefited throughout the years from your classes, workshops, and many publications.

- **Judy Love**, Educational Therapist: Thank you for your many hours spent in reading and rereading these chapters and for your assistance in enhancing the clarity of the descriptions. I especially value the many years we have worked together.

- **Andrea Maher**, M.S., Speech and Language Pathologist: Thank you for reading and commenting on these chapters and especially for adding the perspective of an SLP.

- **Eli Richards**, B.S., Computer Specialist: Thank you for all that you have taught me through your many years of school, including your struggles and your successes. I thank you for being you and for sharing your thoughts and feelings with me. And, in particular, I thank you for all of your computer assistance throughout this project.

- **Irv Richards**, Loving Husband: Thank you for your continuing support and endless patience and encouragement. We are indeed a team. Thank you also for contributing your "Memo To All Teachers" on page 206.

- **Mary Rush**, Artist: Thank you for your drawings of the pictures on pages 117-128.

- **Jeralee Smith**, M.A., Special Education Teacher: Thank you for the hours spent brainstorming ideas and for your suggestions in proofreading many of these chapters.

To all of these people, and to those unnamed whom I've interacted with throughout the years, I value your professionalism and your commitment to education. Thank you for valuing children.

Regina

Memory and the Brain

"Learning is the process by which we acquire new knowledge about the world."

"Memory is the process by which what is learned can be retained in storage with the possibility of drawing on that at some later time" (Squire, 2002, p. 387).

There is a distinction between learning and memory, but these two functions are so intricately linked that they continuously influence each other. To understand one process, it is necessary to understand the other. Our goal for students is that they increase their learning and memory while gaining an understanding of how they learn. If that goal is met, students can pursue learning as a lifetime endeavor.

Memory is critical for everyday functioning. Because it enables us to learn by experience, it is an essential process for survival. The context of an experience facilitates remembering: a meaningful context is mandatory because the brain continually seeks to make meaning. This context is as much a physiological process as it is a cultural one. Communication within the brain takes place as the neurons "talk to" each other. This communication occurs through synaptic impulses and connections, which is the physiological basis for memory. The probability that the synapses will fire in a predictable association with other neurons is increased by experience (contextual meaning) which then changes the way synaptic connections are made.

> Neurons that fire together, survive together, and wire together (Siegel, 2000).

In Chapter 2, we will discuss an information processing model of memory. In preparation for that discussion, it will be helpful to review some basic anatomy of the brain, as this information can be useful in developing instructional strategies and curriculum to help our students learn more effectively. This understanding is useful when working with any student, but is critical in planning strategies for students who learn differently and struggle with tasks of learning and remembering.

The Cells

The central nervous system includes the brain and the spinal cord, structures which are comprised of specific cells: *neurons* and *glial cells*. The brain is analogous to a "three-pound soufflé" and is a fragile mass shaped like a walnut and about the size of a grapefruit. To picture the size of the brain, make a fist with each hand and bring your fists together. Your fists represent the approximate size of your brain.

Glial Cells

Glia is derived from the Greek word that means "glue." Glial cells are helper cells in the brain and outnumber neurons ten to one. They are not conductive cells and are quite different from neurons. They play an important role in the developing brain by forming temporary scaffolding for the neurons during the initial migration process, enabling the neurons to move to a predetermined location in the brain. A discussion of the different types of glial cells is beyond the scope of this book; however, it is valuable to mention that inefficiencies in neuronal migration are implicated in some learning differences, among them, dyslexia.

Dr. Gordon Sherman, a neuroscientist and past president of the International Dyslexia Association, describes changes identified in the brains of children and adults with diagnosed dyslexia. One change involves *ectopias* — small bundles of nerve cells (neurons) and tangled nerve fibers (axons).

Some Brain Statistics

▲ The average weight of the human adult brain is about three pounds.

▲ The relative weight of the cortex at birth is about 12 ounces — about 25% of its adult weight.

▲ The average weight of the cortex at 6 months is 50% of its adult weight.

▲ The average weight of the cortex at age 5 is 90% of its adult weight.

▲ The brain represents 2% of total body weight.

▲ Every minute 1.5 pints of blood traverse through the brain.

▲ There are 100,000 miles of blood vessels, capillaries, and other transport systems.

▲ The brain consumes 25% of the body's oxygen and burns 70% of the body's glucose (Wesson, 2002, 3).

These ectopias are caused by a change during neuronal migration — the journey all newborn neurons undergo to their final positions in the brain. Some newborn cells, though, miss their stops, travel too far, and end up in foreign locations in the cortex, becoming altered in the process and connecting to the rest of the brain in atypical ways.

The fascinating thing about ectopic neurons is that they seem to connect with neurons and other parts of the brain differently. Since most ectopias are in the language networks and the frontal part of the brain related to verbal memory, it is easy to see how a different "wiring" pattern might affect the complex process of learning to read and write (Sherman, 2002).

Neurons

Cells in our central nervous system differ from other cells in our body because they do not generally regenerate. The neurons have an ability to transmit information through a system of networks, thus creating electrical signaling within the brain. They can be referred to as our brain's network communicators.

Neurons exist in several different shapes and sizes and are very small (about 1/1000th of the size of a period on this page). Each contains a cell body with a nucleus, a single axon usually covered by myelin, and several projections called dendrites. Dendrites are like branches or fingers which reach out to receive information from other cells. The axon is like a tail that sends information to other cells. The junction between the axon terminals and specific spots (spines) on the dendrites or cell bodies is called the *synapse*.

Neurons transmit messages at the synaptic junction by means of electrical and chemical signals and release chemicals called neurotransmitters. These amino acids, monoaminos (amines), or peptides serve as chemical messengers from the axon of a sending neuron to a receiving neuron. Some of the most commonly known neurotransmitters are dopamine, serotonin, norepinephrine, and acetylcholine, the latter of which is directly involved in memory. Neurotransmitters are triggered by an electrical signal (action potential) which either excites the target neuron to fire or inhibits it from firing. The more action potentials that arrive at the terminal, the more molecules are released into the gap (synapse). No specific function is carried out by a single synapse between neurons, but rather, behavior and memory are the result of the activity of numerous nerve cells linked together to form complex neuronal networks.

This unique communication ability among neural networks allows for our information processing model that forms the basis of memory. No specific location in the brain stores information. Rather, components are stored in various locations throughout the brain and then circuits or networks of neurons work together to join or coordinate the components of the information. As an analogy, picture a file cabinet containing multiple files or locations of the many small pieces of input/information that coordinate to form a memory. When we experience something new, the brain seeks a familiar existing network into which

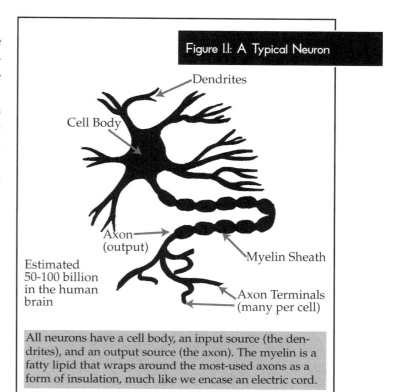

Figure 1.1: A Typical Neuron

Dendrites

Cell Body

Axon (output)

Myelin Sheath

Axon Terminals (many per cell)

Estimated 50-100 billion in the human brain

All neurons have a cell body, an input source (the dendrites), and an output source (the axon). The myelin is a fatty lipid that wraps around the most-used axons as a form of insulation, much like we encase an electric cord.

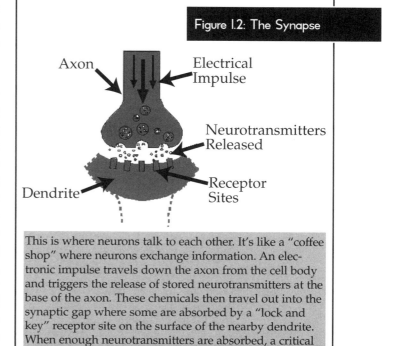

Figure 1.2: The Synapse

Axon

Electrical Impulse

Neurotransmitters Released

Receptor Sites

Dendrite

This is where neurons talk to each other. It's like a "coffee shop" where neurons exchange information. An electronic impulse travels down the axon from the cell body and triggers the release of stored neurotransmitters at the base of the axon. These chemicals then travel out into the synaptic gap where some are absorbed by a "lock and key" receptor site on the surface of the nearby dendrite. When enough neurotransmitters are absorbed, a critical mass is reached (an action potential) and a new charge is generated to travel down the dendrite.

the new information will fit. With a good fit, what was stored previously provides a context for the new information.

A kinesthetic mnemonic: Hold your hand out in front of you, with the palm facing you and your fingers spread wide. Your palm represents the cell body of the neuron. Your fingers and thumb represent the dendrites. Your arm represents the long axon.

1. Rub a finger of your other hand around the "cell body."

2. Touch your "dendrites."

3. Trace the long, tail-like "axon" with your other hand.

> ### Encoding New Memories
>
> Experiences are encoded by brain networks whose connections have already been shaped by previous encounters with the world. This pre-existing knowledge powerfully influences how we encode and store new memories, thus contributing to the nature, texture, and quality of what we will recall of the moment (Schacter, 1996, p. 6).

David Sousa provides a practical example of the number of neurons and dendrites working in the brain.

There are about 100 billion neurons in the adult human brain — about 16 times as many neurons as people on this planet and about the number of stars in the Milky Way. Each neuron can have up to 10,000 dendrite branches. This means that it is possible to have up to one quadrillion (that is a one followed by 15 zeros) synaptic connections in one brain. This inconceivably large number allows the brain to process the data coming continuously from the senses; to store decades of memories, faces, and places; and to come by information in a way that no other individual on this planet has ever thought of before. This is a remarkable achievement for just three pounds of soft tissue! (Sousa, 2001, p. 22)

Jean M. Auel describes the phenomenon of using information in a way unlike any other individual with the novelty leading to problem solving and innovation. In her book, *The Shelters of Stone*, part of the Earth's Children series, the two main characters return home after a long absence. They demonstrate a new use for a spear, which they called a *spear-thrower*.

But the spear-thrower was more than a new use of principles that were innately known. It was an example of an inborn characteristic of people like Jondalar and Ayala that made their survival more likely: the ability to conceive of an idea and turn it into a useful object, to take an abstract thought and make it real. That was their greatest Gift, though they didn't recognize it for what it was (Auel, 2002, p. 202).

Activity 1.1: Labeling the Neuron

Label these parts of a neuron: *dendrite, axon,* and *cell body*. The answers are on page 3.

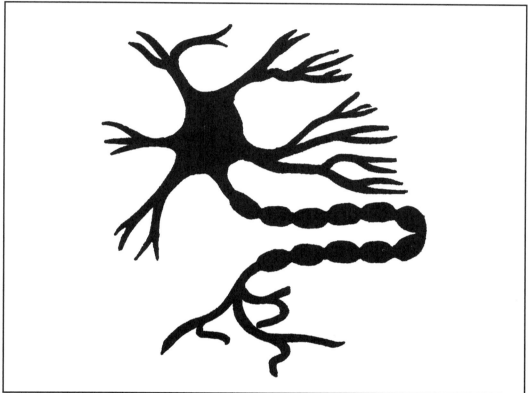

By themselves, neurons are not very smart, but linked with countless other neurons, they form a magical electrical network that produces each thought, feeling, or dream.

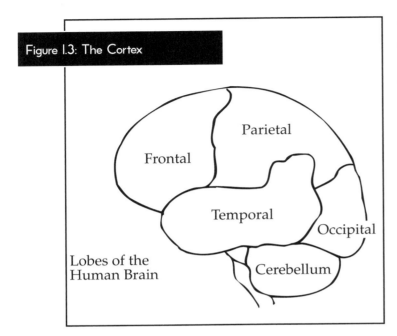

Figure 1.3: The Cortex

Parietal

Frontal

Temporal

Occipital

Cerebellum

Lobes of the
Human Brain

The Cortex

The cortex — the outer layer of the brain — is approximately 1/8th of an inch thick. If it were flattened, it would be about the size of a 2 ½ foot square sheet of newspaper. The word *cortex* is derived from the Latin word for *bark*, which provides a good mnemonic because both the cortex of the brain and the bark of the tree are wrinkled and folded. The deep folds of the cortex enable it to fit in a small space. This area of the brain is sometimes referred to as the "grey matter" and is responsible for perception, awareness of motion, planning, and conscious thought. One analogy that illustrates the power of the brain is that the average brain's capacity is about 10 million books of 100 pages each (Robbins, 2002).

Activity 1.2: Word Association

Match the word on the left with its association on the right. Answers are on page 16.

_____ 1. cortex

_____ 2. glial cells

_____ 3. axon

_____ 4. dendrites

_____ 5. synapse

a. branch-like structure (from Greek word meaning "tree")

b. outer layer (from Latin word meaning "bark")

c. a junction (from Greek meaning "to join together")

d. tail (from Greek word meaning "axis")

e. helper cells (Greek meaning "glue")

The Function of the Cerebral Lobes

The major folds of the cerebral cortex create several different areas called lobes, each with a separate function. The four main lobes have names that correspond to a nearby skull bone of the head. Each lobe has many subdivisions, each with a different role. Coordination and communication via networking within and among cells in different lobes facilitate the process whereby information makes sense and has meaning. As we have already learned, information that is meaningful is most likely to be available for recall and retrieval.

Occipital Lobes

These lobes are located at the lower back central part of the brain and are responsible for processing visual stimuli. The primary visual perception area contains millions of neurons which are further organized into areas designed to process different aspects of vision. Once the incoming information has been perceived, i.e. assembled in these areas, it then travels to the secondary area, the visual association area, and is compared with previous experiences. Visual stimuli do not become meaningful until the entering perceptions are matched with previously stored cognitive associations. For some people, this process generally occurs rapidly; whereas others need more time and may depend on more cures.

Advance notification or priming increases the brain's ability to focus on essential information by providing cues to anticipate critical features or ideas that will be forthcoming. One example of priming includes looking for your child on a crowded soccer field because you know what your child looks like and you know he will be there: you can anticipate the critical features, which makes it easier to locate your child. Another example of priming is presenting the objective of a lesson in advance: this prepares the students to look for critical information and concepts.

Temporal Lobes

These lobes curve forward from the occipital lobes and are located on either side of the brain just above the ears. Their primary function is to process auditory stimuli and some components of long-term memory. At the junction of the left occipital, parietal, and temporal lobes is a group of cells known as *Wernicke's Area*. This area is critical for speech and language and allows us to comprehend what we hear and puts words together with correct syntax when speaking.

Parietal Lobes

These lobes are at the top of the brain and are almost like a flat plate in each hemisphere. They primarily deal with orientation in space and some types of recognition. The two major subdivisions of the parietal lobes play different but complementary roles. The anterior, or front, part of the parietal lobes forms a strip of cells called the *somatosensory cortex*. These cells allow us to receive information from our environment regarding touch, temperature, pain, and position of our limbs. The posterior or rear part of the parietal lobes continuously integrates all the information received from the anterior part and processes it to provide spatial awareness, allowing the brain to know where each part of the body is in relationship to its surroundings.

Frontal Lobes

The frontal lobes occupy 28% of the cortex and perform the most complex functions. They are often referred to as the *executive control center*. Located in the front of the brain, they extend back across the top of the cortex. The frontal lobes allow us to be consciously aware of our thoughts and actions and enable willful movement, planning, attention, and decision-making. The two main categories for frontal lobe functioning are sensorimotor processing and cognition. An important component within the frontal lobes is the prefrontal cortex, also called the association area. It is where the highest forms of mental activities take place.

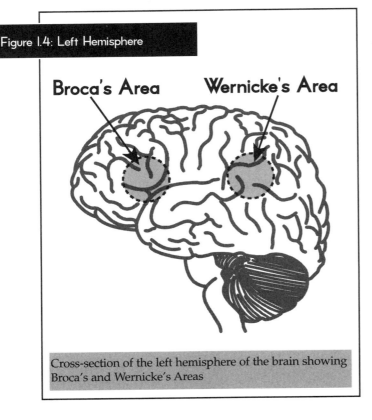

Figure 1.4: Left Hemisphere

Broca's Area   Wernicke's Area

Cross-section of the left hemisphere of the brain showing Broca's and Wernicke's Areas

Between the parietal and frontal lobes is a strip of cells that stretches along the top of the brain and forms a path similar to the headband on a pair of earphones. This path, called the *motor cortex*, is important for directing the neural activity for muscular movements. Just in front of the motor cortex is a supplemental motor area known as *Broca's Area*, a critical part of the cortex that allows us to speak. Broca's area is connected to Wernicke's Area in the temporal lobes by a bundle of nerve fibers.

Any activity in which we engage requires the coordination of many components of our cortex. For example, think about the task of asking for a drink of water. After we decide we want the drink, then Broca's Area, Wernicke's Area, and the motor cortex all must work together to enable us to speak and make our request. This coordination enables us to think about what we want, plan what to say, and organize the speech muscles to say it clearly.

Activity 1.3: Word Association Mnemonic

Develop your own mnemonic to help remember the function of each of the four major lobes.

Occipital _____

_____

Temporal _____

_____

Parietal _____

_____

Frontal _____

_____

Activity 1.4: Brain Kinesthetic Metaphor

Place each hand in a fist, with your thumbs toward you. Bring your fists together so that your fingernails almost touch and your knuckles touch completely. Your knuckles and the outside parts of your hands represent the cerebral cortex. Your thumbs represent the frontal lobes. Your pinkies represent the occipital lobes. The pathways represented by your ring fingers and middle fingers represent the sensory cortex and the motor cortex. Your fists also represent the approximate size of your brain. Your wrists represent the brainstem where vital body functions are controlled: body temperature, blood pressure, heartbeat. Your forearms represent your spinal column.

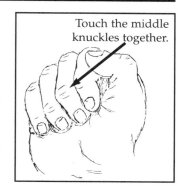
Touch the middle knuckles together.

If you open your hands, as in the picture to the right, the location where your nails touched represents the corpus callosum.

Now, put your fists back together, but spread your palms apart while keeping the knuckles and fingers touching. Look at the tips of your fingers. This represents the limbic or emotional system. This system is deep within the brain and its structures are duplicated in each hemisphere.

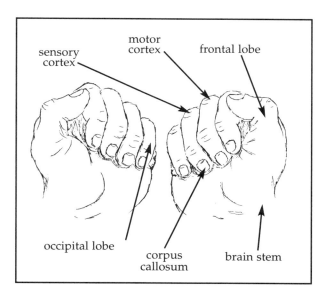
sensory cortex
motor cortex
frontal lobe
occipital lobe
corpus callosum
brain stem

Activity 1.5: Labeling the Cortex

Label the lobes of the cortex: frontal, occipital, parietal, temporal, and the brain stem. (The answers can be found in Figure 1.3 on page 6.)

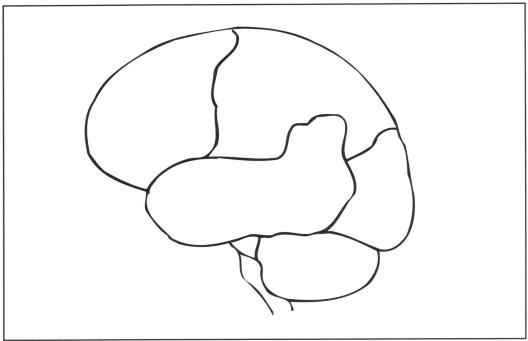

Figure 1.5: Left Hemisphere

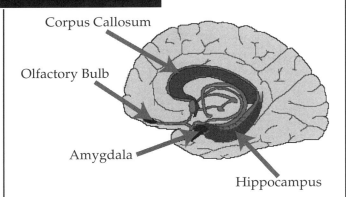

Corpus Callosum

Olfactory Bulb

Amygdala

Hippocampus

The hippocampus and amygdala are bilateral (one on each side). They are recessed into the midbrain and the temporal lobe. The left and right brain do their jobs in subtle but measurably different ways and are connected by the corpus callosum.

Other Brain Structures

Limbic System
The Limbic System lies deep within the brain, above the brain stem. Among its functions is the generation of emotions. "Its placement between the cerebrum [cerebral cortex] and the brain stem permits the interplay of emotion and reason . . . It is intriguing to realize that the two structures of the brain mainly responsible for long-term remembering are located in the emotional system" (Sousa 2001, p. 18-19).

Thalamus and Hypothalamus
The thalamus is named for the Greek word for "inner room or chamber." It

is a small structure, about the size of a walnut that functions like a relay station. Nearly all stimuli from the sensory organs travel first to the thalamus to be sorted and sent on to the appropriate brain area. The prefix *hypo-* means "below," referring to the fact that the hypothalamus is located below the thalamus. This is a small organ about the size of a thumbnail that helps us maintain or regulate normal body states such as temperature, heart rate, eating, and drinking. For example, in a frightening situation, the hypothalamus will activate the body's "fight or flight" response.

Hippocampus

The hippocampus, whose name is derived from the Latin word for "seahorse," is a critical structure that holds memory of the immediate past and sends memory to the cortex. "It plays a major role in consolidating learning and in converting information from working memory via electrical signals to the long-term storage regions, a process that may take days or months. It constantly checks information relayed to working memory and compares it to stored experiences. This process is essential for the creation of meaning" (Sousa, 2001, p. 18).

The hippocampus is involved in the recognition of novelty, a very important processing job for our brains. Neuroimaging studies suggest that we involve a hippocampal response when we encode or input novel information. Metaphors and mnemonics are valuable strategies for introducing novelty.

▲ *A Simple Metaphor*
Imagine that your brain is a computer. You can think of your cortex as your hard drive where memories are stored. Your hippocampus is your keyboard, the means by which you place and access memories in the cortex (Sapolsky, 1998, p. 176). The thalamus, literally and figuratively, decides what buttons to push.

> ### Awakening the Hippocampus
>
> The hippocampus becomes active during a novel event and draws our attention to it. Then another network becomes active, the left inferior frontal lobe. This then enables us to perform elaborative encoding because of a wealth of semantic associations and knowledge (Schacter, 1996, p. 56).

▲ *Stress*
Some stress is valuable because it serves as an activating motivator, and short-term stressors of mild to moderate severity enhance cognition. However, stress that is enormous or prolonged is disruptive to cognition and may lead to the physical destruction of neurons in the hippocampus and thus interfere with learning and memory storage. In a 1996 study, Sapolsky, a leading researcher on the relationship of stress and memory, reported that stress that lasted for weeks led to reversible atrophy in the hippocampus but prolonged stress, lasting for months, led to permanent loss of hippocampal neurons. He concluded that lifelong stress can influence the likelihood of hippocampal and cognitive aging. To prevent the negative side effects of stress, it is beneficial to balance our stress, by providing and experiencing a beneficial number of positive experiences.

Affects of Stress on Memory

There are obscure mechanisms by which moderate, short-term stress makes your memory receptors more sensitive . . . (when our) glucocorticoid levels go from the range seen for mild to moderate stressors to the range typical of big-time stress, the hormone no longer enhances long-term potentiation in that hippocampal slice but begins to disrupt it" (Sapolsky, 1998, p. 183-184).

Amygdala

The almond-shaped amygdala is located near the thalamus and hypothalamus and is also involved in our fight or flight response. It functions like an alarm system and plays a critical role in the control of emotion. By communicating with the hippocampus and other areas of the cortex, the amygdala can identify danger and trigger the appropriate physiological processes.

Cerebellum

The cerebellum, also known as the "little brain," is a large structure that resembles cauliflower and lies on top of the brainstem just under the occipital lobes in the back of the brain. It is a deeply-folded structure that provides the key to coordinating muscle function, balance, body posture, and the body's senses.

New motor movements begin to develop with conscious planning. The cortex can plan and initiate movements but it does not have the neural circuitry needed to calculate the sequences of muscular contractions necessary for the movements.

When the cerebellum receives information (in about one-50th of a second) that the motor cortex has begun to initiate a movement, it computes the contribution that various muscles will have to make to perform that movement and sends the appropriate messages to those muscles. The action has begun. Throughout the action, the cerebellum continuously monitors and modifies the activity in the muscles, making the changes necessary for smooth completion of the action (Wolfe, 2001, p. 24).

Activity 1.6: Labeling the Cerebellum

Activity: return to Activity 1.5 on page 10 and label the cerebellum.

▲ *Motor Patterns*

I observed a developing motor plan (i.e., cerebellular involvement) as my son learned to drive. Initially, his movements were precisely planned: he sat down, put on his seat belt, determined the location of the gas and brake pedals, and then carefully inserted the key and turned the ignition. He could not talk or listen to the radio. The process was under control of several different parts of his cortex and required intense concentration. As his skills automatized, his cerebellum then stored the movement patterns in neural networks and he could call upon them as needed. His body "remembered" the necessary motor patterns without requiring as much conscious thought. As a result, he could then efficiently drive, listen to the radio, and talk to a friend. This automatization occurred because of his many purposeful repetitions combined with high motivation.

Have you ever had the experience of driving home from school while thinking about your plans for the next day and suddenly you realize you're home and don't remember the drive or how you got there? In this situation, the process of driving was a mechanical or automatic motor pattern (hopefully combined with some cognitive awareness of the environment). The process of planning your next day's lesson called upon your active working memory.

Corpus Callosum

The corpus callosum, at 4 inches in length, is the largest fiber system in the brain and is composed of approximately 300 million axons. This bundle of fibers joins the two hemispheres of the brain. The corpus callosum matures slowly and often in a predictable developmental pattern, generally beginning around age 9 or 10. As the corpus callosum is maturing, students begin to do the following (Wesson, 2002):

- process abstractions and perform more complex thinking
- use more insight and consider different perspectives
- perform more multi-step tasks
- lose touch with some of their earlier childhood memories

As a mnemonic, you can perform this chant with students, using each fist to represent a hemisphere of the brain.

Left brain (hold up left fist),
Right brain (hold up right fist),
I use both of them (bring both fists near each other),
Because I have you,
My corpus callosum (bring fists together with nails touching).

The two hemispheres of our brain work together in wonderful coordination but there is also hemispheric specialization. The left hemisphere governs the right side of the body and the right hemisphere governs the left side of the body. In most people, the left hemisphere is primarily involved in language, sequential, and reasoning skills and processes information faster than the right hemisphere. The right hemisphere provides the context or overall meaning, encodes patterns and processes information more globally. "The specializations of each hemisphere develop to their fullest when informed by the opposite hemisphere" (Wolfe, 2001, p. 47). Almost nothing is regulated solely by the left or right hemisphere.

> The two hemispheres are in the same body, only a couple of inches apart. Each half of the human brain shares years of experiences with the other. They eat the same cereal . . . (and thus receive the same changes in their blood supply); they share the same hormones . . . they look at the same TV programs, and they go to the same parties. And neither hemisphere operates anything on its own, any more than we walk with one foot or the other, or whether the area of a rectangle is dependent on its length or width. (Ornstein, 1997, p. 68).

Review

This review will help you consolidate your own synaptic connections.

Challenge Questions

1. If you were a hippocampus, how would you look? _____

   _____

2. If your skin was like your cortex, how would it look? _____

   _____

3. How can you use your hands and arms to represent two neurons and show

   how the dendrites of one approach the axon of the other? _____

   _____

Identify

Earlier in this chapter we reviewed some of the brain structures using a multiple-choice format. That required a recognition process. Now we will use a retrieval process. You will note that this list is much longer, with the goal of providing more extensive review. The answers appear on page 16.

1. cells responsible for network communication _____

2. branches from the cells which reach out to
   recognize information _____

3. the junction between cells _____

4. the name of the outer layer of the brain _____

5. the brain lobes which are the primary processing
   centers for visual information _____

6. the structure responsible for coordinating
   muscle function _____

7. the fibers that connect the right brain hemisphere
   with the left brain hemisphere _____

8. the brain lobes that function as executive
   control centers _____

9. the primary emotional center of our brain _____

10. the structure that sends memory to the cortex _____

Which activity was easier for you: the matching task on page 6 or the retrieval task on the previous page? Why do you think that is? _____

_____

_____

_____

_____

Teaching Tip

Recognition before Retrieval!

Answers for Activities and Review

Activity 1.2 on page 6
1. b
2. e
3. d
4. a
5. c

Identify questions on page 14
1. neurons
2. dendrites
3. synapse
4. cortex
5. occipital lobes
6. cerebellum
7. corpus callosum
8. frontal lobes
9. limbic system
10. hippocampus

The Process of Memory

Chapter
2

Memory is both dynamic and active and is under control of the central executive of our brain. This highly complex process involves multiple components simultaneously. Our discussion of this system will describe the functional components of memory. The goal is to explain the process in a more concrete manner. Consequently, categories and analogies will be used to represent the major components by which we encode, store, retrieve, and integrate information. These are *not* intended to represent different structures or distinct stages within the process.

When thinking about our students and learning, several key points are valuable to keep in mind.

- Things can go wrong at any stage of the memory process. If we identify the breakdown point, or the point where the process went wrong, we can develop better tools to help that student create strategies and enhance his memory and learning.
- Learning requires collaboration of the proper memory functions.
- Many components are rapid, integrative, and multidimensional; but consolidation is a slow process.
- "Vastly more extensive and strenuous use of memory is required for school success than is needed in virtually any career you can name." (Levine 2002, p. 91)

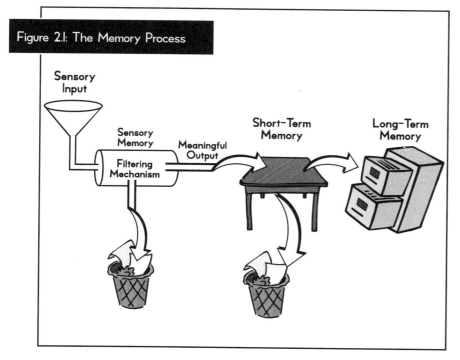

Figure 2.1: The Memory Process

Sensory Input

Sensory Memory

Filtering Mechanism

Meaningful Output

Short-Term Memory

Long-Term Memory

In the graphics in Figure 2.1 and Figure 2.6 (page 33), the functional components of memory are identified as:

- sensory memory
- short-term memory
- long-term memory
- retrieval

Sensory Memory

Everything begins as sensory input from the environment. Our sensory system takes in information through its receptors: sight, sound, touch, movement, taste, smell, gravity, and position. A great deal of sensory information is simultaneously input. If we were to pay attention to all of this, we would experience sensory overload. For example, most of us rarely attend to the feeling of our clothes on our body or the position of our big toe as we sit and read. We have a mechanism to filter out and discard irrelevant or unnecessary data. This same filtering mechanism also organizes relevant data into meaningful patterns.

> Memory is a net; one finds it full of fish when he takes it from the brook; but a dozen miles of water have run through it without sticking.
> — *Oliver Wendell Holmes, Sr. (1809-1894)*

This process can also be compared to the function of a sieve or filter. Since 99 percent of all sensory information is discarded almost immediately upon entering the brain, what remains is generally (and hopefully) the most valuable and important (Gazzaniga, 1998). The representation of the sensory memory in Figures 2.1 and 2.2 uses a filtering mechanism, similar to a common filter like a water filter.

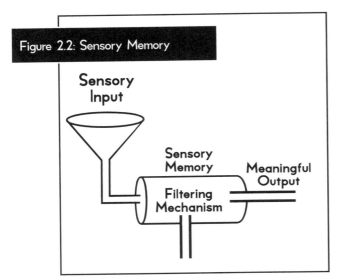

Figure 2.2: Sensory Memory

Our sensory memory results from a complex input mechanism which is actually more of a registry than what is usually thought of as memory. It is our special way of paying attention to ongoing events and it has a major impact on subsequent memory for them. This encoding or inputting process helps us get information into the brain and serves as "a procedure for transforming something a person sees, hears, thinks, or feels into a memory" (Schachter, 1996, p. 42).

Our sensory memory is a system that holds information while a decision is made about what to do with it. Different terms often refer to varying forms of input. For example, *iconic memory* relates to visual stimuli (the light ray) whereas *echoic memory* refers to auditory stimuli. The function of our sensory memory is limited by that factor of time, usually milliseconds to a few seconds. Immediately after the sensory input, a slight delay occurs to enable us to develop an appropriate strategy to assist with storage. We recycle the information while we simultaneously plan and organize efficient strategies. Unless the image is actively shifted to short-term storage, it fades away or decays and hence, it is "dumped."

The initial registry process is very brief: most incoming sensory information first travels to the thalamus. This structure operates like a switchboard and determines the importance of information, usually in just milliseconds (1/1000th of a second). Sensory memory is also quite brief, but slightly longer than the registry process. For example, iconic memory may only last for a few milliseconds, whereas echoic memory may last up to 15 or 20 seconds.

Attention
Sometimes our memories may exist as fragments of experiences. This may occur if we are distracted as an event unfolds and while the sensory information is coming in. In such cases, we may later have difficulty remembering details of what happened, although we may still have a general memory of the event. Memories can be built from fragments of

experience, but these are frequently not durable. The key to learning is to help students process information more in depth so that it will be established as a durable memory rather than as a fragment or series of fragments.

There is no such thing as "not paying attention." The brain is always paying attention; however, attention is selective. We do not control this initial processing stage on an awareness level, but we can use conscious effort to direct our attention (or our students' attention) to specific stimuli by incorporating attention-getting factors into our presentations, such as the following:

- novelty
- intensity
- movement

Our brains are programmed to pay attention to the unusual, to something that is of a differing intensity, or to something that moves. Intensity can change visually (bright light) or auditorily (ringing a bell). There are many different ways to incorporate novelty, intensity, and movement. Divergent thinking and creativity are the keys to developing new ideas and strategies; however, the brain also has a tendency towards habituation. For example, with repetition, a stimulus is no longer novel and can be filtered out as unimportant. Hence, what is novel one day may lose its novelty with repetition and will need to be changed. Variety is the key.

Meaning and Patterns

We also have some direct control over other factors that will influence whether the brain initially attends to arriving information and whether this information will be sustained in the memory process. These are factors such as *meaning* and *emotion*.

It is very difficult (and perhaps impossible) to sustain attention on something that we can not figure out and that makes no sense to us. Pat Wolfe proposes a thought-provoking question on this issue:

> Consider students in a classroom confronted with information that doesn't match anything they previously stored. Their brains look for an appropriate network to help to make sense or meaning of this information. If nothing can be found, the information is discarded as meaningless. Without being facetious, is it possible that much of what we teach in schools fits this description, and we shouldn't be surprised that our students' brains often refuse to attend (Wolfe, 2001, p. 86)?

The brain seeks meaning through patterns. The process of perception is the meaning we attach to information as it is received through the senses. To assign meaning to what we perceive, we need prior knowledge and expectations. When information comes in, our brains check existing neural networks of information. If the new information is something that activates a previously stored neural net, then there is a match. This matching of new input to existing information is referred to as *pattern recognition*. For example, the letter **a** can be written in a variety of different fonts: a α α **a**. If we had never seen the letter **a** before, and if we did not know what it represented, the symbols would be meaningless. There would be no recognition. On the other hand, because we are familiar with this symbol, we can generalize a specific representation of the letter **a** to the general pattern, even though the specific font may vary.

Emotion

Another way to draw attention to what needs to be remembered is through the process of emotion, as the brain is biologically programmed to first attend to information that has strong emotional content. Good moods enhance the ability to think flexibly and with more complexity, thus making it easier to find solutions to problems and to remember information (Goleman, 1995, p. 85). Positive emotional experiences can help make the information more meaningful. The key is to develop positive hooks to capture the important information. Priming activities (setting expectations) and meaningful strategies are some ways to develop these important hooks. For example, by having fun acting out a particular history event, you increase students' chances of remembering that event because it is more likely to hook into their emotional and motivational network.

Research supports the idea that it is beneficial to develop activities that engage students' emotional and motivational interest. Such activities result in stronger memories of that information because emotional arousal usually results in the release of adrenaline (also called epinephrine). In one study, blocking the adrenaline soon after viewing an emotionally laden picture resulted in decreasing recall of the picture. In discussing this type of research, Joseph LeDoux states the following:

> This suggests that if adrenaline is released naturally (from the adrenal gland) in some situation, that experience will be remembered especially well. Since emotional arousal usually results in the release of adrenaline, it might be expected . . . that explicitly conscious memory of emotional situations would be stronger than the explicit memory of nonemotional situations (LeDoux, 1996, p. 206).

Negative emotion has the opposite effect. Working memory is critical as we deal with information and tasks because it is the capacity of attention that holds in mind the facts that are essential for completion of the task or problem. The prefrontal cortex is the brain region responsible for this function:

> Circuits from the limbic brain to the prefrontal lobes mean that the signals of strong emotion — anxiety, anger, and the like — can create neural static, sabotaging the ability of the prefrontal lobe to maintain working memory. This is why when we are emotionally upset we say we "just can't think straight." (Goleman, 1995, p. 27).

Short-term Memory

To establish a durable memory, the incoming information must be prevented from being dumped by being encoded more thoroughly, or deeply. This is accomplished by associating it meaningfully with knowledge that already exists in memory. This process of short-term memory is represented by the middle section of Figure 2.1 on page 17. Short-term memory is represented as a table because we actively work on the input to elaborate it. Just as we work on a table to organize and create something, we can work on the input to organize and create a memory. That is, we can use rehearsal and mnemonic strategies. If the information is not established as a durable memory, it is dumped and goes into the trash.

The goal of short-term memory is to structure the input so it moves into long-term memory in a meaningful and memorable format. While this short-term storage process is of short duration, the memory is maintained for a longer period of time than it is during the sensory memory process. Many scientists refer to this mediating process as *working memory*, the conceptualization we will use in this book. Technically, working memory occurs simultaneously throughout all phases of the memory process. Because memory is an active, dynamic process, working memory and mediating strategies help to organize storage and retrieval throughout the entire process (Feifer and De Fina, 2002, p. 87).

This working aspect of memory storage holds small amounts of information for a brief period of time: it's like holding information while we use it or think about it, just as we use a tabletop to hold our supplies as we create something. For example, when we look up a number in a phone book, we can repeat it through a rote memory process and hold it long enough to dial the number. Then we may forget it. To establish the memory as a more durable memory, it must be encoded more deeply by associating it meaningfully with knowledge that already exists in memory. This is where strategies become very valuable. For example, we might sing the phone number and/or chunk the digits into meaningful units.

Patterns and Memory

"Since our "thinking cap" (the neocortex) is strongly influenced by patterns, not facts, remembering information is maximized when it is provided in contextual, episodic event-oriented situations which include motor learning, location changes, music, rhythm, and novelty . . . We do poorly when we "piecemeal" learning into linear, sequential facts and other out of context information lists" (Jensen 1995, p. 26).

Activity 2.1: Recall Activity

The following activity is based on memory research studies. Try it with a friend and discuss the results.

Ask your friend to listen to and answer each of the following questions as you read them:
▲ Is **coat** a type of clothing?
▲ Is **apple** a type of food?
▲ Is **Toyota** a type of car?
▲ Is **collie** a type of food?
▲ Is **book** a type of car?
▲ Is **Popsicle** a type of food?

Now do the same with these questions:
▲ Does the word **shirt** contain more vowels or more consonants?
▲ Does **Honda** contain more vowels or more consonants?
▲ Does **bread** contain more vowels or more consonants?

▲ Does **blanket** contain more vowels or more consonants?

▲ Does **school** contain more vowels or more consonants?

▲ Does **elephant** contain more vowels or more consonants?

Thirty minutes later have your friend try to recall each of the target words (indicated by the boldface). Many people find it easier to recall the target words in the first list because they need to think about the meaning of the word in order to answer the question accurately. This represents more collaborative encoding. Many people can answer the questions easily in the second list without attending to the meaning of the word and, therefore, may not encode the word as deeply.

During workshops, I have fun performing word recall activities similar to the one above with a large group. Participants on one side of the room answer the first type of questions and those on the other side of the room answer the second type of questions. We then determine which group of participants tended to recall the largest number of words from their list. With a large group, the pattern is often quite obvious: it is generally easier to recall more semantically encoded words than words that are not semantically encoded. In a related activity, I later read a list of words, many of which are the same words as previously presented, but I also include some related but different words. I ask the participants if each word was one of the target words they heard earlier. This taps recognition memory rather then retrieval memory and some people achieve better accuracy with a recognition activity. However, there may also be some confusion with the words that are similar. For example, using the activity above, I may present the word **quilt** and some people answer affirmatively that it was in the list because of its categorical similarity to the word **blanket** (which was in the list).

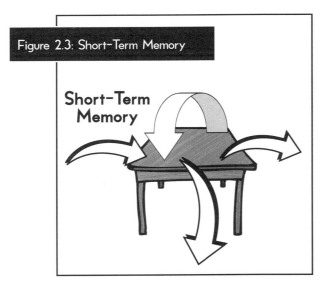

Figure 2.3: Short-Term Memory

Short-Term Memory

High levels of performance can be promoted by certain types of semantic encoding. Semantics refers to the study of words or understanding and use of words. Semantic encoding is using words to form various hooks. This permits elaborative encoding which then allows us to integrate new information with what we already know. When working with students it is valuable to help them form meaningful mental associations among the study materials. As you model the strategies, simultaneously teach them to independently use similar associations and self-questioning. This then helps them develop a valuable study strategy.

Active working memory plays a critical role in learning and productivity in school. It is the mental workspace we use to temporarily hold information as we carry out cognitive tasks like reasoning and comprehending. It is a meeting place for short-term and long-term memory. For example, when a student is verbally asked a question, he needs to hold the question for a short time in active working memory while searching for the answer in his long-term memory. It is very frustrating to forget the question while in the process of searching for the answer. This mental work space is analogous to a tabletop, as represented in Figure 2.3.

Activity 2.2: Working Memory

The following activity requires you to draw on your available working memory capacity. Some people will find this task quite challenging or frustrating. In such cases, it may help decrease your frustration, and increase your success, by using a shorter series of numbers.

▲ Repeat these digits: 5 2 8 3 9 4 6.

▲ Now hang onto these digits while reading two sentences from the previous page.

▲ Recall the digits, without looking at them.

Were you able to do this successfully? If so, you drew on ample working memory capacity.

In an interesting study with older adults, it was found that age-related memory differences disappeared when the participants were guided to use pre-existing knowledge to encode information with elaboration and distinction, providing they were later given cues to help them regenerate their encodings. These adults were then able to recall the given information efficiently. Schacter explains these results by emphasizing that "we can still benefit from elaborative encoding because semantic memory holds up well with age." However, we may need to do extra work both during the encoding and retrieval process (1996, p. 291). Similarly, many of our students may need to do extra work during encoding and retrieval to perform at a level commensurate with their peers and with their other skills.

Levine identifies five roles of the working memory system, using the term "active working memory" to emphasize the role of active involvement (2001, p. 77). These five roles are:

- holding an idea in mind while developing, elaborating, clarifying, or using it
- recalling from long-term memory while holding some information in short-term memory
- holding together in memory the components of a task while completing that task
- keeping together a series of new pieces of information so that they remain meaningful
- holding a long-term plan while thinking about a short-range need

Elaboration

To elaborate upon your own understanding of the function of working memory, use the chart on the following page to brainstorm one or more examples for each of these five roles related to working memory. Some examples are presented at the end of the chapter on page 38.

Role of active working memory	Example 1	Example 2
Holding an idea in mind while developing, elaborating, clarifying, or using it		
Recalling from long-term memory while holding some information in short-term memory		
Holding together in memory the components of a task while completing that task		
Keeping together a series of new pieces of information so that they remain meaningful		
Holding a long-term plan while thinking about a short-range need		

Long-term Memory

Here are some definitions relevant to the consideration of long-term memory:

▲ **Consolidation**   the process by which memories are moved from temporary storage in the hippocampus to more permanent storage in the cortex

▲ **Index**   a mechanism under control of the hippocampus that is critical for consolidation and functions as a critical convergent zone for assembling explicit memories

- The index is needed to keep track of all the sights, sounds, and thoughts that come together to comprise an episode and that are tagged in a distributed way by the time, space, and other details of the initial presentation.

- The index keeps track of all this information until a memory engram can be held together by direct connections between the cortical regions themselves.

- The index serves to point to the location of different components of information that are stored in separate cortical regions.

- The index is no longer necessary to recall the specific event once the engram is developed.

▲ Engram	the permanent memory trace that results when brain tissue is anatomically altered by experience
▲ **Long-term Potentiation (LTP)**	a permanent strengthening of synaptic strength and sensitivity that is a result of repeated, frequent firings across a synapse between two associated neurons

- The faster a neuron fires, the greater the amount of neurotransmitter it generates, and the more likely it is to set off its neighbors.

- "As the neighbors fire, the surface of their dendrites change to make them more sensitive to stimulation. This process of synaptic awareness and sensitivity is LTP. Eventually, repeated firing of the pattern binds the neurons together so that if one fires, they all fire, ultimately forming a new memory trace or engram" (Sousa, 2001, p. 80).

> Neurons that fire together, wire together.

▲ **Primacy and Recency Effect**	the phenomenon whereby, during a learning episode, we tend to remember best that which comes first (prime-time-1), second-best that which comes last (prime-time-2), and least that which comes just about past the middle (down-time)

The Hippocampus

The hippocampus plays an important role in long-term memory because storage occurs only after the hippocampus encodes the information and sends it to one or more long-term storage areas. This is the process of consolidation and it is a process that takes time and is distributed throughout the cortex. The hippocampus and related structures serve as a critical convergent zone for assembling the various components of memory. Their role exists only for a short time after the event. The implication of this process is that no single picture exists in mind to correspond to a given event.

The hippocampus routes, retrieves, and sometimes stores data picked up by the senses.

▲ When the senses pick up stimuli from the environment, those inputs travel along neural pathways from the sensory organ to the section of the brain that interprets that type of input.

▲ The input moves to the hippocampus for short-term storage.

▲ If the data is important and is rehearsed, the hippocampus sends codes for the various aspects of that memory to each part of the cortex that specializes in the related aspect.

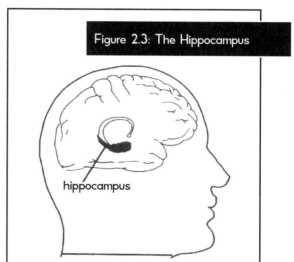

Figure 2.3: The Hippocampus

hippocampus

▲ Here are some examples of codes that might involve cues:
- to recognize a face
- to identify the function of an object
- to visualize a familiar building

In our memory graphics (Figures 2.1 and 2.6), long-term memory is represented by a file cabinet. The specific components of the experience or memory are stored as individual files. It is important to keep in mind that no single file exists to correspond to a given event or memory.

> Long-term memory is a seemingly limitless repository for preserving knowledge, skills, and life experiences. Its massive storage vaults can be drawn upon throughout life. In fact, long-term memory is so enormously vast that there has been debate over whether information ever gets lost from long-term memory or whether, when we can't remember something, it is simply lost in long-term memory. There is plenty of evidence supporting the latter possibility. We are all familiar with the tip-of-the-tongue phenomenon, in which we are trying to remember a person's name and just can't come up with it. Then, three days later, . . . the name suddenly spews forth. It was never actually lost *from* memory; it was lost *in* memory. It may be that we don't forget things, but that we forget where we put them. So it is that the great long-term memory challenge is to store information systematically, to put it where we are most likely to find later (Levine 2002, p. 106).

Long-term memory consolidation occurs in part because people talk about things and events contained in past memories. The older the memory, the greater the opportunity for "post event rehearsal," which acts in turn to promote the direct connections between the critical storage areas that eventually allow assembly of the "jigsaw puzzle that constitutes an event" (Schacter, 1985, p. 87). We also know that there is no guarantee that storage will be permanent, as for example, after a lesson. This is true even if students may seem to have acquired the new information or skill from a lesson. This is why students may appear to have "learned" the concept but then seem to be "clueless" the next day.

Consolidation
Teaching something new too soon can disrupt the consolidation of previous learning, especially if the new information or task is similar to the old. Research is not specific enough to tell us how much time is needed for consolidation; but nevertheless, this time factor would vary considerably among students and for different types of information. Even though we cannot specify any specific length of time that is necessary between introduction of concepts or skills, we do know that consolidation takes time. By building elaborate rehearsal strategies into our instruction, students will be able to process the information more in-depth and thus increase the strength of the learning while also allowing time for consolidation.

A Valuable Teaching Tip

Too much, too fast — it won't last!

Consolidation is undoubtedly enhanced by rehearsal. When we "replay" experiences (talk and think about them), we are providing more opportunities for consolidation. Perhaps this is why instruction that allows students to hook new information to previous experiences increases the strength and complexity of their neural connections and, therefore, the retention of the information (Wolfe, 2001, p. 125).

As teachers, we need to pay greater attention to consolidation time. Sousa gives an example applicable to motor skills. When a learner practices a new skill (for example, swinging a baseball bat),

> Rehearsal enhances consolidation.

the motor cortex (across the top of the brain) coordinates with the cerebellum to establish the pathways that will consolidate the movements to perform the skill. "After the learner stops the practice, it takes about six hours (down-time) for this consolidation to occur. Further memory pathways are established as the learner sleeps. Practicing the skill the next day will be much easier and more accurate." He indicates that if the learner immediately practices a second, similar skill (for example, swinging a golf club) the pathways for the two skills become confused and the learner is not able to perform either skill very well. He identifies two important implications:

▲ Avoid teaching two motor skills that are very similar to each other in the same day. When in doubt, make a list of their similarities and differences. If the similarities far outweigh the differences, it is best not to teach them together.

▲ When the time comes to teach the second skill, teach the differences first. This ensures that the differences are recognized during prime-time-1, which is the most powerful position for remembering (Sousa, 2001, p. 116).

While Sousa's example refers to swinging a baseball bat and a golf club, the same advice applies to fine motor skills such as learning correct letter form. Similar letters, such as the **b** and **d** or **m** and **n** should be taught at different times, with the differences presented at the beginning of the session that teaches the second letter in each pair.

This same process can be generalized to the teaching of concepts. When two similar concepts need to be taught, do so at different times. When teaching the second concept, begin with the differences. This decreases the potential for a student to confuse the concepts. When the similarities overwhelm the differences, it is easy to attach the same retrieval cues to both concepts. Then, when the student uses those cues later to retrieve the information, retrieval could produce either or both concepts, causing a struggle to identify which is correct. Focusing on and practicing the differences provides students with cues to separate the two similar concepts and identify them correctly in the future. Examples of some concepts which have more similarities than differences are the following sets: latitude and longitude, simile and metaphor, acronym and acrostic, vibration and pitch, or series and parallel circuits.

Categories of Long-term Memory

Different memory systems help create different types of jigsaw assembly mechanisms for long-term memory. Two basic categories of long-term memory are *declarative* and *nondeclarative*.

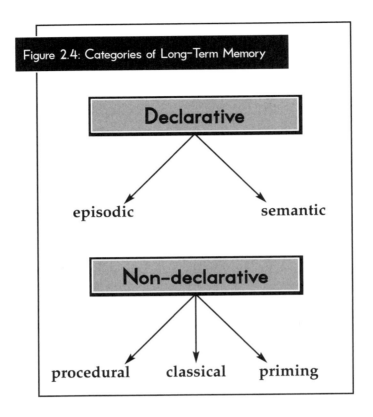

Figure 2.4: Categories of Long-Term Memory

Declarative

episodic   semantic

Non-declarative

procedural   classical   priming

Declarative memory is knowing "what" and is sometimes referred to as *conscious* or *explicit memory*. It requires conscious processing and involves the remembering of events, names, facts, music, and objects. It is generally processed by the hippocampus and cerebral cortex.

Non-declarative memory is the process of knowing "how" and is sometimes called *implicit* or *procedural memory*. There are several forms, including procedural memory, classical memory, and priming memory. This is an aspect of memory experienced through performance rather then through recall.

▲ *Declarative Memory: Episodic Memory*
Episodic memory, also referred to as *source memory*, is the memory of the time and place of events: the "when" and "where." Examples include remembering a specific ride at Disneyland on your 12th birthday or remembering a special surprise presented to you by your class. It has also been referred to as *autobiographical reference* (Squire and Kandel, 2000).

An example of declarative memory:
Think about a significant event in your life, such as the wedding of a good friend. Try to recall an important person who was with you. What does that person look like? What happens once you have the context in mind? Frequently, other components of the memory then come together. The reason is that one part of the memory, i.e., the context and/or a significant person, brings to mind other aspects of the memory. This is how

declarative memory works: it requires conscious processing but once the context is brought to mind, there is almost effortless recall of associated components.

▲ *Declarative Memory: Semantic Memory*
Semantic memory is knowledge of facts, rules, and concepts that may or may not be related to specific events. Semantic memory includes words, symbols for words, rules for manipulating words, and meanings of words. It also includes rules of grammar, math, and chemistry. Many of these facts, rules, and concepts are organized into categories and may be independent of a particular time or place. For example, knowing the year in which I graduated college (a semantic memory) is very different from remembering my experiences during my senior year (episodic). Similarly, recalling that 9 x 5 = 45 is a semantic memory whereas remembering the experience of chanting the times tables during a car ride with my best friend is an episodic memory. Another example of semantic memory involves categorization, such as remembering that my dog is a collie and collies are dog and dogs are mammals. This categorization helps me create a pattern (mammal) that contains several categories and categories within categories.

▲ *Non-declarative Memory: Procedural Memory*
Procedural memory allows us to learn new skills and to learn how to do things. It is knowing *how* rather than knowing *what*. To store these types of memories, we do not need to "declare" or name anything, and we may not be able to verbalize what we're doing. Sometimes skills and habits can be developed or improved upon in the absence of any direct awareness that the performance is improving. Procedural memory skills and habits are typically acquired over time through repetitive practice and may involve motor skills, perceptual skills, or cognitive skills.

- Examples of motor skills include activities such as driving a car, tying a shoelace, riding a bike, throwing a ball, swimming, writing in cursive, or turning on the computer.

- Examples of perceptual skills include discriminating colors, reading, performing math calculations, or identifying different instruments heard in music. For example, when I first learned to read I moved my eyes very slowly from word to word. But with practice and skill development, I learned to move my eyes much more quickly. "Skilled readers move their eyes about four times a second, taking in the meaning of more than 300 words a minute" (Squire and Kandel, 2000 reported in Wolfe, 2001, p. 115).

- Cognitive skills involve figuring out a procedure for solving a problem. These are different from cognitive concept building because cognitive skills are performed automatically and rely on procedural memory rather than declarative memory. An example is solving a story problem in math.

Remembering how to do things is vital in all school subjects and activities. Once procedural memory skills become practiced and automatic, the memory becomes efficient and can be performed with little or no direct thought or conscious recall. Practice, rehearsal, and the depth of the encoding are critical to aid this development. Our ability to perform many skills without conscious thought has been referred to as "memory without record" by Jerome Bruner (Squire and Kandel, 2000). Students who fluently express their ideas in writing often have developed this level of automaticity for letter form: for example, they no longer need to think directly about how many humps are needed for the letter **m**. In contrast, students who struggle to get their ideas down in print may be performing the motor movements related to letter form on a less-than-automatic basis.

It is interesting that some automatic procedures form an unconscious habit that becomes difficult to access in any way except by performing it. For example, every time I try to recall my parents' phone number, I find my fingers need to perform the specific movements as on the touchpad of the telephone. Another example is the touch typing habits of a trained typist. When asked to verbally describe the location of a specific letter on the keyboard, I find it is difficult for me to do so without moving my fingers in that pattern.

Procedural memory is involved in the development of habits and behavioral routines that we perform every day. Some interesting research has shown that monkeys with brain damage (lesions to the medial temporal lobes) may have poor memory for recent events and experiences but can learn new habits at a normal rate. When given hundreds of practice trials, the amnesic monkeys gradually learned what to do in order to obtain a food reward, even though they had little memory for what happened on any particular trial (Mortimer Mishkin in Schacter, 1996, p. 188). While our students are very different in this regard, this example does show that procedural memory differs from episodic memory while also providing an answer to explain a common memory question repeatedly asked by parents and teachers: "Why does he remember precise details of his trip to Disneyland but can't remember his times tables?"

▲ *Non-declarative Memory: Classical Memory*
This aspect of memory is a form of learning sometimes referred to as *classical conditioning*. In famous studies by the Russian physiologist, Ivan Pavlov, a dog heard a specific tone several times (a conditioned stimulus). Each was followed immediately by a food reward (the unconditioned stimulus). In time, the tone began to elicit the same response formerly elicited by the food, i.e., salivation (the conditioned response). The animal learned that the tone signaled the immediate appearance of food. Classical conditioning enables us to learn about the causal structure of the world. We form associations between the events that are associated in our environments. One type of association involves body movements; for example, if an object approaches close to our eye, we tend to blink. Another type is involuntary conditioning, which involves the involuntary response systems of the body, such as heart rate and pupil size.

There are many examples of classical memory, or reflexive learning, through our day. For example, if we approach a hot object such as a stove, we draw back. We can encourage reflexive or automatic memories through structured repetition, using what some call "overlearning." Overlearning, however, must be done in a purposeful, meaningful format. The more practice that occurs, the easier it will be for the learning to become automatic. Games like hopscotch and other quick-reaction activities can help store and retrieve memories. The automatic nature of rap can trigger this type of memory for both the physical motions and auditory cues.

I remember Joey, an entering fourth grader in our classroom. One of his mother's concerns was that after many years of different attempts and practice, he still was unable to recall his phone number. She knew she could obtain a bracelet, but she felt both his self-esteem and his safety would be enhanced if he could remember this number. At the end of the first day, he excitedly ran to his mother and recited his phone number. She was, of course, excited and delighted.

What was the secret to Joey's wonderful success in learning his phone number? Several components were incorporated into activities as he worked to learn this sequence of numbers.

- He chunked the numbers into 3 small groups.

- He learned one chunk at a time, using a rap rhythm.

- He wrote each chunk of numbers on the chalkboard using rainbow writing (writing over the numbers using different colors of chalk).

- He then wrote the numbers large and clearly on the chalkboard and jumped on a trampa while reciting the numbers. (A trampa is a small, 36-inch mini-trampoline. See Figure 4.10 on page 79.)

Through the use of patterns, multisensory involvement, physical activity, and rehearsal Joey was able to develop an automatic, or reflexive, recall of this important sequence of numbers. He organized the information into a meaningful pattern on his "tabletop" (short-term memory) and was then able to use his practiced cues to retrieve it when desired, as shown in Figure 2.5. The increase in his self-esteem set a very positive tone for his approach to his new school during the coming year.

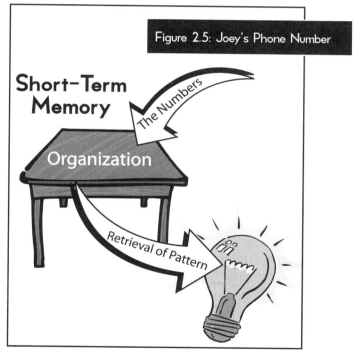

Figure 2.5: Joey's Phone Number

▲ *Non-declarative Memory: Priming Memory*
Priming is also called *implicit memory* and involves being influenced by a past experience, often without awareness of remembering that experience. Priming is an important aspect of memory because many events in our daily lives are predictable and, consequently, blueprints of objects encountered once are likely to be encountered began. For our ancestors, it was advantageous if objects processed and analyzed sometime earlier could be processed and analyzed more quickly on their second encounter. This is an ability that would make animals more successful in avoiding predators because it would make the brain "more available for the important task of processing and analyzing entirely novel stimuli" (Squire, 2002, p. 393).

Sometimes priming occurs independent of conscious memory (Schacter, 1996, p. 167). An example of such a manifestation of priming is evident in plagiarism lawsuits. A

Memory and Perception

The ultimate long-term effect of memory is to change the actual neural structure of part of our cortex. For example, over time, "changing the neural structure of the visual cortex alters the machinery of perception" (Wolfe, 2001, p. 123).

highly publicized case several decades ago involved the former Beatle George Harrison's 1970's hit song, "My Sweet Lord." His melody nearly duplicated the tune of a 1962 classic by The Chiffons', "He's so Fine."

When a lawsuit was brought against him, Harrison conceded that he had heard "He's So Fine" prior to writing "My Sweet Lord," but denied he had intentionally borrowed from the earlier song. Reasoning that the resemblance between the two was simply too strong to be the product of coincidence, the trial judge "held that Harrison's work did infringe through what the courts felt must have been unintentional copying of what was in Harrison's subconscious memory" (Schacter, 1996, p. 167).

Examples of priming also include situations in which we are aware of the events of the priming cue. These may be instances when we directly intend to prime our future memories, such as providing ourselves with reminders, reading the questions at the end of the chapter prior to beginning the chapter, or setting an alarm clock. Once we see or experience something — especially more than once — we prime our ability to recall it later. Teachers can take advantage of the benefits of priming by using it as a valuable teaching strategy for all ages. One example is providing an overview at the beginning of a lesson.

Retrieval Memory

The process of memory involves a large network throughout our brain, and therefore, any specific memory is not stored in any specific location. The process of recall and retrieval involves reconstruction or reactivation of elements of our past experiences which reside all over our brain.

We use an index process to aid in this reconstruction. Retrieval begins with activation in the short-term memory loop as the brain activates the index to begin to look for a cue to use in searching for the components of the information within the long-term memory storage. To recall a memory we need "an activation of all these separate sites in unison, creating an integrated experience" (Damasio, 1994). Once the cues are located and the separate sites become activated in unison, the memory of the experience or concept returns to short-term memory to be organized within the active working memory system and then retrieved. If it is determined to be unnecessary or useless, it is trashed.

Retrieval can be activated by appropriate self-talk as a student re-verbalizes the information and/or talks himself through specific retrieval strategies. Teaching such strategies enables the student to "learn how to learn." This is a gift we can give to students that is perhaps the most valuable of gifts.

One of the many available descriptions of the retrieval system describes two aspects of retrieval: *associative* and *strategic* (Schacter, 1996, p. 68).

32

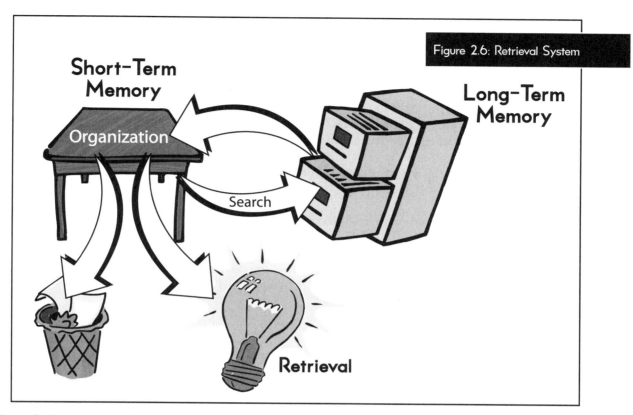

Figure 2.6: Retrieval System

Short-Term Memory — Organization

Long-Term Memory

Search

Retrieval

▲ **Associative Retrieval**
- This is an automatic reminding process that depends on the hippocampus and related medial temporal lobe structures.
- It occurs when a cue automatically triggers an experience of remembering.

▲ **Strategic Retrieval**
- This is a slow, deliberate search of memory which depends on regions of the prefrontal cortex and the right frontal cortex.

Another conceptualization of the retrieval process is depicted by Mel Levine. He represents the memory system using an analogy of a factory. Levine's "Memory Factory" depicts a floor plan that maps different areas for different memory functions. There is also a "Retrieval Robot" who is able to adjust the speed of the assembly line:

> Some information is recalled slowly, such as when students do homework. On other occasions a moderate rate is called for, such as when answering questions or participating in a class discussion. There are also the frequent occasions when the instant (automatic) retrieval is critical. This is especially the case when someone is engaged in simultaneous retrieval (remembering several things almost at once), a demand that is most often imposed in writing (2000, p. 9).

Among the many areas on the floor of the Factory is an "output area" to which information is delivered. There are "delivery vehicles" which enable the information to move through the Factory and these are labeled as listed on the following page:

▲ muscle output

▲ language output: words

▲ behavior output: actions

▲ insight output

> The mind's cross-indexing puts the best librarian to shame (Begley, 1986).

One of the great values of the Memory Factory is its utility in demystifing the memory process for students, parents, and educators. It graphically explains the concept that there are many different types of memory and many different memory situations. This helps explain why a student may be superb in remembering tiny minute details of a trip to Disneyland but also be unable to readily recall the multiplication tables.

Knowledge of aspects that contribute to more efficient retrieval of memory is highly significant in a teaching situation. Such knowledge will enable teachers and therapists to encourage their students to be systematic in their uses of memory, perhaps by asking themselves what strategy they can use to study for a given situation. Teachers also need to use this knowledge to develop strategic "hooks." The remainder of this book is devoted to strategy development.

Review

A brief review will help consolidate your synaptic connections regarding some of the information discussed in this chapter. As you review and answer these items, think about cues you might use to trigger your hippocampus to "send a code" to your long-term memory system so that it will be easier for you to retrieve the information at a later time.

After you answer these questions on another sheet of paper, discuss your responses with a colleague.

Challenge Questions

1. What are functional components of the memory process?

2. Name three elements that can be used to help direct attention to a specific stimulus and give examples of each.

3. Describe working memory and give one example of a task requiring working memory.

4. Is long-term memory a dynamic process or a static process? Why?

5. What structure encodes information and sends it to a long-term storage area: the hippocampus or the hypothalamus? Develop a mnemonic to help yourself remember the correct answer.

6. Complete the visual organizers on pages 36-37 in order to describe and identify the forms or types of declarative and non-declarative memory. Give an example of each type of memory.

7.   State two examples of procedural memory.

8.   What initiates retrieval memory? Describe an example of this process.

9.   When, and in what situation, might you say the following to a child:

>   "Your brain wants to be right, so you often think and answer very quickly. But you may miss some important steps. That's why it sometimes takes you longer to learn something. We are going to work together to find a way to help you slow down and go through all the right thinking steps, so you won't miss any of them. You will find that you will also eventually be able to think more quickly, while also remembering all of the steps."

10. When might you discuss Levine's concept of the Memory Factory with a student?

> Downtime is as important as the time you spend hunkered down doing your work.
> — *Maya Angelou, American writer and poet*

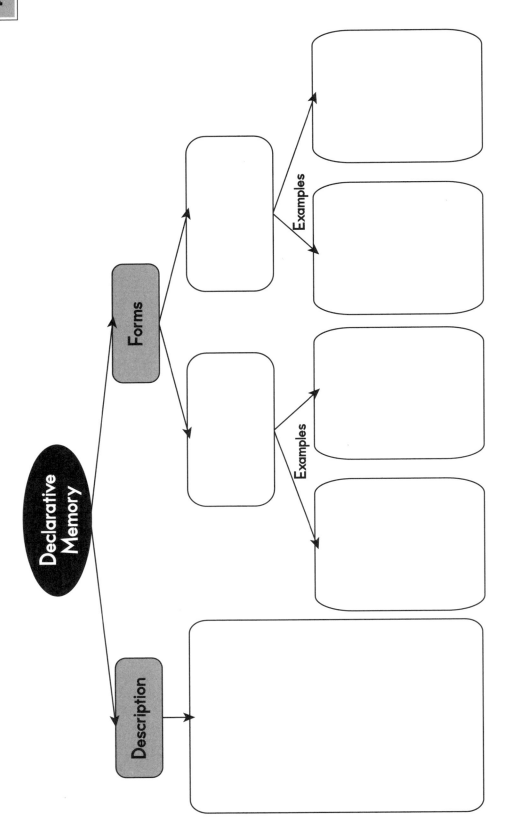

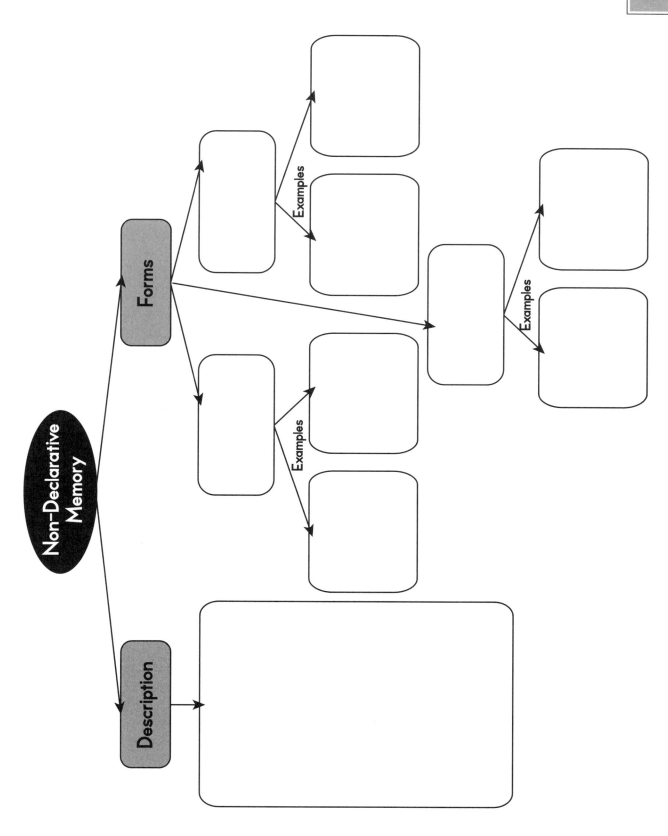

Elaboration Chart Examples (page 24)

Role of active working memory	Examples
Holding an idea in mind while developing, elaborating, clarifying, or using it	Remembering the beginning of an instruction while listening to the rest; remembering the ending while performing the beginning.
Recalling from long-term memory while holding some information in short-term memory	Retrieving information to answer a question while also remembering all the parts of the question; remembering where you are going and why you are going there while also figuring out how to get there.
Holding together in memory the components of a task while completing that task	Amber at age 10 stated, "There is no room for all that stuff inside my head. Every single time I try to write, I forget what I am doing. If I think about one thing like spelling, then I forget all about something else, like punctuation; or else, when I have to think hard to figure out what I'm going to write, my handwriting gets really messy" (Levine, 2002, p. 99).
Keeping together a series of new pieces of information so that they remain meaningful	Sounding out a multisyllable word: remembering the first syllable while working on subsequent syllables and then combining all the syllables to blend them into a word while flexing the sounds (manipulating, accenting); remembering the math procedures and specific facts while performing a multi-step math problem.
Holding a long-term plan while thinking about a short-range need	Rushing through math, resulting in a messy paper with careless errors: the child feels that she must work fast or else she will forget what she is doing.

Memory in the Classroom

Chapter 3

Memory is a complicated, multi-departmental operation that does its work at many diverse brain sites, a lot of which have not even been located by neuroscientists. Nothing is ever learned without tapping into some component of memory. A child may be able to understand a fact, process, or concept as it is being explained or demonstrated; but without memory, none of it can be retrieved and applied. Without the collaboration of the proper memory functions, learning fails (Levine, 2002, p. 91).

As teachers, clinicians, and parents, we want our students to enhance their memory skills. Understanding the process of memory facilitates our efficiency in teaching strategies and enables us to better identify the breakdown points when students struggle. It is also valuable to help students understand the memory process and be able to identify their own breakdown points so they may then make sense of why some tasks are easier and some are more difficult.

Helping students understand these memory issues is an aspect involved in demystification of the learning process. As students learn to better understand their own learning patterns, they can become self advocates. As such, they will be able explain to themselves and others why they may need to spend more time in using specific strategies. Many students avoid using strategies that require more time; however, if they understand the purpose and value of doing so, it makes it easier for them to accept the concept of investing additional time in their learning.

Mel Levine discusses the concept of demystification throughout many of his writings and states, "Students with memory problems have a critical need for demystification which reassures them that: 1) they are not stupid (i.e., they just have trouble storing certain things in their minds); 2) when they grow up, the memory strain will not be so bad; and 3) they can work on improving their memory capacity for schoolwork and learning (1998, p. 97). The following are examples of some demystification statements that can be used to help a student clarify his struggles with a component of memory (2002, p. 92).

▲ **Sequential Memory**
- "It's really hard for you to put things in your memory in the right order. That's why when the teacher tells you to do several things in a row, you get all mixed up."

▲ **Active Working Memory**
- "A lot of times you forget what you're doing while you're in the middle of doing it. It would be like a television screen where parts of the picture disappear in the middle of a program."

▲ **Access to Long-term Memory**
- "Your memory is like a closet with a sticking door. It's hard for you to remember things in school because the door keeps getting stuck. We have to figure out how to make the door open more easily!"

Different Aspects of Memory

> Nobody has a perfect memory the way some people might have perfect pitch, nor, for that matter, is anyone shackled with a totally incompetent memory. We should always ask, "memory for what?" (Levine 2002, p. 92)

When I ask teachers in workshops to think of different kinds of memory activities that relate to academics, common answers are short-term and long-term memory or auditory and visual memory. The global memory process, as presented in Chapter 2, provides us with a general framework; however, there are also many specific types of memory tasks directly related to academics.

Activity 3.1: Types of Memory Tasks

Think of as many different types of memory tasks as you can. Make your list on a separate sheet of paper or in the margin. How many did you think of? If you came up with more than 8 different types of memory, you are quite knowledgeable. If you came up with more than 10, your knowledge is superior.

Following is a chart listing different memory activities, with a brief description of each. This list is not absolute and only represents some of the more common types of memory demands and challenges that face our students.

Only the first two columns of the chart are completed. Think about each type of memory and, in the third column, write a relevant example that relates to your students. (You might work with a partner for this brainstorming activity.) In the remaining columns, check (✔) the processing component(s) that are relevant to this type of task, keeping in mind that answers may vary, depending on the structure and format of the task. (Some suggestions are in a completed chart on pages 59-60.)

Type of Memory	Description: This is memory for ...	Classroom-based Example	Sensory memory	Short-term memory	Long-term memory	Retrieval memory
Visual Memory	Recognizing something previously seen					
Auditory Memory	Recognizing something previously heard					
Episodic Memory	Events learned or experienced in the past					
Automatic Memory	Input that is so fast you don't have to think about what you need					

Type of Memory	Description: This is memory for . . .	Classroom-based Example	Sensory memory	Short-term memory	Long-term memory	Retrieval memory
Procedural Memory	Finding stored facts and skills you need in a timely manner					
Procedural Memory	Knowing how to perform an action in sequence					
Motor Memory	Knowing how to perform an action with your muscles					
Associative Memory	Information that is stored together					
Factual Memory	Knowledge					
Interpretive Memory	Organizing and pulling together language information					
Recognition Memory	Knowing that something is familiar					
Simultaneous Memory	Access to multiple facts or procedures all at once					
Cumulative Memory	Access to what was learned earlier as a basis for new information					
Categorical Memory	Classifying knowledge into pre-existing groups					
Sequential Memory	Information or procedures containing components in a certain order					

Identifying Breakdown Points

Academic memory challenges follow the processing procedures related to sensory memory, short-term memory, and consolidation as discussed in Chapter 2. When a student encounters a memory challenge and struggles with an academic task, it is valuable to think about the type of demands being encountered. Is the student's struggle related to sensory memory and attention? Working memory? Short-term memory? Consolidation? Is the struggle related to the type of memory demand, such as sequential or motor demands? Is it a retrieval struggle related to the format or the chunk size of the task? These are some of the issues we will be discussing throughout this book.

When a student struggles to recall information, we automatically assume that "memory" is the culprit. However, other issues may be involved. The student may remember the information but not be able to readily retrieve it in the format being requested. Or, the student may not have understood the information as initially presented and then she may be recalling her misunderstood concepts or facts.

The activities presented in Chapters 4-8 of this book are generalized memory strategies that may be modified to assist students in a variety of different tasks. Many interventions will be suggested with a goal of helping the reader to develop a "bag of tricks" to use, as required by the developmental needs of the student and the given situation. When a problem or inefficiency occurs, it is useful to analyze where the student is cognitively at that moment the problem occurs, i.e., the breakdown point, and then select an appropriate strategy that will help the student. The chart in Figure 3.1 provides a few examples of some possible breakdown points that may be exhibited by your students.

Figure 3.1: Examples of Breakdown Points

Description of task	Student's response	Possible breakdown point
Example 1: A full page of two place multiplication problems	Correctly computes problems on the first two lines and then begins making many errors	**Format:** Chunk size is too large. Student experiences cognitive, visual, or motor fatigue. This is a result of trouble with the volume of the parts within the activity.
Example 2: Copying information from the chalkboard	Looks up every few seconds	**Multi-tasking:** Student cannot hold a chunk of visual information while also transferring it to a motor response. This results in poor output.
Example 3: A spelling test	Cannot recall the words (but can remember little details of events from long ago)	**Pattern recognition:** Student struggles with phonological patterns (but has excellent episodic memory).

42

Mel Levine identifies six sometimes overlapping areas of weakness that contribute to learning problems. The student can encounter a breakdown because of any one of these difficulties (Levine, 2002, p. 248):

1. *Trouble mastering skills (as in Example 3 on the previous page)*
   All academic skills are composed of groups of specific subskills. These become stronger the more they are used; however, they must be adequately understood and learned at the initial levels.

2. *Trouble acquiring facts or knowledge (as in Example 3 on the previous page)*
   Having a well-stocked storehouse of knowledge makes learning more meaningful and relevant. Knowledge provides attachment points for new information.

3. *Trouble accomplishing output (as in Example 2 on the previous page)*
   Output problems result in low levels of productivity. There are many possible underlying reasons for this phenomenon, but "there is no such thing as a lazy kid."

4. *Trouble understanding*
   Many developmental aspects can inhibit a child's ability to understand the language of school, even if the child knows the answer and/or information.

5. *Trouble approaching tasks systematically*
   A poor systematic approach to learning is often seen in students who are generally disorganized. Levine calls them "nonmethodologists": they're devoid of strategies that might make work easier and more successful for them.

6. *Trouble with the rate and amount of demands (as in Example 1 on the previous page)*
   These students have minds calibrated to function at a slower than average pace. Sometimes the rate and volume demands outpace the growth of a student's capacity to handle them.

It is hoped that the strategies in Chapters 4-8 of this book will also be utilized in a global format to encourage students to use strategic learning. This will increase the efficiency and productivity of their learning because strategies encourage recall of a pattern. Furthermore, the use of strategies can enable us to incorporate an aspect that is novel, humorous, visual or kinesthetic (movement patterns). These enhancements then serve as excellent attention-getters for the concept.

> Strategies can be used to introduce a concept in a way that will stick and provide a palette for the student to use as he works to expand his understanding of the concept (Richards, 2001, p. 85).

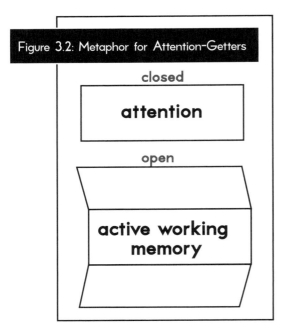

Figure 3.2: Metaphor for Attention-Getters

closed

attention

open

active working memory

Attention-Getters
Hold a sheet of paper in landscape format (with the long side horizontal) as in Figure 3.2. Fold it evenly in thirds. On the top outside portion write the word "attention." Open the folds, and on the inside portion write the words "active working memory."

This tri-fold shutter paper represents the concept that attention is critical for opening the doors to active working memory. There are many ways that we can extend the sensory input so that it can move more efficiently into active working memory. Then, when we are at the stage of active working memory, we need to seize the moment and work with the students' different learning styles. Examples of some relevant strategies that students can use to help activate attention and extend the sensory input include the following:

▲ whisper the information under your breath

▲ form pictures in your mind's eye (a visual scratch pad)

▲ perform a corresponding motor action

▲ repeat the information using a rhythm or tune

As teachers, we can help open the doors of attention by incorporating a variety of attention getters to initiate an activity. Some variables to consider include:

    ▲ predictability and patterns (for meaning and emotion)

    ▲ novelty, intensity, and movement

    ▲ the Big 4 memory facilitators:
        • systematic learning
        • active learning
        • structured activities
        • systematic presentation

    ▲ sensory modalities

In initiating an activity, it is valuable to incorporate different aspects of memory, such as *visual memory* (images), *episodic memory* (stories), and *emotional memory* (feelings). This helps students set up a pattern or framework and it provides predictability and expectations. An example would be to begin an activity with a related story as preparation to teach the concepts of *circumference, diameter,* and *radius*. This activity is appropriate for upper elementary and middle school students, but similar activities can be devised for concepts presented to younger or older students, as students of all ages enjoy fun stories. Begin by reading the story *Sir Cumference and the First Round Table* (Neuschwander, 1997) to your students. In this story, Sir Cumference and his wife, the Lady of Di from Ameter, have an adventure as they try to develop an adequate table for the Knights. Their son, Radius, who is half as tall as his mom, Lady Di, comes up with the solution of a round table. After reading the story, the students can discuss and then role-play the events portrayed.

Additional strategies for promoting attention relate to the concept of priming. For example, overtly reinforcing the student who is actively paying attention to the task at hand triggers, or primes, the other students to also pay attention. Often, it's in "small ways that we make big differences in learning." Pam Robbins highly values priming and suggests focusing learners' attention by using priming such as in the following strategies:

▲ Provide advance organizers.

▲ Post outcomes or key results areas.

▲ Use bracketing.

▲ Eliminate distractors.

▲ Ask for expectations.

▲ Generate previous experiences related to the topic.

▲ Consider **KWL** charts: (What do you **K**now? What do you **W**ant to know? And, after the lesson, What have you **L**earned?)

Memory Facilitators

While a wide variety of different activities may serve as memory facilitators, key features cluster into four categories. The "Big 4" memory facilitators are:

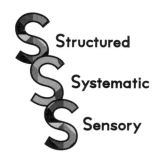

Structured

Systematic

Sensory

▲ active learning

▲ structured activities

▲ systematic presentation

▲ sensory modalities

Active Learning

One of the best memory facilitators is *active involvement*. The more we are involved with the material or information to be learned, the more efficiently we will consolidate and then recall it. This does not always mean that we need to be physically active when learning. However, we do need to be actively receiving and participating in the information. When we passively receive information, either auditorily or visually, there is a tendency to remember (consolidate) less and forget more. When we are more actively involved, we then interpret and process more efficiently. Receiving information both visually and verbally enhances recall and provides a complementary dimension to the information. To further enhance processing depth, some students also need to manipulate or experience the concepts or procedures.

Activity 3.2: Involvement in Learning

The following chart provides some examples of active and passive involvement within specific activities. Use the last column to brainstorm and discuss additional active involvement examples of each task.

Task	Passive Involvement	Active Involvement	Additional Examples of Active Involvement
Reading a chapter	Move your eyes over the print from beginning to end.	Preview the chapter; then read, take notes, and use self-questioning.	
Learning how to perform a new math computation	Listen to the teacher's explanation and watch her compute a problem; then compute 2 similar problems.	Watch someone compute a problem and use manipulatives to explain each step; then perform the same manipulations and steps for that problem and two similar problems.	
Knowing a German shepherd dog is a mammal whose original purpose was as a herd and work dog	*Maintenance rehearsal:* Repeat the information several times.	*Elaborative rehearsal:* • what I learned about mammals last year • other mammals • image of my friend's German shepherd • what I know about herd dogs • thinking about why a working dog would make a good family pet	

Structuring Activities

Structuring an activity means progressing in an organized manner so that the student knows the expectations. It may involve presenting a global picture of the activity, also called priming, prior to the individual steps. For example, in an art activity, especially if the activity has many steps, students would benefit by first seeing the finished product and then having each of the individual steps demonstrated as they perform the activity. Starting with a global understanding will enhance their recall of each substep within the sequence. This applies to working with students of all ages.

A form of structuring an activity is the concept of a pattern: our brain likes to organize input into patterns. Some students with learning differences, especially language-based learning disabilities, have an even greater need for information to be presented in patterns so that they can structure and organize it for better consolidation and recall. Patterns help develop understanding and enhance a concept because it is difficult (and often impossible) to remember something that is not understood. Structuring involves helping students elaborate upon the information, as in the German shepherd example included in the chart for Activity 3.2.

> "The brain craves information only as a means of forming or creating conclusions or patterns of meaning" (Jensen 1995, p. 25).

In discussing patterns, Mel Levine states:

> Pattern recognition can be very user-friendly and gratifying. If you take a trip to a town you have not seen in four years, on arrival you begin to recognize various features of the metropolis that you never thought you'd remember. You are uplifted by your own exemplary memory performance . . . In school, recognition can be elusive because recurring patterns most often are partially obscured by superficial differences that are potentially misleading. A competent student has the ability to penetrate the superficial differences to recognize the underlying recurring pattern (1998, p. 83-84).

When working with students who learn differently, it is our job to help the students learn to recognize patterns by "penetrating the superficial differences." For example, within math word problems, teach students to look past the details that may lead them away from the underlying pattern and cues that define the necessary process for successfully completing the word problem. These cues may reoccur throughout different word problems and it is critical that the student develops sensitivity to these verbal patterns.

A Valuable Teaching Tip

When developing activities,
keep in mind the three S's:
Structured, **Systematic**, and **Sensory**.

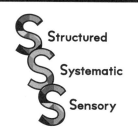

When activities are structured, they progress systematically and with some predictability. Having a system helps students develop their own patterns, which in turn helps all the components of memory. Increasing the cognitive complexity of a task provides a form of structure while also ensuring that instruction stimulates and develops the students' higher order thinking capabilities. One system, Bloom's Taxonomy of Educational Objectives, has been used for four decades. The six levels of complexity are show in Figure 3.6 on page 56.

Systematic Activities

Systematic activities and strategies follow a plan and encompass a basic pattern. The pattern might also be generated by making a connection between a new concept and something that is familiar.

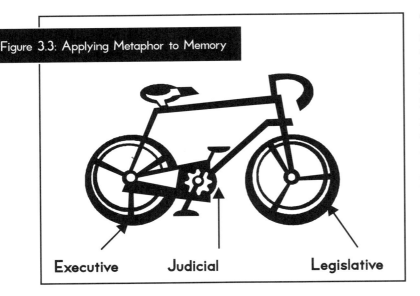

Figure 3.3: Applying Metaphor to Memory

Executive   Judicial   Legislative

The use of analogies and metaphors are very helpful in in creating connections between familiar material and new information. For example, one of my students was having difficulty remembering the three branches of government for his high school government class. He happened to be an avid bike rider and enjoyed working on the mechanics of his bike. Because he understood the importance of patterning and making systematic connections, he decided to compare the three branches of government to the three parts of his bicycle. In drawing his picture and representing the relationships, he developed a deeper understanding of the concept and understood the interaction of checks and balances among our three branches of government. He was then able to visualize how each branch had its own function and needed to work in an integrated manner for the good of the "whole."

A valuable memory facilitator that encourages being systematic is *staging*, which is performing a task in a step-by-step manner. Staging particularly helps expand active working memory capacity. By segmenting a complex, multi-layer task into its individual steps, greater focus can be placed on each component. Doing so then enhances the student's retrieval of more details.

The process of proofreading a written paper is an example of a task that requires a great deal of working memory efficiency. There are a large number of components to recall and utilize in a simultaneous manner. In using a staging approach, the student proofreads the paper for one critical aspect at a time. This requires proofreading more than once, but each proofing will focus on a different attribute, such as capitalization, punctuation, spelling, organization, word usage, or whatever other critical elements were identified for the particular task. Many mnemonic strategies are available to help cue the necessary components. One example, **COPS** is a reminder to proofread in four separate steps: once each for **C**apitalization, **O**rganization, **P**unctuation, and **S**pelling. Each letter in the acronym **COPS** represents one of the steps.

Jensen refers to the concept of staging as *chunking*, using a computer term that means bundles of information. To "chunk up" is to find the next larger bundle of the similar kind. As an example, suppose a student makes a statement such as, "All this work for just 2 homework points! It's just not worth it." To chunk up, help the student move from the level of the assignment to the benefits in life it can bring and/or in future concepts within the class. Say, for example, "You're right. This may require a great deal of energy on your part; however, doing it can bring you pride in yourself and better grades. You'll realize these concepts are stepping stones to the next. Then you'll be glad you did it."

To "chunk down" is to break the bundle of information into smaller units. This requires putting the information into a pattern or a framework that is easier for the student to understand. As an example, suppose a student says, "I just don't understand math." To chunk down, help the student understand the subtasks in math, perhaps by saying, "It seems as though you understand addition quite well. Now we are working on subtraction. Can you help me figure out what specific part of subtraction you do not understand?"

An important component of systematic instruction relates to literacy areas. Researchers such as Moats, Lyons, and Torgesen refer to the need for systematic instruction to help students better understand the system of reading and spelling while also enhancing their ability to remember and apply the instruction. Describing specific details regarding systematic reading and spelling instruction is beyond the scope of this book. However, the relevant methodology has been thoroughly delineated in many other books including, Moats and Lyons (1996), Moats (1999, 2000), and Torgesen (2000).

Sensory Involvement
▲ Multimodal

Sensory involvement encourages students to use a variety of sensory channels during activities. Termed *multimodal instruction* or *practice*, it is valuable for students of all ages and in many different types of activities. The more varied experiences a student may have with a concept, the more neural pathways will be developed. Increased pathways and neural networks will enhance efficiency, understanding, recall, and timely retrieval. Increased activity also facilitates the elaboration of patterns. A simple example is the use of colored pencils or pens, which enhances the visual input and emphasizes the critical features. Jensen states that "there is strong evidence to suggest that colored pens make information easier to recall than what's recorded by a thin-line ballpoint pen or pencil" (Jensen, 1995, p. 190). Therefore, using different colors to present information to students can be very valuable in enhancing students' sensory involvement. Similar advantages occur when students use colored markers when creating visual organizers or highlighters when taking notes.

> "Any system utilizing two or more of the brain's natural memory processes is considered a complex, and therefore successful, learning strategy" (Jensen, 1995, p. 182).

An example unit involving the study of volcanoes might incorporate a variety of sensory modalities in activities such as the following:

- Creating a visual organizer describing the characteristics of volcanoes, using a variety of colored markers
- Reading and/or listening to stories that include events related to a volcano eruption
- Watching a movie about a volcano
- Building a volcano that actually erupts (using baking soda)
- Role-playing being a volcano, incorporating the various steps that lead up to an eruption

To elaborate on the student's understanding of a volcano, students who have studied an event such as the American Revolution may connect their knowledge about volcanoes with a different sort of eruption, such as a revolution. Ask students to brainstorm and list the similarities and differences between a volcano and a revolution. On the surface these two concepts appear different, but there are actually many similarities, and it is useful for students to discover these patterns and connections. A Venn diagram, as in Figure 3.4, can be created as the students brainstorm their ideas. As they state a characteristic of either a revolution or a volcano, they also determine if it is an aspect that is similar or different compared to the other one. If the characteristic relates to only the volcano or the revolution, it is placed in the appropriate column. If it relates to both concepts, the characteristic is placed in the center, intersecting location.

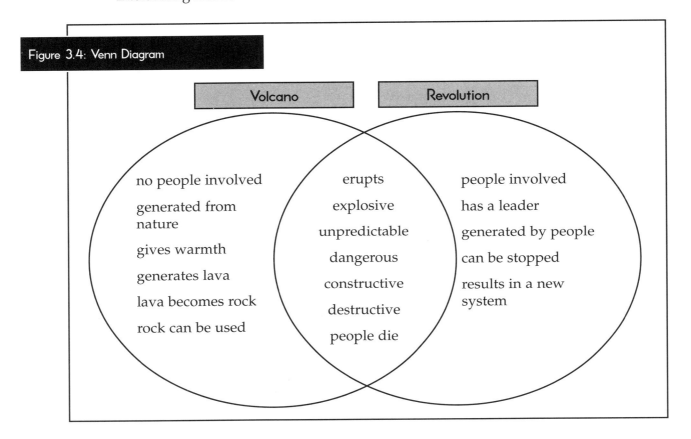

Figure 3.4: Venn Diagram

Volcano

no people involved

generated from nature

gives warmth

generates lava

lava becomes rock

rock can be used

erupts

explosive

unpredictable

dangerous

constructive

destructive

people die

Revolution

people involved

has a leader

generated by people

can be stopped

results in a new system

A Valuable Teaching Tip

When attempting to facilitate memory,
don't "pack and stack": allow time for elaboration and consolidation.

▲ Music

The use of music facilitates connections and stimulates both sides of the brain. It appeals simultaneously to both the rational and emotional parts of the brain (Teele, 1999, p. 65). The benefits involve both cognitive and non-academic areas. Music supports relaxation, creativity, self-discipline, memory, and motivation. Several studies have also shown that listening to music can stimulate the parts of the brain that are responsible for memory recall and visual imagery (Nakamura, et. al., 1999, p. 222-226, 275). Music-making activates and synchronizes neural firing patterns that orchestrate and connect multiple cognitive brain sites. Thus, the brain's efficiency and effectiveness is enhanced. The key systems impacted are well-connected between the frontal, parietal, and temporal lobes, as well as the cerebellum. The value of music-making to spatial reasoning, creativity, and generalized mathematical skills has been well established (Jensen, 2000b, p. 30).

Mathematics appears to be an academic area closely connected to music. Music relies on fractions for tempo and time divisions for pacing, octaves, and chord intervals. Further mathematical concepts that apply to music include patterns, counting, geometry, ratios and proportions, equivalent fractions, and sequencing. Sousa reports several studies supporting the relationship of music to mathematics, including one from 1998 with low socioeconomic students. The students who took music lessons from 8th through 12th grade scored significantly higher on standardized tests than those low socioeconomic students who were not involved in music. Mathematics scores more than doubled and history and geography scores increased by 40 percent (Sousa, 2001, p. 227).

Rhythm may be incorporated into many aspects of learning and at many grade levels. A statistically significant correlation between reading and spelling ability, and the ability to detect rhythm was reported by researchers working with groups of children averaging

Visualization and Verbalization

A study by Crowley and Siegler indicates that comprehension and memory increase when students receive a visual demonstration of a new learning task followed by a verbal explanation and then cemented with a reiteration of the technique in the learner's own words. The application to our teaching of this information is that observation followed by explanation and then a self explanation, or re-verbalization, allows learners to analyze and internalize the information in multiple modalities. This provides the brain with the chance to make sense of what has been seen.

Scientists know that when we observe or read something, increased activity occurs in the left frontal, temporal, occipital, and parietal lobes of the brain. These are key areas that search for meaning, patterns, and context in what we see. Without meaning, there is no learning. The subsequent verbal explanation, followed by self-explanation, allows the brain to make the necessary neural connections for meaningful learning to occur. An application for the classroom is that we can strengthen neural connections with a three-step process of observing, listening, and asking for an explanation in the learner's own words (Crowley and Siegler, 1999). A student who is made aware of his self-talk and how it impacts learning has been given a powerful lifelong learning tool.

age eight. A six-month follow-up study to determine if this relationship was causal involved two groups. The experimental group was exposed to music skill instruction in visual, auditory, and motor areas. The control group received instruction in discussion, narrative, and storytelling skills for the same length of time. At the end of the six months, the experimental group showed statistically significant gains (as compared to the control group) in reading (Douglas and Willatts, 1994).

The use of music and rhythm enhances our brain's memory system in two important ways:

- It activates our attentional systems.
- It activates multiple memory pathways for both explicit and implicit memory.

> "The more educators use music to assist in the learning of other material, the more quickly and accurately the material will become embedded. Instead of relying strictly on lecture, educators who use more movement, singing, and music will improve learning efficiency and retention" (Jensen, 2000b, p. 75).

Our attentional system is regulated by the interplay of many brain areas, including the frontal lobes, formations that surround the thalamus, and the thalamus. The thalamus functions as a gateway or organizer for incoming sensory stimuli and has been referred to as "the gateway to the cortex." Hence, listening to music or using music and rhythm with information, will strengthen one or more of our memory systems.

▲ Movement

Movement is valuable for many reasons, not the least of which is the benefit of enhancing attention. How many of us while reading, studying, or working periodically stop and stretch, walk around, or get up for a cup of coffee or soda? Our skin is our largest sensory organ and it develops from neurons. This gives it a natural and direct connection to the central nervous system. Because of this connection, movement facilitates retrieval and generates positive learning states. Movement helps increase cognitive function while also helping students get rid of "the wiggles" or kinesthetic energy. It allows for cognitive downtime which then provides an opportunity for synaptic consolidation of the information.

As a metaphor, the brain can be compared to a busy city where people are constantly moving from area to area. There is a great deal of rapid transportation along the main highways (the arteries in the brain) and along side streets (the veins in the brain). To arrive at a location, more than one way may be chosen. For the city to function efficiently, a variety of systems and networks are necessary, and these need to be constantly interacting. Jensen reminds us that intelligence is not "merely a mental phenomenon and that the mind cannot be educated without the participation of the body. The body frames the learning context for the mind. It is no longer mind or body: we now know it is the complex interplay between mind and body that engages the learning brain" (2000, p. 15).

> "Quite simply, music is good for you — physically, emotionally, and spiritually. It can strengthen the mind, unlock the creative spirit, and miraculously, even heal the body" (Jensen, 1995, p. 220).

The cerebellum stimulates many more areas of the brain than previously thought. This includes areas of the brain associated with cognitive functioning, as there is constant interaction between movement and learning. How many of us learned to ride a bike by reading a book about it? There are more neurons with axons that leave the cerebellum, communicating with other parts of the brain, than the reverse. The cerebellum (our movement-maker) does not passively wait for a command, but rather actively participates in our lives. There's also a pathway from the cerebellum back to parts of the brain involved in memory, attention, spatial guidance, rhythm, perception, and body positioning. This suggests that it is not just our conscious mind telling our "brain's engine" what to do, but the reverse is also true. "Amazingly, the part of the brain that processes movement is the same part of the brain that processes learning" (Jensen, 2000, p. 22).

Many studies have shown that children who exercise do better in school. Eric Jensen, in reporting many of these studies (1998, p. 82-87; 2000, p. 77-83), describes an interesting one from Scripps College in Claremont, California in 1991. Students who exercised 75 minutes a week demonstrated quicker reactions, thought better, and remembered more information (Michaud, 1997). Also, neuroscientists at the University of California at Irvine discovered that exercise triggers the release of a brain-derived neurotrophic factor called BDNF. This is a natural substance that enhances cognition by boosting the ability of neurons to communicate with each other (Kesslak, et al., 1998).

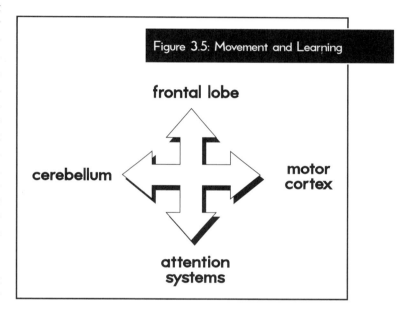

Figure 3.5: Movement and Learning

frontal lobe

cerebellum

motor cortex

attention systems

Many researchers agree that exercise reduces stress by lowering cortisol levels that have been shown to kill brain cells, especially brain cells in the hippocampus, a critical area for long-term memory formation (Jensen 2000, p. 80). Therefore, physical activity is good not only for the heart, but also for the brain because of its high need for glucose and oxygen.

For some individuals, the body may appear to be a regular barometer of cognitive events. Common expressions such as "getting a feeling in my bones" or having a "gut reaction" to a person or idea suggest this metaphor of a barometer. Kinesthetic imagery can also be valuable and may be frequently used for various aspects of cognitive development and memory.

A look at some of the world's most brilliant thinkers illustrates how kinesthetic imagery functioned as an important part of their creative process. Albert Einstein, asked to comment on his own problem-solving methods, reported: "The words or the language, as they are written or spoken, do not seem to play any role in my mechanism of thought. The psychical entities which seem to serve as elements in thought are certain signs and more or less clear images . . . The above-mentioned elements are, in my case, of visual and some of muscular type." An example of this kind of kinesthetic thinking is the fantasy Einstein had as an adolescent in which he conceived of himself riding on the end of the beam of light. This high-speed mental thrill ride allowed Einstein to experience at a visceral level the conditions under which time and space exposed their relativity (Armstrong, 1993, p. 88).

Movement can boost brain function and increase learning. Some basic strategies that can be used involve asking students to respond to an aspect of the instruction by using their bodies. A common example is asking students to raise their hands to indicate understanding. A modification can be used by asking them to hold up fingers to indicate their understanding: one finger would indicate just a little understanding, whereas raising five fingers would show complete understanding. Other examples of encouraging students to provide body answers could be activities such as the following:

- During instruction, say to the students, "If you understand what I've just said, put your finger on your nose. If you don't understand, scratch your head."

- During a grammar lesson, say to students, "If you think this sentence has parallel construction, raise your hands high like a referee indicating a touchdown. If you think the construction of the sentence is not parallel, put your hands together over your head like the peak of the house."

- Use the game of Charades to encourage students to pantomime specific concepts or terms from your lesson. This activity requires them to translate information from linguistic or logical symbol systems into bodily kinesthetic expression.

- Incorporate hands-on activities into lessons, such as using Cuisenaire rods in math, performing experiments in science, building dioramas, or expressing complex concepts by creating sculptures or collages.

- Use the body as a reference point in activities. Here are some examples:
  - ✔ Finger counting
  - ✔ Finger multiplication
  - ✔ Air writing letters and representing midline (waist), tall letters (head), and letters with a tail
  - ✔ Representing the continents with a rhythm related to body parts (activity presented on pages 161-164 in Chapter 6)

Remember that movement helps students build more durable memories. The sensorimotor stimulation helps grab attention and encourage motivation, consequently boosting memory. Movement plays a major role in cognition and memory as there are many more axons that carry impulses away from the cerebellum to areas of cognition than the reverse.

Specific Procedures

A variety of procedures will be incorporated within the strategies presented in Chapters 4-8 of this book. These strategies include mnemonics — memory tricks that facilitate recall of information, facts, or procedures. Different categories of mnemonics will be incorporated throughout the strategy suggestions. The strategies presented are not designed as a cookbook approach, but rather as suggestions to guide you in helping students develop particular strategies for specific situations. Adapt and modify the strategies to increase their appropriateness for different age levels or learning situations.

Format

As educators, we must be aware of the format used during instruction so that we recognize how students learned the information. It is valuable to provide the same stimulation for assessment. If the stimulation or format of the assessment is going to differ, it may be necessary to help some students with this transition. Many students are able to make this transition easily and effortlessly. But some students with learning differences learn in ways that are more format bound, and such students need specific structured help with this type of transition.

Here are two general guidelines:

▲ Teach a new concept using the format that best facilitates the ability of the student to grasp the concept.

▲ Review the concept using the format that will be necessary for testing, helping the student make the appropriate transitions as necessary.

The issue of format is a common reason students may appear to have memory problems. For example:

▲ A student studies her spelling words all week with a parent but then fails her spelling test in class.

- *Why did this happen?*
  Practice during the week consisted of verbal practice: while doing the dishes or driving the car, Mom dictated the words and the student spelled each verbally. However, in the classroom, the teacher dictated the words for the student to write. This difference in modality format necessitates a different perceptual preparation.

▲ At home, the student writes spelling words in a practice test with 100% accuracy but fails the test in class.

- *Why did this happen?*
  While writing spelling words at home, Mom waits until the student finishes one word before giving the next word. In the classroom, the teacher progresses at a given rate and the student cannot process and retrieve the sequence of letters fast enough. This is a difference in speed format.

▲ A student recites the multiplication facts perfectly for Dad at home, but is unable to pass the test at school on the same facts.

- *Why did this happen?*
  There are several possibilities and one needs to determine if the format changed in modality, speed, or level of distraction.

Complexity and Difficulty
It is important to discriminate between the difficulty of a task and increasing its complexity. These differences should be kept in mind as you expand and vary activities suggested within this book.

Complexity and *difficulty* are words that have often been used interchangeably to describe different mental operations. However, there is a critical difference between these two concepts. The concept of *difficulty* refers to the amount of effort that the learner must expand within a given level of complexity to complete the task. It is possible for a learning task to increase in difficulty without increasing its complexity. An increase in difficulty would involve increasing the number of responses required, increasing the output level (retrieval instead of recognition), or increasing the number of repetitions required. A decrease in difficulty involves the opposite: decreasing the number of required responses, decreasing the output level, or decreasing the number of repetitions or the chunk size.

The concept of *complexity* describes the level of thought or the thought process that is being used. This can be related to levels of higher order thinking skills such as those described in Bloom's Taxonomy. Strategies that encourage students to compare and contrast, or choose an option and defend their choice are examples of increasing complexity. Strategies that use a lower or decreased level in the Taxonomy decrease the complexity of the task.

The six levels of Bloom's Taxonomy of the cognitive domain, in decreasing order of complexity are represented in Figure 3.6 (Bloom, 1976; Armstrong, 2000, p. 117).

Figure 3.6: Levels of Bloom's Taxonomy

Level	Definition	Example
Evaluation	appraise, assess, judge	determining the value or utility of information using a set of standards
Synthesis	imagine, compose, design, infer	weaving together component parts into a coherent whole
Analysis	analyze, contrast, distinguish, deduce	discovering and differentiating the component parts of a larger whole
Application	practice, calculate, apply	the capacity to transfer knowledge from one setting to another
Comprehension	summarize, discuss, explain	the ability to translate, paraphrase, interpret, or extrapolate material
Knowledge	define, label, recall	rote memory skills: knowing facts, terms, procedures, classification systems

Teaching Tips

To help students increase memory efficiency, teach them to do the following:

▲ Identify the task format.

▲ Identify the type of memory demand.

▲ Develop a strategy that matches.

When a memory challenge occurs, analyze for the breakdown point considering the various components of the memory function:

▲ sensory memory

▲ short-term memory

▲ working memory

▲ consolidation

▲ storage

▲ retrieval

Above all:

▲ Grab attention with intensity, novelty, and movement.

▲ Make connections and develop patterns.

▲ Value the importance of strategies as a lifelong skill.

▲ Have fun!

Don't just strive to
Motivate your students.

Instead,
Lead them to an
Addiction
Of their own:
Greatness.

> Neurons that fire together,
> wire together.

Review

In Chapter 1, we reviewed parts of the brain using a recognition activity (the multiple choice format on page 6) and a retrieval activity (the short answers on page 8). These activities relied on semantic memory; to form such memories requires practice and rehearsal, and hence, is an unnatural way to learn and remember things. In contrast, contextual memory is more natural because it helps to integrate information within patterns. The formation of this natural memory is motivated by curiosity, novelty, and expectations and encourages "the information [to be] stored in a fabric or weave of 'mental space'" (Jensen, 1995, p. 262). In the consolidation activity on the next page, we will review the parts of the brain using a more global, pattern-oriented format.

Review Activity

Create a visual organizer, using colored pens or pencils, to represent the parts of the brain that we have discussed. The format has been started. Complete the visual organizer using these parts of the brain. They are listed in alphabetical order.

▲ amygdala   ▲ hippocampus

▲ brain stem   ▲ limbic system

▲ cerebellum   ▲ occipital lobe

▲ cortex   ▲ parietal lobe

▲ frontal lobe   ▲ temporal lobe

A visual organizer in hierarchy format is started below. You may use this format if desired. Use the information in Chapter 1 to check your answers if necessary.

The Brain

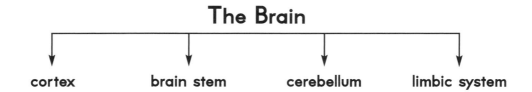

cortex   brain stem   cerebellum   limbic system

Activity 3.1 Examples (pages 40-41)

Types of Memory Tasks

Following is a sample completed chart from the activity on pages 40-41. Your examples may differ from the ones suggested. Each of these types of memory tasks could be structured for different memory components. For example, a visual memory task of recalling a spelling word could be considered *short-term*, *long-term*, or *retrieval*. A different example of tracing a spelling word would be *sensory input*. The motor memory example of forming cursive letters consistently and neatly is listed as *long-term* and *retrieval* because the example stated "consistently." A short-term example would have been copying a model of a letter. In deciding which type of memory component to select, base your answer on the *specific classroom-based example* you choose.

Type of Memory	Description: This is memory for . . .	Classroom-based Example	Sensory Memory	Short-term Memory	Long-term Memory	Retrieval Memory
Visual Memory	Recognizing something previously seen	Recalling the correct spelling of a word		X	X	X
Auditory Memory	Recognizing something previously heard	Recalling and completing a verbal direction	X	X		X
Episodic Memory	Events learned or experienced in the past	Answering questions about a chapter read days ago or writing what you did last summer			X	X
Automatic Memory	Input that is so fast you don't have to think about what you need	Writing your name		X	X	X
Procedural Memory	Finding stored facts and skills you need in a timely manner	Recalling a strategy previously used			X	X
Procedural Memory	Knowing how to perform an action in sequence	Remembering and using the steps for addition or multiplication			X	X

Activity 3.1 Examples (pages 40-41), *continued*

Type of Memory	Description: This is memory for . . .	Classroom-based Example	Sensory Memory	Short-term Memory	Long-term Memory	Retrieval Memory
Motor Memory	Knowing how to perform an action with your muscles	Remembering and using the steps for addition or multiplication			X	X
Associative Memory	Information that is stored together	Recalling the dates for the signing of the Declaration of Independence			X	X
Factual Memory	Knowledge	Recalling the causes of the Civil War			X	X
Interpretive Memory	Organizing and pulling together language information	Summarizing a paragraph from a chapter recently read	X	X		X
Recognition Memory	Knowing that something is familiar	Walking in the classroom and going directly to your own desk	X		X	
Simultaneous Memory	Access to multiple facts or procedures all at once	Writing a factual paragraph, including correct facts, spelling, punctuation, and capitalization		X	X	X
Cumulative Memory	Access to what was learned earlier as a basis for new information	Progressing in foreign language class	X	X	X	X
Categorical Memory	Classifying knowledge into pre-existing groups	Recalling information about many mammals	X		X	X
Sequential Memory	Information or procedures containing components in a certain order	Recalling the sequence of steps for long division from yesterday's lesson	X		X	X

Language Arts Strategies: Reading and Spelling

The suggested strategies in this chapter will provide ideas and recommendations for practicing various skill components related to reading and spelling. The goal of the strategies is to utilize elaborative rehearsal that will increase the students' consolidation, and ultimately, recall and retrieval. The assumption is made that basic reading and spelling concepts have been previously taught to the students and that the activities in this chapter will be used to enhance consolidation of the concepts and skills. The suggestions are not designed as a complete systematic teaching program, and it is important to be cognizant of developmental levels to ensure that students have the necessary background to elaborate upon each concept.

Phonological Awareness

Phonological awareness involves sensitivity to sounds within words for structure and meaning. This critical foundation facilitates understanding of the language patterns necessary for decoding (reading) and encoding (spelling). In general, moving beyond pure rote memorization helps develop memory patterns that are more readily consolidated. This is especially true for phonological awareness skills, as rote memorization generally prepares the student to perform the activity at a given moment in time. It may not enhance a generalized awareness of sounds within words or enable a student to process sounds or patterns more efficiently. The activities in this chapter endeavor to enhance a student's awareness of patterns within our language system by using a variety of memory facilitators.

Phonological awareness is a vital skill that enables a conscious awareness that words are composed of separate sounds. It is the ability to identify, manipulate, and remember strings of speech sounds. Phonological processing ability accounts for much of the difference between good readers and poor readers and between novices who will learn to read easily and those who will struggle (Moats, 2000, p. 42).

The highest level of phonological awareness involves automaticity and a facility in self-correcting errors when reading or spelling. When students plod through a reading task with only minimal phonological awareness and manipulation skills, they struggle with comprehension and read slowly. Their spelling is generally poor and can be characterized by confusions such as *towbeller/bell tower*, *runroader/roadrunner*, *reserve/reverse*, and *Pacific/specific*.

The human brain is designed to pay attention to the meaning of the message between speakers, not to the specific sounds in words. Becoming aware of the speech sounds in our language is a process of exposure and understanding. We must acquire information about a level of language processing that we constantly use although we generally do not have to dissect the language. "Words and phonemes are segments in a stream of language that flows continuously without pauses for acoustic breaks. Speech sounds are unsegmented in words; that is, they are not spoken as separate units. Speakers almost never say words as a series of discrete segments, and if they do, the segments in isolation do not sound as they do in words . . . Our brains know what is coming next in a word and make adjustments in articulation of individual segments so that the sequence is amalgamated into one speech gesture — a word" (Moats, 2000, p.22).

Figure 4.l: 9 Phonological Awareness Levels

Early Literacy Auditory Levels
1. Rhyming and Alliteration
2. Sound Awareness and Rhyming Production
3. Segmenting Sentences into Words

More Advanced Auditory Levels
4. Auditory Blending and Analysis
5. Syllable Segmentation
6. Phoneme Segmentation
7. Phoneme Manipulation

More Advanced Levels Integrating Auditory Activities with Letters/Words
8. Syllable manipulation
9. Higher Levels of Phoneme and Syllable Manipulation: Sound Games Using Vocabulary and Humor

---

It is important to keep in mind that phonological awareness skills must be initially taught with auditory input and without sound/symbol relationships. The reader desiring a more thorough analysis and explanation of phonological awareness development is referred to other sources such as *The Source for Dyslexia and Dysgraphia* (Richards 1999), *Speech to Print: Language Essentials for Teachers* (Moats 2000) and *A Basic Guide to Understanding, Assessing, and Teaching Phonological Awareness* (Torgesen 2000). A sequence of phonological awareness levels is listed in Figure 4.1 (Richards, 1999, p. 109).

Repetition and practice are essential for our brains to build the necessary networks and remember how to manipulate the sounds. Some students require more practice than others for this aspect of phonological memory to become automatic. Critical components to incorporate within activities for phonological awareness development are as follows:

▲ Students must experience the concept or process and manipulate the sounds: not perform the activity as a rote task.

▲ Repetition is important but the repetition should be goal directed.

▲ Students need auditory input and do not develop phonological awareness and manipulation skills through visual activities such as workbook pages or worksheets.

▲ Students must understand the prerequisite concepts.
  • Be cognizant of developmental levels within each chosen activity.
  • For example, if a student confuses *beginning* and *end* it will be necessary to train the meaning of these words before practicing activities that depend on their understanding.

▲ Pictures and cue cards are valuable to help enhance a student's active working memory, i.e., his ability to hang on to multiple components while performing the task.

▲ The more concrete and structured the activity, the easier it will be for students to develop automatic patterns.

▲ The fewer the components within a task, the easier it will be to process the sounds.
  • Less demand on the active working memory system will facilitate the efficiency of the sensory memory system.

▲ As students achieve facility and automaticity, it is then necessary to slowly increase the difficulty of the task.

Activity Suggestions for Phonological Awareness

These sample activities are suggestions for increasing phonological awareness skills. Adapt the activities to your students' developmental and interest levels as needed. Follow these suggestions to enhance the activities:

▲ Be creative!

▲ Modify the activities to fit the needs of your curriculum.

▲ At all times, remember to respect the age-appropriate needs of your students. Often older students may be particularly sensitive to activities that appear "babyish."

▲ As a convention within these activities, letter names appear in **boldface**, and letter sounds are written in brackets, as in /t/.
   • Caution: Pronounce isolated sounds clearly, i.e., say /b/, not /buh/.

Table (or Standing) Activities for Segmenting Sounds Within Words

Purpose: to provide a fun activity for students to reinforce and review the concepts of sound positioning and sound segmenting using pictures to reduce the demands on active working memory.

Preparation: Distribute pictures of items that represent one-syllable words, such as *hat, sun, book, mat, dog, bike,* and *bun.*

Tasks:

1. *Sound Isolation:* Students take turns holding up a picture and stating the first sound of the word. A student might hold up a card and say, "The first sound in *hat* is /h/" (initial sound).
   ✔ *Repeat the activity using final sounds:* Students take turns holding up a picture and stating the last sound of the word; for example, "The last sound in *hat* is /t/."
   ✔ *Repeat the activity using medial sounds:* Students take turns holding up a picture and stating the middle sound of the word. A student might say, "The middle sound in *hat* is /a/."

2. *Blending:* The teacher places six or seven one-syllable word picture cards in front of the students and says the sounds that make up one of the words (/d/–/o/–/g/). The student selects the picture that represents the word.
   ✔ To decrease the difficulty, have students make their choice from among two or three pictures instead of from six or seven.
   ✔ To increase the difficulty, provide more pictures from which to choose or eliminate pictures completely, thus making it a retrieval activity.

3. *Segmenting Sounds — Single-Syllable Words*
   ✔ The student selects a picture and segments the sounds. For example, choosing *bun,* he says, "/b/–/u/–/n/" or choosing *bike,* he says, "/b/–/ī/–/k/."
   ✔ Segmenting and blending may be combined by having students work in pairs or groups: one student segments and the other blends that word while the first student provides feedback.

4. *Segmenting Syllables — Multisyllabic Words*
   ✔ The teacher says a syllable: /ab/ or /prō/.
   ✔ Facilitate the activity by beginning with a syllable that creates a prefix.
   ✔ Students segment the syllable into individual sounds: /a - b/ or /p - r - ō/.
   ✔ The teacher elicits suggestions of words that begin with the syllable.
   • /ab-/: *absolute, abandon, abbreviation, abdomen*
   • /prō/: *prologue, probation, probe*

5. *Blending Sounds from a Syllable and Generating Complete Multisyllable Words:* The teacher says sounds that create a syllable: /c – a – m/ or /s – c – ō – p/.
   ✔ The student blends the sounds: /cam/ or /scōp/.
   ✔ The teacher elicits suggestions of words that begin or end with the target syllable.
   • /cam-/: *camouflage, camel, camera*
   • /-scōp/: *telescope, microscope, kaleidoscope, periscope*

Note: Activities 4 and 5 are valuable for older students as they may resent using only simple, one-syllable words for practice.

Movement Activities Using Pictures

Purpose: to provide a fun activity which reinforces students' abilities to listen to sounds within words and to determine sameness and difference.

Preparation: Select students to each hold a picture of an item that represents a one-syllable word such as *hat, mat, bike, sun, bun, bag, nine, nose, rose.* (To decrease the difficulty, begin with only three words but progress to a larger number of choices.)

Tasks
1. *Rhyming:* Three students come to the front. Each selects a word. Two students select words that rhyme and the third student selects a word that does not rhyme with either of the other two. Each holds up his picture. Other students identify which one is different or which one is "odd man out."
   ✔ *hat, mat, sun* (sun)
   ✔ *sun, bike, bun* (bike)

2. *Isolation:* Three students come to the front. Each selects a word. Two students select words that begin with the same sound, and the third student selects a word that begins with a different sound. Each holds up her picture. Other students identify which one is different or which is the "odd man out." This activity can also be used to isolate final and medial sounds.
   ✔ Initial sounds:
   • *bun, hat, bike* (hat)
   • *nine, nose, sun* (sun)
   ✔ Final sounds:
   • *bag, sun, nine* (bag)
   • *rose, nine, nose* (nine)
   ✔ Medial sounds:
   • *bike, nine, nose* (nose)
   • *bag, bun, mat* (bun)

Filler Activities to Reinforce Phonological Awareness

These are simply examples; feel free to expand upon their basic design:

1. *Line-up Activities:* Students line up by the initial sounds in their names.
   - Ask all children whose names start with the /t/ sound to line up.
   - Ask, "Is there a student whose name starts with the same sound as Susie's?"

2. *Identification Activities:* Have all children wearing a shirt that has a color that starts with a certain sound (/b/) to stand up.

3. *Singing:* Modify songs to reinforce the concept of playing with sounds.
   - ✔ Sing "If You Think You Know This Word" to the tune of "If You're Happy and You Know It, Clap Your Hands" (Yopp, 1992, p. 699) (Richards, 1999, p. 121).
   - ✔ Sing "Who Has a /d/ Word to Share with Us?" to the tune of "Jimmy Cracked Corn and I Don't Care" (Yopp, 1992, p. 700) (Richards, 1999, p. 123).
   - ✔ Sing "What's The Sound That Starts These Words?" to the tune of "Old McDonald Had a Farm" (Richards, 1999, p. 124).
   - ✔ Sing "I Like to Eat, Eat, Eat" to the tune of "Three Little Angels" (Richards, 1999, p. 137).

Syllable and Sound Manipulation Activities[1]

Purpose: to provide students with practice in recognizing and manipulating syllables. The general principle in effect here is that recognition precedes retrieval.

Preparation/Considerations:
- ✔ These activities will be easier for students if they are first presented with a multiple-choice format from which to select their responses.
- ✔ As they progress in skill and awareness, the format can be changed so that they need to retrieve their answers without the benefit of provided choices.
- ✔ As they become accustomed to the activity and format, students can create words and phrases for other students to manipulate.

Tasks:
1. *Spoonerisms:* Select a phrase from a paragraph related to current content students are studying and have the students create spoonerism phrases.
   - ✔ Spoonerisms are phrases, sentences, or words that have some sounds swapped. This often happens by accident, especially if the speaker is speaking quickly. However, many students with learning differences, and especially those with sequencing issues, may also experience Spoonerisms. Purposefully creating Spoonerisms enables students to practice manipulating sounds within words while having fun and also enhancing their phonetic flexibility. It provides a tool for more active learning.
   - ✔ Spoonerisms can include phonetic transposition, transposition of large parts of words or whole words, and transposition of initial sounds within a word. Some Spoonerisms make sense, linguistically, as well as the original phrase (go and take a shower/go and shake a tower), whereas others do not (the speed of light/the leed of spight). Examples of Spoonerisms are on the next page.

[1](Richards 1999, p. 146-151; Lederer 1990; fun-with-words.com)

- Spoonerize the first and last names of classmates: John Dear (*Don Jeer*), Jennifer Jordash (*Jornifer Jendash*)
- Fighting a liar (*lighting a fire*)
- You missed my history lesson (*You hissed my listory messon*).
- Wave the sails (*Save the whales*).
- Come and look out the window (*Come and wook out the lindow*).
- To bridge the gap (*To gap the bridge*)
- Criminal (*Crinimal*)

2. *Sniglets:* Students combine 2 separate or unrelated word parts to create a new word which they then define. This is a valuable and fun activity for the older student who needs extra work in sound manipulations.
   - ✔ *Aquadexterous*: possessing ability to turn the bathtub faucet on and off with your toes
   - ✔ *Rovealert*: when a dog starts a neighborhood network of barking
   - ✔ *Gyroped*: a kid who cannot resist spinning around on a diner stool
   - ✔ *Chalktrauma*: a body's reaction to someone running his fingernails down a chalkboard

3. *Ink Pink Games:* One student (or team) offers a concise, clear definition and a second student (or team) must translate that definition into 2 words that rhyme. The first student indicates the number of syllables required for each word in the answer: "Ink Pink" for one-syllable words, "Inky Pinky" for two-syllable words, "Iinkity Pinkity" for three-syllable words, etc. (Lederer, 1990, p. 135; Richards, 1999, p. 149-150). Here are some suggestions for using Ink Pinks:
   - ✔ Create a multiple choice format to teach the task.
   - ✔ Use retrieval activities once students are more familiar with the manipulations.
   - ✔ If they become "stuck," provide examples leading to the correct response for one of the words, as in Figure 4.2 for the definition "an inexpensive land vehicle."
   - ✔ Examples of "Ink Pink":
     - grass strength (*lawn brawn*)
     - an inexpensive land vehicle (*cheap Jeep*)
     - meat robber (*beef thief*)
     - stupid finger (*dumb thumb*)
   - ✔ Examples of "Inky Pinky":
     - a comical hare (*funny bunny*)
     - an untippable piece of furniture (*stable table*)

Figure 4.2: Ink Pink Dialog Cues

Student:	An old car
Teacher:	You're right, a car is a land vehicle; but I'm thinking of a different word that is a land vehicle.
Student:	A truck
Teacher:	Another good word. But, not the one I'm thinking of. I'm thinking of a word that is a vehicle that goes on land as well as on roads.
Student:	Could it be jeep?
Teacher:	Right! Now, we need a word that rhymes with *Jeep* and has how many syllables?
Student:	One
Teacher:	Right. Who can think of a word that has one syllable and rhymes with Jeep and means "inexpensive"?
Student:	Cheap. Oh — a cheap Jeep!

- vegetable for talking bird (*parrot carrot*)
- unreliable dill (*fickle pickle*)
- gruesome tale (*gory story*)

✔ Examples of "Inkity Pinkity"
- elastic bushes (*rubbery shrubbery*)
- how to save the environment (*pollution solution*)
- display of sweets (*confection collection*)
- frozen bike (*icycle bicycle*)

✔ Examples of "Inkitity Pinkitity"
- bubbly teenager (*effervescent adolescent*)
- royal cloth (*imperial material*)
- star war (*constellation altercation*)

✔ *Doggie "Inky-Pinky"*: the challenge is to categorize the answers. In this case all answers contain either the full or abbreviated name of a dog breed, although they may contain one, two, or three syllables. As before, the two words of the answer must rhyme and both contain the same number of syllables.
- damper sporting dog (wetter setter)
- cup for a toy (pug mug)
- funny-looking large working dog (goofy Newfie)
- Southern home for a non-sporting dog (Dalmatian plantation)

4. *Word ladders:* The task is to change one letter at each step, keeping the other letters in the same order, with a goal of changing the first word into another word that means the opposite.

✔ Use a vertical list with an arrow between each word pointing to the next word.
- To make the activity more concrete, use a graphic such as a picture of a ladder.
- Draw a ladder and have the students place a different word on each rung of the ladder, as in Figure 4.3.

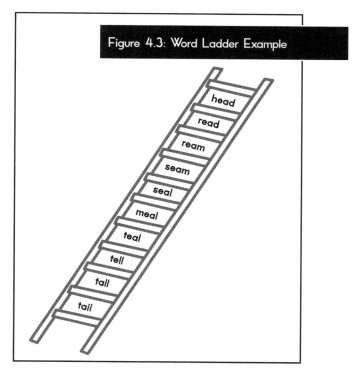

Figure 4.3: Word Ladder Example

head
read
ream
seam
seal
meal
teal
tell
tall
tail

✔ Select words from the students' typical reading materials.
- Decrease the difficulty by using fewer words and providing cues, such as the final target word and/or the number of steps to be used.
- To increase difficulty, use more words and provide fewer or no cues.

✔ Examples of sequences
- lead — gold (3 steps)
  lead, load, goad, gold

- try — win (4 steps)
  try, toy, ton, tin, win
- flour — bread (6 steps)
  flour, floor, flood, blood, brood, broad, bread

Where to Start?

Looking for suggestions on where to start with these new strategies? Here are some ideas.

Remember: It is always critical to take into account your students' developmental levels and learning styles. Where you choose to begin may differ from these suggestions based on the specific needs of your students.

▲ Suggestions for early-elementary students:
- standing activities using pictures
- modifying songs to reinforce the concept of playing with sounds

▲ Suggestions for upper-elementary students:
- segmenting sounds
- blending sounds

▲ Suggestions for middle-school students:
- segmenting syllables with multisyllabic words
- blending sounds from a syllable and generating multisyllabic words

▲ Suggestions for high school students:
- spoonerisms
- sniglets

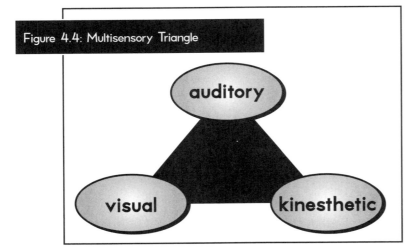

Figure 4.4: Multisensory Triangle

Sound/Symbol Correspondence

Often the traditional exposure and practice provided by reading programs enable students to learn the associations between sounds and symbols. However, some students, especially those who learn differently, may require more exposure to form the important associations and consolidate the matches. For sound/symbol correspondence to become automatic, students must be able to form reliable associations between the information that is *auditory* (what they hear), *visual* (what they see), and *kinesthetic* (what they say and write), as represented in Figure 4.4, The Multisensory Triangle.

Key Words

A common technique involving key words can be used to cue a relationship between a sound and its symbol. In this strategy, a given sound of a word, usually the initial sound, represents the target symbol. Consistency is important and repetitive use of this technique has been shown to develop automaticity in many programs (Gillingham, 1998), (Slingerland, 1977), (Richards, 1997). In the key word technique, a consistent word is provided for each target sound and students practice linking auditory, visual, or kinesthetic input until the associations become automatic. This repetition in a systemized and structured manner helps establish critical memory links, and then the key word easily functions as a cue that aids retrieval of the sound/symbol association.

It is important to realize, however, that just memorizing the sound (or sounds) that goes with each letter is not sufficient for development of phonological awareness, phonetic analysis, or reading fluency. Automaticity of sound/symbol correspondence is only one step in the hierarchy, although a very important and critical step.

Visual Mnemonics

Memory Foundations for Reading (MFR) is a program to teach key words by combining principles of visual mnemonics with sentence cues (Richards, 1997). Some students find the additional associations and visuals useful in establishing memory patterns. For some, visual mnemonics are easier to retain and retrieve than a paired link of a word and a sound. While MFR provides ready-made visuals and related sentence cues, alternate pictures can also be created using different key words.

To remember sounds for the short vowels, a picture is used showing a little boy with an apple sitting on an umbrella. The sentence cue is "Apple Ed is on umbrella." Many students can easily visualize the picture which then leads them to recall the sentence, "Apple Ed is on umbrella." Then they have a tool, such as the word *apple* to help recall and retrieve the sound: the short vowel **a** has the same sound that begins the word apple: **a** – apple – /a/.

Elaboration and development of multiple neural networks can be encouraged as students practice a variety of activities to reinforce the associations. The activities need to help them link the sound to the symbol using different sensory channels.

Neural Network Development Activities for Sound/Symbol Associations

1. *Auditory Links*
   ✔ The student hears the sound and says the letter name.
   - *Teacher:* What letter says /i/ (as in the word *in*)?
   - *Student:* The letter **i**
   ✔ The student hears the letter name and says the sound.
   - *Teacher:* What sound does the letter **a** make?
   - *Student:* The sound is /a/ (as in the word *apple*).

2. *Visual Links*
   ✔ The student sees a card with a letter and says that letter's name.
   - *Teacher:* (Shows a card with the letter **z**.)
   - *Student:* **Z** says /z/.

✔ The student sees a card with a letter and says the sound that goes with the letter (or for more elaboration, the student may say the sound and the key word).
  • *Teacher:* (Shows a card with the letter **m**.)
  • *Student:* **M** says /m/. (Or, "**m**, /m/, *monkey*")

3. *Kinesthetic Links*
  ✔ The student hears a letter name (or sound) and writes that letter in the air while saying the name (or sound).
    • *Teacher:* The letter is **j**.
    • *Student:* (Writes **j** in the air or says, "**J** says /j/."

  ✔ The student sees a letter card and writes that letter in the air while saying its name and sound (and keyword if desired).
    • Teacher: (Shows card with **ch**.)
    • Student: (Writes **ch** in air.) **Ch** says /ch/. (Or "**ch**, /ch/, *chicken*")

4. Additional activities to reinforce the links:
  ✔ Role-play the mnemonic phrases incorporating the key words.
  ✔ Color the pictures related to the visual mnemonics.
  ✔ Create a picture using a letter as a base for the picture and occasionally use this picture instead of a letter card in the visual links.
  ✔ Create a song, rhythm, or rap using the mnemonic phrase and have the written phrase readily visible while singing the song.

Figure 4.5: MFR Picture Example

h**oo**k the m**oo**n
This illustration represents two sounds for the letter combination /oo/.

The first of the three MFR sets presents key words for the primary isolated consonant and vowel sounds. In all, the program presents three interconnecting sets to represent additional patterns among sound symbol correspondences. For example, the letter combination **oo** has two different sounds, the type of pattern represented by set 2: letters with multiple sounds, as in Figure 4.5. The patterns represented by set 3 of MFR provide students with mnemonics for those sounds that have multiple spellings. Example phrases of such patterns include the phrase "Ed has bread" or "money umbrella." When using sets 2 and 3, it is important to go beyond the basic association between sound and symbol and fully discuss how the structure and/or the position of the letter or letter combinations influence the sound. To reinforce sound/symbol correspondence, you may wish to use a visual mnemonic program such as MFR, create your own visual mnemonics, or use individual key words with a corresponding picture for each. Select target sounds based on your students' needs.

The Spelling Process

The necessary components for spelling efficiency involve more than just memorization of the word or the sequence of the letters within the word. To represent these components, the multisensory triangle can be modified, as in Figure 4.6.

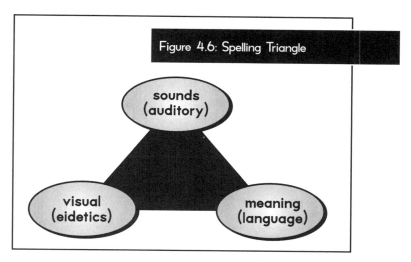

Figure 4.6: Spelling Triangle

The Auditory Component

The auditory component of spelling is critical to enable the student to efficiently hear the sounds within the word, a necessary component before being able to segment the sounds. To spell a word, a student must first segment the word into syllables and then segment each syllable into individual sounds. Then the sounds can be associated with the appropriate letters. For some students, this process is easier to perform in an auditory rather than a written mode. Many of our clinic students complain that they "knew" their spelling words with great accuracy in the car on the way to school when Mom was drilling them; however, they received a low grade on their written spelling tests in the classroom. The reason for this discrepancy often involves the format of the retrieval situation. For some students, their learning may be more efficient in one format (auditory) but they may need to produce the information in a different format (written) in the classroom. In such situations, have the students practice the spelling words in their most efficient learning format but then, once the words are learned, have them practice spelling using the format or situation in which the knowledge will need to be produced in the classroom. Being aware of the importance of format is a necessary component for identifying the breakdown point when a student has difficulty remembering spelling. The same process, regarding the format of the task, is applicable to other academic areas besides spelling.

The Visual Component

The visual component is critical for the process of spelling. This involves recognition and retrieval of eidetics, an important processing skill that incorporates perceptual efficiency; recognition of letters, word parts, and whole words; and the ability to maintain consistency in remembering and using these units. When working with the visual component, it is valuable to ensure that the student understands and can manipulate syllables and the morphological units of words, the small parts of words that are impor-

> *Morphology* is defined as the study of meaningful units of language and how they are combined in word formations.

tant for enhancing and carrying meaning. Students benefit by having an automatic eidetic recognition of units such as *-ing* or *-tion*. At the higher levels of development, eidetics, or visual retrieval memory, is the "capacity to hear or think of a particular word and mobilize an accurate visual image of its spelling. That image contains a correct sequence and a proper overall configuration" (Levine, 1998, p. 389). An important difference between reading and spelling is that spelling requires full visual association, whereas reading can be successful with only partial visual association. Therefore, the process of spelling results in much more stress for the visual memory and active working memory systems than the process of decoding for reading.

While these labels are not vital for students to know, it is important for teachers to understand the critical nature of word parts in visual eidetic development, as this area creates many difficulties and confusions for students. The teacher who understands language and how children are using it can give clear, accurate, and organized information about sounds, words, and sentences. This leads to systematic structured teaching and helps students form critical patterns. "The teacher who knows language will understand why students say and write the puzzling things that they do and will be able to judge what a particular student knows and needs to know about the printed word" (Moats 2000, p. 1).

Figure 4.7: Some Useful Definitions

▲ **Homonyms**
Two or more words spelled and pronounced alike, but with different meanings, as in a *pool* of water or a game of *pool*. Here are other examples:
- I spent last *evening evening* out a pile of dirt.
- There was a *row* among the oarsmen about how to *row*.

▲ **Homophones**
Two or more words pronounced alike, but different in meaning, derivation, or spelling: *to, too, two*.

▲ **Homographs**
Two or more words spelled alike, but different in origin, meaning, or pronunciation, as in *conduct*, the noun (watch your conduct), and *conduct*, the verb (he will conduct the orchestra). Here are some other examples:
- A farm can *produce produce*.
- The dump was so full it had to *refuse refuse*.
- The *present* is a good time to *present* the present.

The Meaning/Language Component

The meaning/language component of spelling is critical so that the task of spelling moves beyond mere rote memorization and into its overall purpose: being able to spell accurately while doing something else. This requires a growing storehouse of words that are available for automatic retrieval. This then "liberates memory, attention, and cognition to engage in more sophisticated intellectual and creative enterprises" (Levine, 1998, p. 389). The meaning/language component coordinates the word parts with the meaning of the total word, and ultimately its use within the context. This is where activities that deal with homonyms, homophones, and homographs are important. Figure 4.7 lists definitions and examples of these terms.

Mel Levine (2002) discusses the relationship between spelling and memory in stating the following:

> Spelling is sometimes considered a triumph of visual memory, since it seems to require recalling the appearance of a word. We now know that this is not at all the case; most spelling occurs through one's knowledge of how

language works . . . There is evidence to suggest that visual memory is actually our built-in spellchecker. You write down a word, then glance at it, and realize it does or does not look quite right. If it doesn't look familiar, you make some modifications. Thus, the visual feedback that you receive comparing a word on paper to your memory of how the word looks provides a second chance and thereby ensures accuracy — if it works (p. 162-3).

> The right hemisphere of our brain tends to organize visual and global information while the left hemisphere of our brain tends to control the processing of sounds and sequential information (Richards 2001, p. 8) (Schacter 1996, p. 54).

Spelling Strategies

Strategies for the auditory component of spelling involve the same types of activities as recommended for phonological awareness and sound/symbol correspondence. Strategy suggestions for the language component are presented in the Vocabulary section of Chapter 5.

Strategies for the visual component revolve around the concept of visualization. Visualization is an efficient memory hook that enhances retrieval because it incorporates visual and spatial skills. Movement related to the concept of the word(s) can also be integrated within visualization activities, ideally involving both sides of the body. Multisensory activities are valuable, as they enable the visual strategies to link the processing components within different areas of the brain by associating the auditory and/or kinesthetic with the visual information. Remember the Big Four Memory Facilitators as you engage students visually:

> Enhancing a student's use of the mind's eye enhances comprehension.

▲ **Active Learning:** Encourage students to be actively involved with the strategies.

▲ **Structure:** Structure the task, paying attention to developmental levels and readiness.

▲ **Systematic:** Present new material in a systematic manner so students can more easily form patterns.

▲ **Sensory:** Involve different sensory systems.

Strategies to Enhance Visual Eidetics

These sample activities are designed to provide suggestions for teachers and parents to adapt to the level needed. Be creative and modify the activities to fit the needs of your curriculum.

Visualizations Using Spelling Mnemonics

▲ *Identify a tricky part of a given word and create a cue to remember that part.*
  ✔ **Ninety** — The **e** is the tricky part: associate the word *ninety* with the word *nine* as in the sentence, "*Nine* typewriters typed *ninety* times."

  ✔ **Pajamas** — The middle stressed vowel retains its sound, but the other two are reduced to a schwa sound (/uh/): associate the syllables with a familiar word as in, "*Pa* and *ma* wear *pajamas*."

✔ **Beach/Beech** — These words are homophones. Create a sentence for each word, associating the tricky part (the vowels **ee** or **ea**) with a related word.
  - A b**ea**ch is by the s**ea**.
  - A b**ee**ch tr**ee** is in my yard.

▲ *Analyze the word components.*
  ✔ Find a small word within the larger more troublesome word.
   - Know**ledge** gives you the **edge.**
   - **Hide** from the **hide**ous monster.

  ✔ Consider the word's derivation: Sometimes it is easier and more logical to spell the shorter, more common form of the word and create a sentence that relates the target word to another word based on its root.
   - Large **muscles** make you very **muscular** (**musc-** in *muscle — muscular*).
   - **Scholastics** are for **scholars** in **school** (**schol-** in *scholastics — scholars*).

▲ *Use alternate mnemonics for words that are generally tricky.*
  ✔ Mispronounce the syllables to focus on the individual components.
   - **Wednesday:** Wed – nes – day
   - **together:** to – get – her

  ✔ Create an acronym so that the first letter of each word in a sentence spells out the target word.
   - **A r**at **i**n **t**he **h**ouse **m**ight **e**at **t**he **i**ce **c**ream (*arithmetic*).
   - **B**alls **a**lways **z**oom **a**cross **a** **r**oom (*bazaar*).

  ✔ Group words with the same unusual spellings together in a single sentence:
   - For **gn-**: The **gn**arled **gn**ome **gn**ashed his teeth as he **gn**awed a **gn**at.
   - For **-ough**: I th**ough**t I'd b**ough**t en**ough cough** syrup to make it thr**ough** this r**ough**, t**ough** winter.

Visualizations Using Word Parts

▲ Encourage students to manipulate and associate various suffixes within a pattern as related to a similar vowel sound, with a goal of developing automatic recognition of endings.
  ✔ The *LiPS* program (Lindamood, 1998, p. 363-366) presents a variety of activities using word endings, called the "Ending Grid."
   - In *LiPS*, students use the discovery method to develop expectancies for suffixes (endings) that begin with a similar sound, such as the /u/ sound in **-on** (*lemon*), **-an** (*human*), **-a** (*banana*), **-ous** (*famous*), **-al** (*final*), **-ent** (*parent*) and **-ence** (*sentence*).

▲ Enhance any word or word part visualization activity with air writing.
  ✔ Imagine writing each letter in the air in color or using colored strips of spaghetti.
  ✔ Imagine writing each letter in the air using colored Silly String.

Visualization of Words Using Trails of Intersecting Lines

▲ The challenge is for the student to visually track each line (without using any finger), remember each successive letter, and then mentally combine the letters to spell the word. Two examples are provided in Figures 4.8a and 4.8b.
  ✔ To make the trails easier, use fewer lines and color code the lines.
  ✔ To make the trails more challenging, use more lines all of the same color.

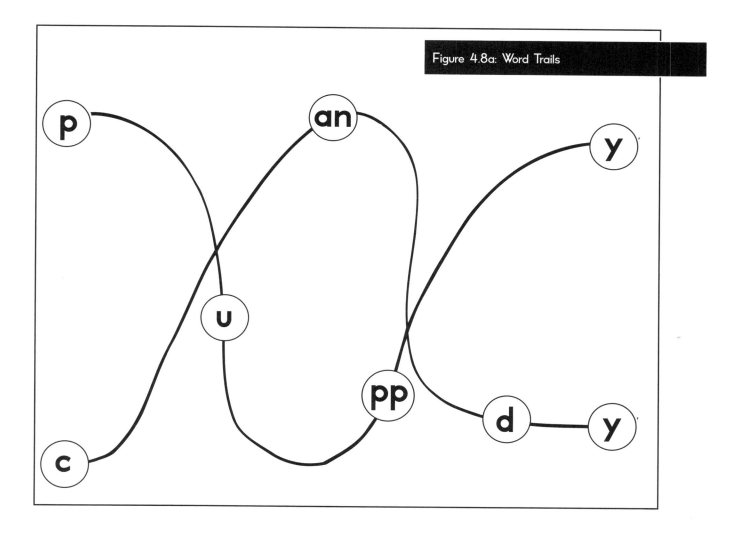

Figure 4.8a: Word Trails

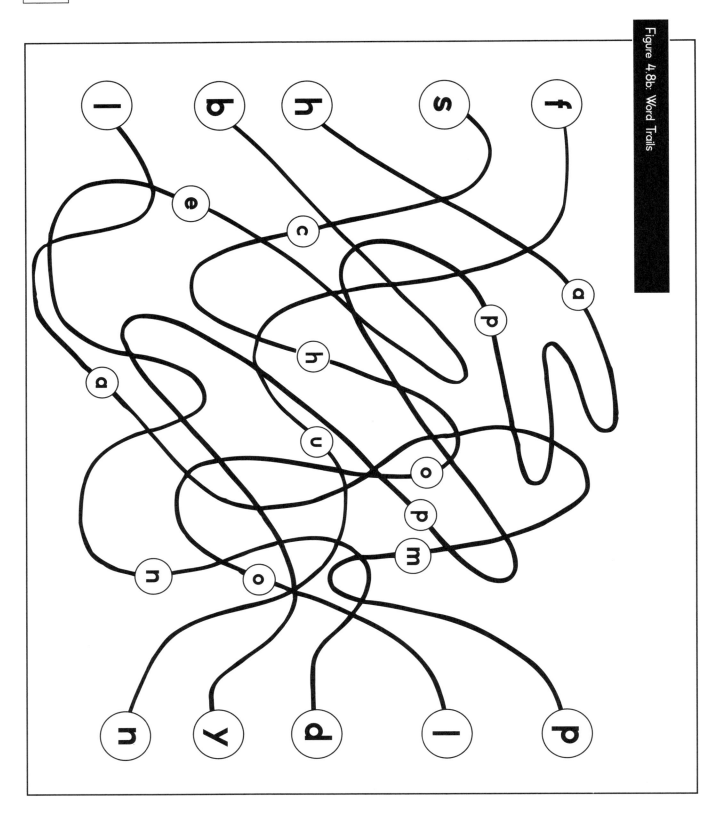

Figure 4.8b: Word Trails

Kinesthetic and Tactile Activities

Kinesthetic and tactile activities can be used to reinforce written activities, such as appropriate letter formation, word parts, or whole words. *Kinesthetic* refers to incorporating movement while *tactile* refers to the sense of touch. These related terms are often used interchangeably, but actually they refer to different sensory processes. The activities in this section reinforce motor memory while also enhancing visual eidetics. If letter names are stated simultaneously, a more complete linkage is formed between the auditory, visual, and kinesthetic systems.

Textures and Skin (Arm or Hand)

▲ Students write letters or words on a variety of textures to reinforce the sensory input, using a finger instead of a pencil.
  ✔ light sandpaper
  ✔ blue jeans
  ✔ a box filled with about one inch of rice
  ✔ carpet or tile
  ✔ edibles such as chocolate pudding or whipped cream

▲ Students write on the palm of their nondominant hand, using the index finger of their other hand.
  ✔ Students write cues to reinforce (and remember) the sensory input of an important word, such as a person's name or a key concept term.
  ✔ With longer conceptual terms, students might only write the first letter of each syllable as they repeat the word several times, clearly stating each syllable as a chunk.

▲ Students write the letter or word directly on top of their nondominant arm.

Tapping Letters and Syllables

▲ *Arm:* Students spell the word by sequentially tapping each letter on their nondominant arm while simultaneously saying the letters aloud.
  ✔ Teacher says a word, such as *possible*.
  ✔ Students say the word in syllables: pos – si – ble.
  ✔ Students then spell the word, one syllable at a time, tapping each letter on arm while spelling: p – o – s / s – i / b – l – e.
  ✔ Students repeat the whole word.

▲ *Desk:* Before attempting to spell a word, students lightly tap out each syllable on their desk. Options for tapping include the following:
  ✔ Tap with the side of the fist while holding a pencil and saying each syllable aloud.
  ✔ Tap with the whole fist without holding a pencil while saying each syllable aloud.

▲ *Finger spelling:* Students learn the American Sign Language and spell part or all of a word using finger spelling. Examples for specific words are:
  ✔ *terrible*: while spelling the word aloud, finger spell **r–r** and then **b–l–e.**
  ✔ *moment*: finger spell **m–e–n–t.**

✔ Some students prefer to spell the whole word simultaneously with their fingers, while others may find it too distracting to manipulate the entire word, as it places too much demand on their active working memory system. These students prefer to concentrate on the tricky part(s) of the word.

Figure 4.9: Air Writing

Air Writing

▲ Students write each letter of the word in the air as they spell the word aloud (See Figure 4.9).
   ✔ Students use fairly firm arm movements, avoiding having their arm in a rigid, straight position.
   ✔ Students use two fingers as their "pointer" or pretend pencil.

Singing and Rhythmic Activities

▲ *Choral spelling*
   ✔ Write five words on the chalkboard.
   ✔ Students chant each letter of each word in a rhythm, without pausing between words.
   ✔ Option: use a metronome to maintain rhythm.
   ✔ Many variations may be used.
      • Students chant each letter, saying each consonant loudly and each vowel in a whisper.
      • Students stand or sit in a circle and bounce a ball to each other (in random order).
         — The person who catches the ball states the next letter.
         — Progress through each letter in the words.
      • Students chant each letter, standing up for each vowel and sitting for each consonant.
      • Students sit in a circle, chant the letters, and thrust one arm toward the center of the circle each time they say a vowel.
      • Students sit in a circle, chant the letters, standing up for each consonant and sitting down for each vowel.
      • To increase the difficulty, include more words in the list.
▲ *Songs to reinforce spelling of a word*
   ✔ Sing a familiar song with a repetitive beat that has the same number of beats as the number of letters in the target word, singing one letter for each beat.
      • Sing (spell) a five-letter word to the tune of "You Are My Sunshine."
      • Sing (spell) a six-letter word to the tune of "Happy Birthday to You."
      • Sing (spell) a seven-letter word to the tune of "Twinkle Twinkle Little Star."

▲ **Jumping in rhythm**
- ✔ Use a trampa (36″ round rebounder or exerciser as shown in Figure 4.10) and combine jumping in rhythm with spelling and visualization.
  - Toss a ball to the child in order to increase levels of working memory needed.
- ✔ Students orally spell words while jumping in rhythm.
- ✔ Students read each letter of words written on the chalkboard while jumping and maintaining a consistent rhythm.
- ✔ RSV: Read-Spell-Visualize
  - Write five words on the chalkboard.
  - The student reads each word, jumping separately for each syllable (*read*).
  - The student reads each letter in each word while jumping in rhythm on the trampa (*spell*).
  - The student repeats the *spell* step until she feels she can visualize the words on the chalkboard in her mind.
  - The student turns (so that she cannot see the chalkboard) and spells the letters in each word while jumping, visualizing the words on the chalkboard in her mind (*visualize*).
  - Have the student check her responses by looking at the chalkboard.
- ✔ RSV performed with sentences
  - Write a short sentence on the chalkboard.
  - The student reads each word, jumping separately for each syllable (*read*).
  - The student reads each letter in each word while jumping in rhythm on the trampa (*spell*).
  - The student repeats the *spell* step until she feels she can visualize the words on the chalkboard in her mind.
  - The student turns (so that she cannot see the board) and spells the letters in each word while jumping, visualizing the words on the chalkboard in her mind (*visualize*).

Figure 4.10 Jumping in Rhythm

Where to Start?
Looking for suggestions on where to start with these new strategies? Here are some ideas.

Remember: It is always critical to take into account your students' developmental levels and learning styles. Where you choose to begin may differ from these suggestions based on the specific needs of your students.

▲ Suggestions for early-elementary students:
  • visualization of words using trails of intersecting lines
  • writing letters or words on a variety of textures

▲ Suggestions for upper-elementary students:
  • visualizations using spelling mnemonics
  • tapping letters and syllables on arm or desk

▲ Suggestions for middle-school students:
  • tapping letters and syllables on arm or desk
  • jumping in rhythm

▲ Suggestions for high school students:
  • tapping letters and syllables on arm or desk

Interactive Centers

A variety of these activities can be modified into brief interactive center tasks for students. The appropriate materials are placed on a table and students are given a list of 5-7 activities from which to choose. Students work with a partner and each partner "verifies" that the other student has performed the activity appropriately with all of their spelling words. As a variation and to simplify or shorten the activity, students may choose only a given number of their spelling words to perform using their chosen activity. To increase their involvement, have students perform more than one activity.

Suggestions for Interactive Spelling Centers

▲ Write your words big on a piece of paper.

▲ Spell your words using magnetic letters.

▲ Have someone write your words on your back as you guess each word.

▲ Air-write your words very big, using your whole arm while saying each letter.

▲ Write your words with your finger on a baking sheet covered with one inch of shaving cream or chocolate pudding.

▲ Write your words with your finger on a baking sheet covered with one inch of salt or baking powder.

▲ Write your words on the pavement using a squirt bottle filled with water containing a small amount of food dye in it or use sidewalk chalk.

▲ Spell your words while doing jumping jacks.

▲ Spell your words while jumping rope.

▲ Spell your words while bouncing a ball.

▲ Spell your words while tossing a beanbag from one hand to the other hand.

▲ Create a visual picture with your word: write the word using a variety of different colors of marker and add small drawings to illustrate the meaning of the word.

▲ Create rainbow words with each of your words by tracing over the word five times using five different colors of chalk on the chalkboard (or use different-colored markers on a paper).

▲ Spell out your words using Play-Doh or Wikki Stiks.

▲ Write your words on a bumpy surface such as tile, carpet, blue jeans, or fine sandpaper.

▲ Use a piece of window screen and use a crayon to write your words over the screen onto a piece of paper.

▲ Write your words in a column going down, with only one letter on each line.

▲ Write your words in a column going up, with only one letter on each line

Spelling Compensations

One of the most important spelling compensations that a struggling student can use is one that will enable her to find the correct spelling while also encouraging her to analyze the pattern and sounds in the word and match this analysis to the visual recognition of the word parts. An electronic resource such as a speaking Franklin Language Master is useful for accomplishing this goal because it recognizes words phonetically and, with the speaking component, will pronounce the words in the list of choices. For example, it will easily recognize and correct misspelled words such as *fizishin* (physician*)*, *fotogruf* (photograph), *gome* (gnome), *austrinut* (astronaut), and *tertty* (tardy).

There are many models of Franklin Electronic Resources, but my favorite at this time is the Franklin Language Master 6000b because of its option of a large font size and its good speech clarity.

A speaking electronic spell checker may be used for multiple purposes:
▲ To reinforce phonetic analysis of the sounds and recognition of patterns by encouraging students to focus on each sound and/or syllable as they spell a word
    ✔ The student must input the words using good logic.

▲ To connect phonetic spelling with accurate eidetic spelling
    ✔ The students selects the appropriate match.

▲ To provide additional multisensory input when checking the word using the auditory mode
    ✔ The student makes connections between the visual pattern and auditory sound of the word.
    ✔ The student avoids confusion caused by misreading words in the choices.

▲ To encourage the process of decision-making when given choices of similar-looking words
    ✔ The student solidifies connections related to the patterns within the word.

▲ To compensate for sequencing problems in dictionary work or when using a the-saurus

▲ To spell check words identified by a word processing program as misspelled

Students may benefit from using an electronic device either before or after writing a sentence or paragraph.

▲ Before writing, the students may use the speaking spell check to:
   ✔ Brainstorm exciting vocabulary words they might want to include.
   ✔ List important words directly related to the concept or ideas to be written about.
   ✔ The student lists these words and uses the spell check for each word or just for some of the words, depending upon her level and the teacher's goals.

▲ After writing the draft, the students may use a speaking spell check to:
   ✔ Proofread and correct some or all misspellings in their sentence(s).
   ✔ Correct only some words to avoid overload.

Teacher-directed activities can also be created to help students focus on syllables, prefixes, or suffixes. Many models also provide suggestions for synonyms and antonyms.

Syllabification

The activities in this section are designed to reinforce students' understanding and recall of the six primary syllable types. An activity should be performed only after students understand the concept for each syllable type selected in the activity. The activities may be adjusted to include only two-syllable types or all six patterns. Modify the techniques to fit the needs of your group and use the activities as suggestions for additional ideas and procedures to accomplish the same goals. Increase the difficulty by increasing the number of patterns (syllable types) used and decrease difficulty by using fewer patterns within an activity. The six primary syllable types are listed in Figure 4.11.

Figure 4.11: The Six Syllable Types

1. **Closed:** a syllable with a short vowel, ending in one or more consonants
   ✔ **bas** as in **bas**ket
   ✔ **ket** as in bas**ket**

2. **Open:** a syllable that ends with a long vowel sound that is spelled with a single vowel
   ✔ **pro** as in **pro**gram
   ✔ **ba** as in **ba**by

3. **Vowel-consonant-e:** a single vowel that has a long sound, followed by a consonant and then a silent -e
   ✔ **cake**
   ✔ **flate** as in de**flate**

4. **Consonant-le:** an unaccented final syllable containing a consonant plus the letter **l** and a silent -e
   ✔ **-ble** as in fa**ble**
   ✔ **-dle** as in fid**dle**

5. **Vowel team (and diphthong):** a syllable with a vowel sound that uses a vowel combination for spelling
   ✔ **aw** as in **aw**esome
   ✔ **ai** as in r**ai**n
   ✔ **ee** as in fr**ee**dom

6. **R-controlled:** any syllable in which the vowel is followed by the letter **r**, with no vowel causing a long vowel sound, as in **pare**
   ✔ **sort** as in con**sort**
   ✔ **par** as in **par**don
   ✔ **ter** as an en**ter**tain

Syllable Strategies

Clap Syllables

▲ Say a two-syllable word.
  • Students clap once for each syllable they hear.
  • Repeat with other multi-syllabic words.
▲ Students hum the word or place their hand under their chin as they say the word.
  • Students count the "sections" they hear as they hum or feel their chin move.

Syllable Sort

▲ Provide students with a large paper divided into three columns. Label each column with a different syllable type.
▲ Students search through a passage from one of their books looking for examples of each syllable type listed on their paper.
▲ The goal is to find six examples of each targeted syllable type.
▲ Using Post-it notes, students write the words located that represent each of the selected syllables, underlining the target syllable type.
▲ Students place each Post-it note in the correct column on their paper.

Three-Letter Word Play

▲ Give students 14 words, each containing three letters: arrange the words into columns, organizing the words so that a word from one column will combine with another word in the second column to create a new six-letter word.
▲ For example, the 14 words in Figure 4.12 can be combined to create the following words:
  ✔ budget
  ✔ carpet
  ✔ goblet
  ✔ impair
  ✔ manage
  ✔ notice
  ✔ warden

Figure 4.12: Sample Words	
bud	imp
age	man
car	get
air	not
den	let
gob	war
ice	pet

▲ To enhance the challenge for students, present the three-letter words in alphabetical order rather than in columns.
▲ To decrease the difficulty, make the activity more concrete for students by presenting the three-letter words on cards while also having a model of the two columns posted for easy viewing. The cards will allow the students to manipulate the words as they work to combine the single syllable words into two-syllable words. Also, consistently place the first syllable in the first column.
▲ *Adaptation*: write the words on large cards, giving one card to each of 14 students. Have the students arrange themselves to create seven new two-syllable words.

Syllable War

▲ This game is played like the card game "War," wherein the top card in each person's pile is revealed and the person with the highest card wins all piles.
  ✔ Create a deck of simple picture cards representing words with one to five syllables.
  ✔ Deal the cards evenly to two to four students, depending on the number of cards. If desired, students may work together in pairs. Each player places the cards picture side down in a pile.
  ✔ Each player turns over his top card and determines the number of syllables in the word.
  ✔ The player whose word contains the largest number of syllables takes the exposed cards.
  ✔ A syllable war occurs when the words exposed by both players have the same number of syllables. That player calls "syllable war." Each player then turns over the next card. The player with the largest number of syllables then takes all exposed cards.
  ✔ The number of cards used in the deck will determine the approximate amount of time required for the game.
  ✔ Increase the challenge by using all written words on the cards.
  ✔ Decrease the challenge by using pictures and words on each card.
  ✔ Decrease the difficulty by limiting the number of syllable choices; for example, use only one-, two- and three-syllable words.

Where to Start?
Looking for suggestions on where to start with these new strategies? Here are some ideas.

Remember: It is always critical to take into account your students' developmental levels and learning styles. Where you choose to begin may differ from these suggestions based on the specific needs of your students.

  ▲ Suggestions for early-elementary students:
    • clap syllables
    • syllable war with pictures

  ▲ Suggestions for upper-elementary students:
    • syllable sort
    • syllable war

  ▲ Suggestions for middle-school students:
    • three-letter word play
    • syllable war

  ▲ Suggestions for high school students:
    • syllable sort with multi-syllabic words

A Story About Angel

I first met Angel when she was in sixth grade. She was a bright young lady who came to my clinic and enthusiastically described her enjoyment of history. She was able to discuss many of the concepts and stories she learned in class as well as current events. She understood math patterns and kept up well with her math class work, as long as she had compensations to recall facts (multiplication grid, number line) and someone to read all the words to her. Her difficulty, and it was a major one, was that she could not read. She did not understand the difference between a vowel and consonant and she knew only a few sounds for common letters. Her reading level was at middle first grade level, primarily because she had memorized some common words.

Angel was experiencing some obvious difficulties with memory of sequential and paired information. She demonstrated excellent strengths when dealing with episodic memory, which enabled her to enjoy her history class and remember the stories. Her visual memory was superb for pictures and patterns but she struggled greatly with visual memory of sequential symbols. Auditory memory was difficult for her in many areas, but especially with sequential tasks. She demonstrated excellent procedural memory in areas of sports and math steps. The challenge was how to help her hang onto and consolidate paired sequential information, such as sound symbol relationships.

Angel readily grasped and applied visual mnemonics using the MFR program. For example, the short vowels were taught with the mnemonic, "Apple Ed is on umbrella." Many kinesthetic strategies were also incorporated to help her feel the sequence of sounds in her mouth as she said them (Lindamood 1998). This helped her connect her kinesthetic patterns to her weaker visual and auditory input modes. She also greatly enjoyed using the trampa, especially with the RSV activity. The remedial plan was quite successful and Angel learned to read efficiently, although slowly.

Many years later Angel returned to my office, but this time she was bringing her six-year-old daughter as the client. It was quite interesting to observe Angel as she completed the intake form. As she was writing, she would periodically whisper, "Ed, /eh/ e." When asked, Angel explained that she continues to confuse certain sounds such as the short vowel sounds for the letters **e** and **i**, consonants such as **s** in a word like *rose*, and **tch** as in *hatch*. Consequently, she remembers and still uses some MFR pictures, especially "Apple Ed is on umbrella," "Saw rose," and "Chickens hatch."

Conclusion

Angel's memory was enhanced by using movement, novelty, visual mnemonics, and multisensory activities incorporated into a systematic, well-sequenced remedial program. Keywords provided a definite "key" that opened the door to reading for Angel.

Some students find the use of keywords to be cumbersome, saying, "It's one more thing to remember!" However, other students such as Angel, rely substantially on being able to use the necessary cues. It is significant that she continued to use some of the necessary strategies many years later. She knew that the strategies enabled her to be successful!

Language Arts Strategies: Reading Comprehension

Chapter
5

There are one-story intellects,
two-story intellects, and three-story intellects with skylights.
All fact collectors who have no aim beyond their facts are one-story men.
Two-story men compare, reason, generalize,
using the labor of fact collectors as their own.
Three-story men idealize, imagine, predict —
their best illumination comes from above the skylight.

— *Oliver Wendell Holmes (Lazaer, 1991b)*

Efficiency in understanding what is read is a valuable and necessary component for learning. We cannot recall ideas that we have not adequately understood. We need to first comprehend ideas at the input level so that we can fit them in to a larger framework to elaborate and develop concepts. This applies to academic learning as well as much of the generalized lifetime learning outside of formalized education. We perform a positive service for our students by teaching them how to learn so that they develop lifetime skills that will enable them to keep up with the continuing flood of new information and higher language demands that they will be exposed to throughout their lives. Our students need to be encouraged to become "two-story" and "three-story" students, rather than just staying on the first "floor." They need to enter at the first level by using memory strategies efficiently. As they put those strategies to work, they are able to work on increasing the complexity by moving up to "second-story" and then eventually to the "third-story" type tasks.

Reading comprehension tasks are excellent opportunities to incorporate "The Big 4" memory facilitators. This chapter uses these strategies within three primary sections: vocabulary strategies, reading comprehension strategies, and text organization strategies. Each section contains strategies designed to enhance processing depth and decrease passivity. The activities encompass a variety of learning levels, and you are encouraged and cautioned to adjust them to the specific needs of your students, attending to their developmental levels and learning styles.

> **The Big 4 Facilitators**
> Active Learning
> Structured
> Systematic
> Sensory

Vocabulary Strategies

One of the least efficient vocabulary learning techniques for many students, especially those who may struggle with the language of learning, is for them to look up words (as in a dictionary) and then memorize the definitions. This type of task becomes one of rote memory and is often performed in a passive manner. While this practice may help some students pass a vocabulary test, it rarely encourages them to develop an adequate understanding of new words. Consequently, they are unable to retrieve or use the words when writing or speaking.

The goal of vocabulary development should be to help students understand word patterns that enhance vocabulary meaning while they also develop an ability to use more elaborate and semantically-loaded words within their daily lives and in academic activities. Two teaching tips can help students understand new words in a way that they can use and generalize:

▲ Provide a way for them to interact with the meaning of the word.

▲ Ensure they understand the pattern of the words and meaning of the patterns.

Muscle Memory

One way to develop muscle memory, sometimes called motor memory, involves motor involvement and sensory cues. When these approaches are used with new vocabulary words, students are encouraged to better understand the meaning patterns as they interact with each word. The following tasks demonstrate how adding movement to a task can enhance memory. Try these tasks with a partner, or have your students perform them with partners. Discuss how each approach affects memory effectiveness.

Task 1: Memorizing Vocabulary Words

Task 1a: Present this list of 6 words to a colleague or partner, showing the list for only 6 seconds. It may be very difficult to remember them all:
- right angle
- nestle
- tripod
- distract
- calmly
- monkey

Task 1b: Cover the list and ask your partner to recall as many words as possible.

Task 2: Using Vocabulary Words

Task 2a: Act out a meaning for each of the words below while your partner mimics the movement and repeats the word. You may use the suggested movements, or you may adapt the movement to one that makes more sense to you. Proceed through the list fairly quickly, in about 12 to 15 seconds.

right angle	*Arrange thumb and first finger to make a 90 degree angle.*
nestle	*Place one hand within the other and rub or caress it.*
tripod	*Have one hand represent a table by holding hand flat and use three fingers on the other hand to represent the 3 legs.*
distract	*Look all around without focusing on any specific point.*
calmly	*Act completely calm and relaxed.*
monkey	*Make a monkey-like gesture.*

Task 2b: Ask your partner to remember as many words as possible. If he struggles to remember a word, provide the related movement as a memory cue.

Task 2c: Check for meaning by performing each movement and having your partner state the word and its meaning.

Task 3: Discuss Vocabulary Words and Activities

Discuss with your partner which activity was more efficient in helping to recall the words and why. What cues and/or strategies made the recall easier?

Pantomime Meaning of Words

Muscle memory is an important tool that enhances memory capabilities because it utilizes the primary neural pathways — visual, auditory, kinesthetic, and tactual — while also associating these pathways within a conceptual framework. Muscle memory has been found to be valuable for athletes at many levels, including at the Olympic level, and it is a common technique used by coaches and piano teachers.

Encourage students to use the advantage of muscle memory by creating their own gestures for vocabulary words, using gestures that will remind them of the meaning of the word as in Task 2 above. This is a strategy that may be used to introduce new vocabulary at any grade level, from early elementary through high school[2].

There are many other ways that muscle memory can be elaborated upon in the classroom. For example, combine pantomime with visualization strategies to encourage students to develop a visual image and describe or draw that image.

Understanding Word Patterns

Understanding that words are composed of parts and that these parts provide cues as to the function and meaning of the word facilitates the development of a concept related to the word's meaning. Some students, especially those with language-based learning difficulties, try to learn each new vocabulary word as an isolated unit. They fail to perceive the patterns, similarities, and differences that contribute to a word's meaning.

Students can become more efficient in understanding word meaning and the categorical nature of words when they have some appreciation of the word parts (morphology) and the relationship of a word to similar words. Knowledge about the structure of words, especially when combined with syllabification techniques, can greatly help in understanding and sounding out longer, unfamiliar words.

Our brain seeks to form patterns. The following activity suggestions are designed to help students form patterns when dealing with vocabulary. The overall goal is to enhance their understanding of individual words, as well as their overall ability to retain and appropriately retrieve vocabulary words. These activity suggestions are presented as models to be used in developing additional activities directly related to your classroom content areas. As with all activities and strategies within this book, ensure that the students understand the concepts involved through directed teaching activities before having them practice the concepts using the following reinforcement activities.

> "A morpheme is the most elementary unit of grammatical form that has both sound and meaning" (Moats 2000, p. 60).

[2](Activity adapted from Stetkevich, 2002)

Activities with Prefixes and Suffixes

Number Prefixes

1. Present a word such as *unicycle*. Ask students if they recognize any clue that identifies the number of wheels on this vehicle (**uni-** means "one").

2. Some students pantomime the meaning of a word containing a number prefix, focusing on the prefix, while others try to guess the word's meaning.

3. Students draw or use Lego blocks to represent the meaning of number prefixes in given words.

4. Students draw or use Lego blocks to represent the meaning of number prefixes in words selected from a reading passage.

5. A listing of number prefixes can be found on page 114.

Multiple Prefix Use

1. Students write (or dictate) a sentence for each of two or three different words that has the same prefix (such as **pro-**):
   ✔ I have a *program* that describes the events.
   ✔ There was really good *produce* at the market today.

2. Have students write a second sentence using each word:
   ✔ The students put on an exciting *program* for the parents.
   ✔ The farmer wanted to grow lots of different kinds of *produce*.

3. As a group, discuss commonalities among words that have the same prefix.

4. When students write their second set of sentences, the task may be structured in various ways and the chosen structure will determine simplicity or complexity of the task. You can do any of the following:
   ✔ Be flexible and accept any correct meaning for the word.
   ✔ Restrict the sentences to the same conceptual meaning.
   ✔ Require a different conceptual meaning.

Prefix or Suffix Search

1. Students search their reading materials to find six words containing a given prefix or suffix:
   ✔ For example, given the suffix **-ling**, students may find *duckling*, as in "The *duckling* followed its mother across the street."

2. Students determine the meaning of the given prefix or suffix, using a Franklin speller or a dictionary:
   ✔ **-ling** means "connected with" or "having the quality of being young/small."

3. Students write a sentence for each word. Their sentence should differ from the sentence in their book but maintain the same conceptual meaning:
   ✔ "The *duckling* was only a few days old and walked funny."

4. A chart listing some common suffixes can be found on page 115.

Activities Focusing on Word Relationships

Related Roots

1. Students use their reading materials to search for pairs of related words based on morphological patterns. Explain that the focus is on similar roots for the words.

2. Students act out and explain the meaning of each word pair.

3. Examples of words with similar roots:
   ✔ *doubt — dubious*
   ✔ *sheep — shepherd*
   ✔ *holy — holiday*

4. Students play a game of Charades or Pictionary with some of the words.

The Knowledge Tree

Verbal knowledge is organized in networks of associations that have definable structures. A significant value of a knowledge tree is it enables new words and concepts to be known in relation to one another, not as isolated units. "New verbal information is learned in accordance with prior knowledge. Effective teaching elaborates various connections among better-known and lesser-known words, deepens and enriches existing knowledge, and seeks to build a network of ideas around key concepts that are well elaborated" (Moats, 2000, p. 112). Helping students develop these associations provides a vehicle to increase the complexity of the task and increases their understanding and ability to use a wider range of vocabulary words.

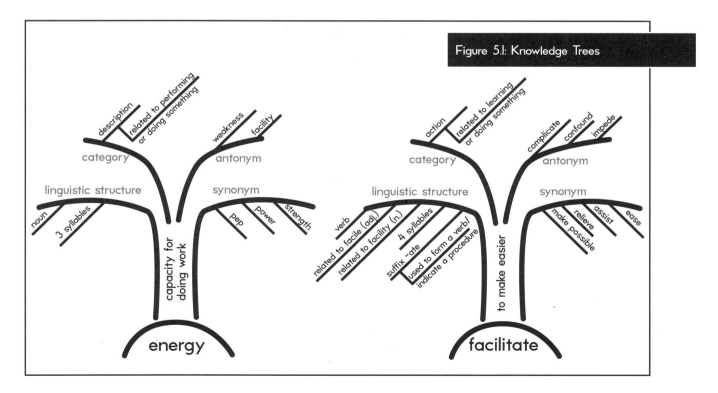

Figure 5.1: Knowledge Trees

1. Students create a knowledge tree, wherein the root of the tree forms the base word, the trunk is the definition, and the branches are the elaborative connections. Examples of components that may be included as branches include:
   ✔ synonyms
   ✔ antonyms
   ✔ related categories
   ✔ alternate meanings (multiple meanings)
   ✔ examples
   ✔ linguistic structures: syllables, prefix, root, suffix
   ✔ related body gestures

2. A simpler knowledge tree will have fewer characteristics.

3. Examples of two knowledge trees using four branches (linguistic structure, category, antonym, and synonym) are in Figure 5.1 on the previous page. The second tree includes more components within each category.

Vocabulary Mapping

1. This activity is similar to a knowledge tree but it is more concrete; therefore, it provides an easier tool for some students to perceive relationships among the words.

2. Build from an example (E) to characteristic(s) (C), and then provide a definition (D).
   ✔ A vocabulary map for the word *milk* is provided in Figure 5.2:
      • E: common drink
      • C: good for you
      • D: Milk is a common drink that is good for you.
   ✔ A similar vocabulary map for the word *dog* would include the following components:
      • E: common pet
      • C: has four legs and barks
      • D: A dog is a common pet that has four legs and barks.

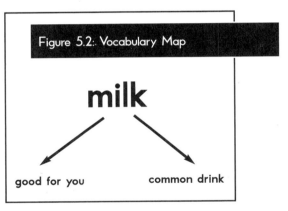

Figure 5.2: Vocabulary Map

milk

good for you   common drink

3. An example of another format that accomplishes the same goal is on page 116, The Vocabulary Word Map (Jones, 2002).

Vocabulary Mapping with Multiple Meanings

1. Give students a basic word such as *run*.

2. Students "map" as many meanings as they can. There are several different formats for visual organizers that may be used: the critical component is that the different meanings are organized visually because then the activity is more concrete and memory is facilitated.
   ✔ Examples of varying meanings for the word *run*:
      • move the legs in a fast gait

- a fast gallop of a horse
- a flaw in a stocking
- a path for skiers
- the flow of sap in trees
- to print a story in a newspaper

✔ The map for the word *run* could be similar to the one in Figure 5.2 for the word *milk*, except it would have eight "branches" instead of just two.

3. A map with only two branches can be used for a word that has two primary alternate meanings, such as *season*.

✔ add spice or flavorings to food

✔ a time of the year

✔ As an extension activity, students can create a single sentence that incorporates both meanings of the word:

- "Next Thanksgiving *season* we will *season* the turkey differently."

Role-Playing Multiple Meanings

1. Read students a book that contains confusions among multiple meaning words such as *Amelia Bedelia* by Peggy Parish. In this story, Amelia is given a list of tasks to perform on her first day as a housecleaner.

   Amelia reads one of the items on her list, "Put out the lights when you finish in the living room." Amelia Bedelia thought about this a minute. She switched off the lights. Then she carefully unscrewed each bulb. And Amelia Bedelia put the lights out [hanging them on the outside clothesline]. "So those things need to be aired out too."

2. Students role-play Amelia as she first responded to the request.

3. Students role-play the meaning intended by the homeowner.

4. Students discuss the differences between the meanings of the two interpretations.

Activities Focusing on Greek Combining Forms

There is substantial Greek influence on our English language. Many words of Greek origin have become common English words, such as *gymnasium, catastrophe, lexicon,* and *thermometer*. As scientists coin new words, they often rely heavily on Greek roots and combining forms as in the words *microscope, psychobiology,* and *synthesizer*. "Greek words can be recognized by their use of combined elements that are analogous to English compounds: each part has equal value in determining the meaning of the word but [each Greek combining form] must exist in combination with others before it can make a word in English" (Moats, 2000, p. 89-90). There are also some Latin combining forms and some words that have a foundation in both Greek and Latin forms. Moats recommends that students begin to study combining forms around 6th grade (Moats, 2000, p. 107).

Somewhat Common Words – Level 1

1. Present students with the words in the left-hand column and generate a discussion of each word's meaning. Test your own knowledge by covering the two right-hand columns to determine how many word parts you can define.

Word	Meaning of Word Parts	Definition
telephone	distant; sound	instrument for transmitting sound over distance
photograph	light; writing	producing images on a sensitized surface by action of light
biology	life; study of	study of living beings and life processes
autograph	self; writing	a person's signature written by hand
biography	life; writing	written history of a person's life
bigamy	two; marriage	marrying one person while still legally married to another

2. Ask students to determine what each of the word parts in the left-hand column below means. Encourage them to use their knowledge of the above words in making their judgments. For example, you might ask, "Since *biography* means 'written history of a person's life,' what might the word part **-graphy** mean?"

Word Part	Definition
tele-	distant
-graph(y)	write, writing
bi(o)-	life
photo-	light
-ology	study, study of
auto-	self
-gamy	marriage

3. Present the new words in the left-hand column below and ask students to determine the meaning of each. Discuss the value of knowing about word parts and how this knowledge helps them analyze and determine the meanings for new words. Again, test your own knowledge by covering the two right-hand columns to determine how many word parts you can define.

Word	Meaning of Word Parts	Definition
monogomy	one; marriage	marriage with one person
geography	earth; recording or writing	study of the natural features of the earth and its climate and products
telescope	distant; see or watch	instrument with lenses or mirrors for viewing distant objects
telegraph	distant; writing	electric system for sending messages by a code over wires
automatic	self; moving	having a self-regulating mechanism
psychology	mind or soul; study of	the study of mind and behavior
photosynthesis	light; combining	formation of carbohydrates by chlorophyll-containing plants exposed to light
biped	two; foot	a two-footed animal

Somewhat Common Words – Level 2

The following activity can be used with high school students to help them further understand the value of morphology and combining forms. I have also used it in many of my workshops with adults because of its effectiveness in highlighting these important concepts.

1. Ask students if they understand the meaning of any of the following words:
   - ✔ *angiocentesis*
   - ✔ *craniotomy*
   - ✔ *cardioplasty*

2. Encourage students to guess or brainstorm possible meanings of whole words or word parts.

3. Then present a chart to your students similar to the one in Figure 5.3. Leave the white boxes blank; the students will complete those.

Figure 5.3: Somewhat Common Words

Nouns	Verbs		
	-centesis (puncture)	*-tomy* (make an incision)	*-plasty* (perform surgical repair)
angio- (vessel)	angiocentesis	angiotomy	angioplasty
cranio- (skull)	craniocentesis	craniotomy	cranioplasty
cardio- (heart)	cardiocentesis	cardiotomy	cardioplasty

Explain that the words in the horizontal gray boxes represent actions, similar to verbs. The words in the vertical gray boxes represent a component similar to nouns.

4. Encourage students to then combine **angio-** and **-centesis** to create *angiocentesis*, and have them write the word in the correct white box. Then have them brainstorm a meaning for *angiocentesis* using their understanding of the word parts or Greek combining forms.

5. Continue brainstorming the words *craniotomy* and *cardioplasty*.

6. As each word is discussed, place it in the appropriate location on the chart.
   - ✔ Encourage the students to discuss how the pattern contributed to their understanding of the meaning of the words.

7. Introduce the remaining words in the white boxes, one at a time.

8. Introduce the word parts **derma-** (skin) and **gastro-** (stomach).

9. Have students use the chart to determine the meaning of the following words:
   - ✔ *dermacentesis*
   - ✔ *dermaplasty*
   - ✔ *gastrocentesis*
   - ✔ *gastroplasty*

Where to Start?

Looking for suggestions on where to start with these new strategies? Here are some ideas.

Remember: It is always critical to take into account your students' developmental levels and learning styles. Where you choose to begin may differ from these suggestions based on the specific needs of your students.

▲ Suggestions for early-elementary students:
  ✔ pantomime meaning of words
  ✔ vocabulary mapping

▲ Suggestions for upper-elementary students:
  ✔ pantomime meaning of words
  ✔ knowledge tree or role-play multiple meanings

▲ Suggestions for middle-school students:
  ✔ pantomime meaning of words
  ✔ related roots in words

▲ Suggestions for high school students:
  ✔ pantomime meaning of words
  ✔ Greek combining forms

Reading Comprehension

The process of learning *how to learn* through reading comprehension involves *metacognition. Meta-* refers to knowing about and *cognition* refers to knowledge or learning. As students develop the many important components for reading efficiency, it is critical that they also understand the purpose of each component and what strategies best apply. Thus, they need to know about (*meta-*) the learning strategy (*cognition*) to increase their awareness of why they benefit from performing a given strategy in a particular manner.

Many students view reading in school as just a task of memorizing answers for a test. Reading needs to be so much more than rote memorization of facts. Students need to realize the value of metacognitive awareness while they are reading, as well as how this awareness directly relates to their ability to remember what they read. Awareness and use of strategies within reading subcomponents increases the capacity of active working memory and facilitates consolidation of information into long-term memory.

Some of the many valuable components to help students learn *how* to learn through reading comprehension are:

▲ previewing

▲ active reading

▲ reading fluency

▲ inferential understanding

▲ organization of information

Many of these components overlap, as the process of reading is an integrated process. For example, active reading overlaps with inferential understanding. The goal of all the strategies presented in this section is to enhance students' abilities to understand, integrate, and retrieve the information. They need to realize that most complex academic tasks have multiple subtasks embedded within them. It is important to preserve all of the subtasks while the task is being executed, which requires active working memory capacity. Mel Levine refers to this preservation of subtasks as "task component suspension" (Levine, 1998, p. 73) because the subtasks must be temporarily suspended (although not forgotten) while other subtasks receive more direct attention.

While there are many subtasks involved in reading comprehension, this book will limit discussion to activities categorized within the above components. It is hoped that the suggestions will serve to stimulate you to develop more ideas to further elaborate upon the concept(s) and that they will facilitate your creation of additional strategies directly related to your specific teaching goals.

Previewing Strategies

Previewing strategies are a primary form of enhancing active reading. Many students have a habit of just running their eyes over the print, but this passive activity rarely generates active understanding and processing depth. Previewing techniques encourage students to survey the text or the chapter prior to beginning to read. Depending upon the material, this may involve looking at chapter headings, reading the questions at the end of the chapter, reading sidebars and highlighted information, and reading captions under pictures. The goal is to develop a general understanding and expectation of concepts and events that may be presented, an activity that many call "priming."

Previewing techniques such as TELLS or developing a KWL chart can be used with either narrative or expository text. Some of the other strategies may be better adapted to one type of text or another. Therefore, students need to understand how to determine what type of text they are reading so that they will know which previewing strategy will be most appropriate.

Many common mnemonic strategies are based on an acronym or acrostic as a reminder of steps to use when previewing or reading a paragraph or story. The value of these strategies is to encourage the student to progress through the activity in an active, step-by-step manner.

Mnemonics

▲ Mnemonics are little tricks you can play with your memory to facilitate remembering facts or steps.

▲ An *acronym* is a sequence of letters that may or may not form a word. Each letter represents one of the words to be remembered. For example, the word FACE helps recall the notes within the spaces on a music staff.

▲ An *acrostic* is a short sentence or phrase wherein the initial letter of each word or each letter in the phrase serves as a reminder for a word to be remembered. The sequence of the letters triggers the correct sequence to be recalled. For example, Roy G. Biv is a name phrase to help recall the colors of the rainbow: red, orange, yellow, green, blue, indigo, violet; and the sentence, "A rat in the house might eat the ice cream," can be used to recall the spelling of the word *arithmetic*.

TELLS

This mnemonic strategy provides a previewing framework for students to use with fiction or nonfiction stories. The acronym TELLS stands for:

✔ Title: Look for clues about the story.

✔ Examine the story for picture or word clues to aid your understanding.

✔ Look at important words or pictures.

✔ Look up hard words you may not know (and/or work with your decoding strategies).

✔ Setting: Identify where and when the story occurred.

KWL Chart

This mnemonic uses a three-column chart. The graphic can be developed by an individual or the group as a preliminary activity to preview a reading or a unit.

✔ Column 1: the **K** (**K**now) column
Students use this column to list what they already know about the concept, information, or story they are about to read. This helps them think about their existing knowledge and opens up hooks onto which they will be able to place their new information.

✔ Column 2: the **W** (**W**ant) column
In this column, students write what they want to know or learn from the information or what they think they will learn. It encourages students to think about the topic while also using some prediction, focusing on the concepts, and determining their purpose for the task. It also can provide an opportunity to think further about the topic and wonder what other related information they might want to know.

✔ Column 3: the **L** (**L**earn) column
This information is completed after the reading task and provides an opportunity to answer questions in column 2 and correct any inaccurate information. Completing this column encourages students to use metacognitive analysis in asking themselves, "What did I learn?"

TP Structures

This mnemonic is a reminder for students to use general previewing strategies to preview the structure of their text before beginning to read. The **T** is a reminder to look at and analyze the **T**extbook structure and the **P** is a reminder to look at the **P**aragraph structure. While this strategy works well with either narrative or expository text, it is particularly useful with more academic information.

✔ **Textbook structure**
  • chapter headings
  • captions under pictures and graphs
  • index

- appendices
- questions at the end of chapters

✔ **Paragraph structure**
- introductory or topic sentence
- keywords
- conclusions

✔ **Be a "detective"**
- The conclusion of this strategy is for students to try and guess the meaning of the passage using only the minimal cues from the structure.
- Be sure students verify the accuracy of their guesses after reading the passage.

Active Reading Strategies

To increase memory and recall of material read, it is critical to accurately process and organize the information. Being active and using chunking while reading are valuable keys that help students increase their overall efficiency and depth of processing. The following strategies are suggestions students can use as reminders to proceed systematically and with purpose through their reading material.

> Chunking is an effective way to enlarge working memory's capacity and help learners make associations that establish meaning (Sousa, 2001, 112).

SQ₃R

This mnemonic strategy cues students to preview the text and then continually ask themselves questions such as, "Do I understand what I am reading?" "How much can I remember?" "Does it make sense?" SQ₃R stands for:

✔ **Survey:** Survey the text.
✔ **Question:** Create questions by restating each heading and subheading.
✔ **Read:** Read to answer your questions.
✔ **Recite:** Recite the answers to your questions (silently or aloud).
✔ **Review:** Review the material to verify or correct your answers.

RCRC

This mnemonic strategy is similar to, but simpler, than SQ₃R. It also encourages students to continually question themselves about their understanding as they move through the text. RCRC stands for:

✔ **Read** a small part of the material one or two times.
✔ **Cover** the material.
✔ **Retell** yourself what you read, i.e, review what you read.
✔ **Check** to see if you remembered it correctly, i.e, compare your recall to the material.

Students can also use a simple "chant and clap" pattern to help remember this mnemonic. In this pattern, students recite the cues while clapping in a 4-beat rhythm.

RC / RC	(left hand taps left knee/clap together)
Help me to / care	(right hand taps right knee/clap together)
Read a / chunk	(left hand hits air [as in a "high 5"]/clap together)
And com- / pare together	(right hand hit air [as in a "high 5"]/clap together)

RAP

RAP is another mnemonic strategy to encourage students to use self-questioning techniques. The letters stand for:

✔ **R**ead the material.

✔ **A**sk yourself questions as you read.

✔ **P**araphrase the information in your own words.

Skim, RAP, Map

This combination mnemonic strategy merges the important previewing technique of skimming with the RAP strategy. The final step is to organize the information into a mind map or other visual organizer.

✔ **Skim:** Skim the material first, looking for clues such as headings, diagrams, charts, and sidebars.

✔ **RAP:** Read, ask yourself questions, and paraphrase the information.

✔ **Map:** Use a mind map to organize the information, either section by section or for the whole chapter.

The Big M and D

This mnemonic refers to the common technique of identifying the **M**ain idea and the supporting **D**etails, or facts for each main idea. It is valuable to have students do this while reading the passage as it encourages greater active involvement.

✔ Accuracy and efficiency are dependent upon the students' ability to understand and adequately utilize skills such as:
  • saliency determination
  • vocabulary determination
  • paraphrasing and summarization

✔ Manipulatives can be used to make the activity more concrete for the students.
  • The general technique is:
    — Use one color to identify the main idea.
    — Use another color to identify the keywords for the facts that support the main idea.

- After reading, use this information to create a visual organizer that summarizes the information.
- Ideas for manipulatives include:
  — Wikki Sticks (similar to colored sticky pipe cleaners)
  — Post-it notes
  — Post-it arrows
  — Hi-Liter pens

QAR Concept Map

To enhance the complexity of tasks and encourage conceptual movement beyond the concrete and into higher order thinking skills, it is necessary for students to become accustomed to answering different types of questions about text.

The importance of complexity is evident in many programs. For example, Wiig and Wilson in *The Learning Ladder: Assessing and Teaching Text Comprehension* (Wiig, 2002) present ten questions after each reading passage. The questions are divided into two sets:

✔ Set A: Using given information
✔ Set B: Going beyond given information

The student's score is based on an overall comprehension percentage, as well as the relationship or balance between the two types of questions.

Students can use QAR as a self-questioning strategy and/or they may develop a QAR concept map. QAR encourages students to recognize that there is a relationship between the type of question that is asked and the type of answers they seek. Understanding this relationship also encourages them to be strategic in the process of answering the questions (adapted from Jones, 2002).

Figure 5.4: QAR Concept Map Format

Right There	Author and You
Think and Search	On My Own

QAR refers to **Q**uestion-**A**nswer **R**elationships. In developing a concept map, students divide their paper into four equal parts resulting in two columns and two rows (see Figure 5.4). They read the questions they will need to answer and then write each question within an appropriate QAR box. In doing so, they will need to think about the type of question that is being asked and how it relates to the type of answer they seek.

✔ **Left column: Text QARs**
The two QAR boxes in the left column are for QARs that are available in the text.

- **Right There:** This QAR refers to an answer that is usually contained within a given sentence in the text. Example questions:
  — What work was John doing on Saturday morning?
  — Where was Sarah's mother going?

- **Think and Search:** This QAR refers to an answer that is within the text, but it may be located within different sentences or it may be stated in parts rather than directly. The student needs to put the information together. Example questions:
  — Tell two ways John expressed his feelings when Matt ruined his paper.
  — How did Tom guess Sharon had put the things on his desk?
  — Can you isolate the most important idea?

✔ **Right column: "In my head QARs"**
The two QAR boxes in the right column are for QARs that are not directly available in the text.

- **Author and You:** This QAR refers to answers that are not directly stated in the text. However, the answer is dependent upon using information within the text and combining that information with other knowledge that the student already knows. Example questions:
  — How else could the choir director have solved the problem of having no soloist?
  — Who else does this legislator remind you of? Why?
  — What would you have done? Why do think this is the best choice?
  — What are some of the things you wondered about as all this was happening?
  — How could you modify this? How would changing the sequence affect the outcome?

- **On my Own:** This QAR refers also to answers that are not in the text and it requires the student to use his own experience and/or knowledge to answer the question. While the question will relate to the text, the answer is not directly dependent upon information in the text. Example questions:
  — In what situations do you think "squealing on somebody" might be appropriate?
  — What would make it possible for you to read another person's reluctance and nervousness from his or her expression?
  — Can we trust the source of this information?

After reading the passage, the student answers each of the questions. It will be important to provide sufficient feedback, scaffolding, and structure to help students develop comfort with identifying the appropriate QAR box for each question, especially initially. Students often discover that their memory for what they read is greatly enhanced once they expand their processing depth by activities such as QAR.

Reading Fluency Strategies

The significance of reading fluency has been receiving much attention in recent literature. Maryann Wolf states that the issue of fluency represents a unique aspect "about the present moment in dyslexia research history." This current emphasis does not represent "a shift away from the phonological paradigm, but rather, an attempt to integrate that knowledge base, both with new findings about a second core-deficit in time- and fluency-related processes, and also with new approaches from the neurosciences" (Wolf, 2001, p. xii).

Reading fluency is dependent upon the reader's ability to read the words accurately which, of course, is dependent upon a large number of other skills. Poor reading fluency will interfere with the comprehension process, as fluency facilitates the rapid integration of the component skills necessary for comprehension. In discussing the value of fluency, Logan states:

> Fluency is not limited to reading connected text quickly and accurately. Instead, it incorporates the development of the component skills of beginning reading such as phonemic awareness and letter-sound association, and the need for a high criterion level of proficiency. Moreover, [the value of fluency] is predicated on the proposition that fluent performance of complex skills and higher-level processes (e.g., word recognition and reading comprehension) requires fluency in the component skills and lower-level processes (Logan, 1997, p. 123-46).

Adequate fluency is dependent upon the process of working memory. To enhance the capacity of students' active working memory within a reading comprehension task, each of the individual components must be as automatic and efficient as possible. One indication that working memory is "overloaded" and interfering with comprehension can be observed in the student who does not readily remember the beginning of a sentence or paragraph by the time he reaches the end.

Several strategies directly related to fluency development will be presented in this section:

- pretraining vocabulary
- repeat reading
- morphological awareness

Pretraining Vocabulary

Being able to read through text without stumbling over individual words facilitates a student's progress in developing fluent text reading. This preliminary technique for enhancing fluid reading involves previewing and pretraining words that may be anticipated as difficult or challenging. The words may be selected by either the student or the teacher. This technique of pretraining vocabulary is one that is strongly promoted by Gillingham in her classic multisensory remedial program (Gillingham, 1968).

✔ Students select specific words from the target passage prior to beginning to read.

✔ Students practice each word, using whatever skills are necessary.
   a. Skills may include phonological awareness, syllabification, morphological awareness, and discussion of the meaning.
   b. The teacher may structure the task by presenting a systematic checklist or students may develop their own system.

✔ Some students may benefit by also using one or more of the active vocabulary development techniques presented previously to enhance understanding of the meaning of the word(s) while also facilitating their decoding ability.

Repeat Reading Strategies

There are different approaches for utilizing the technique of repeat reading. Depending upon the age and skill level of the student, it may be valuable to combine approaches or use different ones at varying points in time. The general principle is that repeating the same word, phrase, sentence, or passage — often several times — improves eidetic recognition, decoding fluency, and prosody. Eidetic recognition is automaticity in recognizing the word. The prosody of language involves the phrasing, stress, expression, pitch, juncture, and intonation that make language flow smoothly.

One value of repeat reading is that as the student repeats the passage first modeled by the adult, there is opportunity for her to experience success since she is able to repeat the words with accuracy, fluency, and awareness of punctuation as used by the adult. Each repetition of the passage by the student leads to more efficient integration of the necessary components.

Repeat Reading with Readiness or Warm-up Activities

✔ This is the approach used in the multisensory program, TREAT, which stands for **Tactile Reading Eidetic Auditory Technique** (Love, 1996). Students first perform a warm-up task using a tactile and/or kinesthetic activity such as letter recognition by touch and/or visual cues, for example, using plastic letters.

✔ An adult then models the selected reading segment, with the length of the segment depending upon the skill level of the student and his ability to recall the visual and auditory input. As the adult reads, she points to each word while the student follows visually. Watching each word as it is selected strengthens the student's eidetic processing.

✔ The student then re-reads the same segment, matching his reading with the rate indicated by the adult's finger as it follows along the print. The adult pauses only if a word is missed or skipped, thus providing immediate nonverbal feedback for each error. This is the student's cue to reread the word.

✔ The process continues (teacher reads and student re-reads) using selections from the same passage until the student reads easily and fluently. If more than one repetition is needed, then the passage may be too long for the TREAT goals and a shorter selection or easier passage should be used next time.

✔ For record-keeping and portfolio information, it is important to develop a system for obtaining and recording data about the student's baseline and progress. The TREAT method provides suggestions for doing so, or the teacher may develop her own system.

✔ At the end of the passage, it is important to ask a variety of comprehension questions to ensure that the student has understood and to help the student integrate the meaning components.

✔ If the student has successfully read the passage fluently with good comprehension, then she progresses to the next section within the material.
— If the student does not successfully read the passage, she moves to material at an easier reading level or new material at the same level.

✔ The goal is for students to be able to use TREAT techniques with material slightly higher than her independent and easy reading level.

More Repeat Reading with Readiness or Warm-up Activities

✔ The adult and student use the same text and the student follows along the printed text with his finger as it is read. If necessary, the adult may place her hand lightly on top of the student's to assist and to ensure that he keeps moving his finger at the appropriate pace.

✔ The adult reads the text, occasionally stopping for the student to read the next word or words.

✔ Repeat the same selection, increasing the number of words that the student reads as the activity progresses.

✔ Eventually, the student reads the entire section by himself. When he successfully reads that selection with good prosody and fluency, he then progresses to the next selection.

✔ At the end of the activity, it is important to ask a variety of comprehension questions to ensure that the student has understood and to help the student integrate the components.

Repeat Reading with A Commercial Program

✔ An overview of the commercial program, *Read Naturally* (Ihnot, 1991):
  • Students read high interest passages at their instructional level and the program combines three strategies: teacher modeling, repeated reading, and progress monitoring. The goal is to encourage readers to spend more time reading by developing greater fluency and comprehension.
  • Students graph their times for cold readings (first time) and hot readings (subsequent times), answer comprehension questions, and summarize the passage.
  • A sequenced series of stories are provided either on cassette tapes or computer CD.

A Caution for Teachers

Fluency should not be used as a total reading program or goal. A study by Berninger indicated that for children with a reading disability, repeated reading alone may not be the best way to increase their oral reading fluency and reading comprehension. She states, "These children critically need to combine explicit alphabetic principal training with repeat readings." In her study, one group of children used the *Read Naturally* program and the other group combined *Read Naturally* with the *Talking Letters Program* (Berninger, 1998). After only 13 hours of tutorial sessions, the *Read Naturally* only group gained 0.6 instructional levels (based on oral reading rate) but lost points in comprehension. The combination group gained 1.6 instructional levels and gained 5.3 points on oral reading comprehension.

Morphological Awareness

Morphological awareness involves an awareness of the components of meaning within words, including prefixes, suffixes, roots, and combining forms. This provides another layer of word analysis that has broad implications throughout the total integrative process of reading. Berninger states,

> This layer contributes uniquely to reading fluency "over and beyond the sizable contribution of the accuracy of orthographic-phonological connections" and it is important to realize that "efficiency, automaticity, and executive coordination may not be the only processes contributing to reading fluency" (2001, p. 395).

In the vocabulary section of this chapter, the multisensory strategies presented suggested active techniques designed to help the students understand some of the patterns that enhance vocabulary meaning. An understanding of the value of patterns is critical for development of morphological awareness since patterns and use of morphological strategies are essential components contributing to fluency development. The same strategies contribute to the development of fluency in reading and should be used quite frequently.

Contextual Analysis

✔ Other strategies, such as analyzing the context and structure of a word, can also enhance comprehension and recall of information. However, it is important that contextual analysis be used only after structured strategies for decoding have been used, and not as a primary strategy or instead of structural analysis.

✔ When students encounter an unfamiliar or unknown word, they can determine and/or approximate its pronunciation and meaning using suggestions such as the following:
  • Look for context clues: familiar words that contain ideas surrounding an unknown word.
    — Read the whole sentence, paying attention to the words directly before or after the unknown word.
  • Look for key words: phrases that define the word or words that might mean the same or opposite (synonyms and antonyms).
    — Look at diagrams or related visuals.
  • Determine if any familiar word parts are in the word.
    — Look for root words, prefixes, suffixes, and combining forms.
  • Guess at the meaning using your new information and determine if the meaning fits within the sentence.

Inferential Understanding Strategies

Inferential understanding and analysis involves using higher order thinking skills, such as encouraged by the QAR concept map strategy. A useful model, developed by Bloom in the 1950s, identifies six levels of complexity of human thought. Even after all this time, Bloom's Taxonomy remains relevant, as it is consistent with the latest research on brain functions. The six levels were discussed in Chapter 3 as a useful framework for consideration in increasing the complexity of tasks. This Taxonomy needs to be especially considered in planning for tasks to enhance students' efficiencies in reading comprehension.

To infer information, students need to organize given data to come to a conclusion about some component that may be missing. As students move from the early grades, where the goal is "learning to read," to the upper elementary grades, where the goal is "reading to learn," there is more demand placed on them for inferential understanding and analysis. However, some students may focus more on the concrete and may not readily understand the concept of inferring. In such situations, a picture strategy can be used, as this bridges the gap between the concrete and abstract.

✔ **Task 1a:** Inferential strategies using three Dog Pictures
Use Dog Picture #1 (on page 117). Ask questions such as the following. As applicable, you may increase the complexity by asking, "What else could it be?" after any set of questions.
- What do you think is in the picture underneath this blank box? What cues led you to that assumption?
- What do you think is going to happen to the dog with the checkered overalls? What cues led you to that assumption?
- What do you think the dog in the striped overalls might be saying? Why do you think that? What cues led you to that assumption?

✔ **Task 1b:** Use Dog Picture #2 (on page 118). Ask questions such as the following. Increase the complexity of the task by asking, "What else could it be?" after any or all sets of questions.
- What do you think is happening in the picture underneath the blank box? What cues led you to that assumption?
- What do you think the dog with the dark pants and striped shirt is saying? Why do you think that? What cues led you to that assumption?
- What do you think will happen? What cues led you to that assumption?

✔ **Task 1c:** Use Dog Picture #3 (on page 119). Ask questions such as the following. Increase the complexity of the task by asking, "What else could it be?" after any set of questions.
- What do you think is in the picture underneath this blank box? What cues led you to that assumption?
- Do you think the three dogs are working hard? Why or why not? What cues led you to that assumption?
- What do you think will happen now? What cues led you to that assumption?
- What do you think the dogs will do next? What cues led you to that assumption?
- Could this ever really happen? Support your answer.

✔ **Task 1d:** Students compare their guesses to the events portrayed in the three Dog Pictures without any covers (pages 120-122). Then have them role-play the dogs' actions in the series of pictures.

✔ **Inferential strategies using three rabbit pictures**
Another set of pictures using three rabbits are on pages 123-125 (with a cover) and 126-128 (without any covers). The rabbit pictures may be used to generate inferential analysis through questions similar to those used with the dog pictures. As an extension activity, have students search for other pictures that would be appropriate to "cover" so that they can create similar tasks for their peers.

Where to Start?
Looking for suggestions on where to start with these new strategies? Here are some ideas.

Remember: It is always critical to take into account your students' developmental levels and learning styles. Where you choose to begin may differ from these suggestions based on the specific needs of your students.

▲ Suggestions for early-elementary students:
  ✔ TELLS
  ✔ KWL chart

▲ Suggestions for upper-elementary students:
  ✔ RCRC
  ✔ Pre-training vocabulary or Repeat reading

▲ Suggestions for middle-school students:
  ✔ Repeat reading
  ✔ QAR mapping or Inferential strategy using three Dog Pictures

▲ Suggestions for high school students:
  ✔ TP Structures
  ✔ Skim, RAP, Map

Organization of Information

To be able to later recall information that was read at an earlier time, and to do so with under-standing and accurate retrieval, it is valuable for students to use strategies that encourage them to actively consolidate, integrate, and organize what they have read. This helps provide them with a hook with which they can hang on to the information and concepts. The more efficiently that the students are able to connect with the material, the more efficient will be their total process.

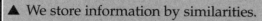

▲ We store information by similarities.
▲ We retrieve information by differences.

Since the brain likes patterns, it seeks similarities. Visual organizers help integrate information by organizing similarities, as well as differences. We store information by similarity because the brain uses similarity to create neural networks. Differences are also important because we tend to retrieve information by differences.

> Long-term memory most often stores new learning into a network that contains learning with similar characteristics or associations, as perceived by the learner. This network identification is one of the connections made in working memory during rehearsal and closure. To retrieve an item, long-term memory identifies how it is dif-ferent from all the other items in that network (Sousa, 2001, 143).

This section presents a variety of visual organizers which can be used in many different situations, as illustrated in Figure 5.5. Some advantages of visual organizers are that they are generally easy to use, help students organize their thinking, and can be easily adjusted to individual preferences. They may include pictures and are often nonlinear, in contrast to the more linear or sequential structure of a traditional outline. The visual nature of the graphic makes it possible to see connec-tions between aspects of the information that may not be as obvious in a more linear form. The

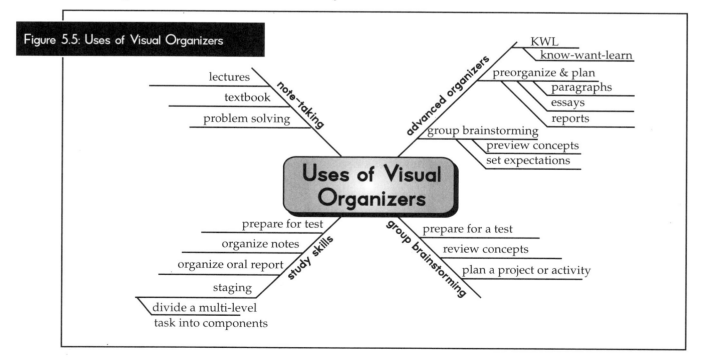

Figure 5.5: Uses of Visual Organizers

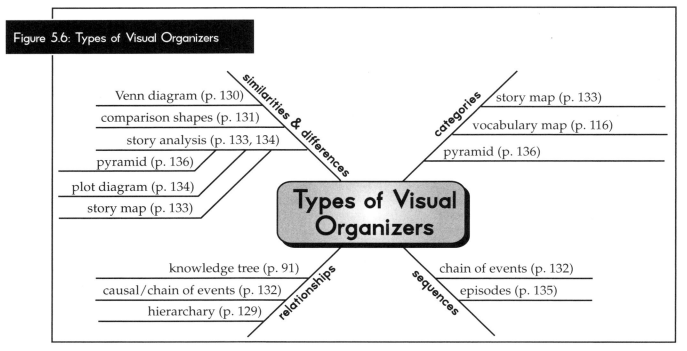

Figure 5.6: Types of Visual Organizers

Venn diagram (p. 130)
comparison shapes (p. 131)
story analysis (p. 133, 134)
pyramid (p. 136)
plot diagram (p. 134)
story map (p. 133)

similarities & differences

story map (p. 133)
vocabulary map (p. 116)
pyramid (p. 136)

categories

Types of Visual Organizers

knowledge tree (p. 91)
causal/chain of events (p. 132)
hierarchary (p. 129)

relationships

chain of events (p. 132)
episodes (p. 135)

sequences

process of creating a visual organizer often generates visualization. This is important because enhancing a student's use of the mind's eye increases comprehension and boosts retention.

Paradoxically, one of the greatest advantages of a visual organizer is that it is seldom needed again. Lazear agrees with that assertion, saying, "The very act of constructing a map is so effective in fixing ideas in memory that often an entire map can be recalled without going back to it at all. A mind map is strongly visual and uses so many of the natural functions of memory that frequently it can simply be read off in the "mind's eye"" (1991, p. 66). Wolfe suggests that visually mapping information mirrors the structure used by the brain, which may be why it is so productive for enhancing students' storage and retention of information. She reminds us that the "various aspects of a memory, or of a learned fact, are not stored in a single, specific location in the brain, but are stored in networks of networks. Images are stored in the visual cortex, sounds in the auditory cortex, and so forth" (2001, p. 158). Similarly, a visual organizer creates networks. Another significant value of developing a visual organizer is that it helps to chunk information. For example, when planning a multi-level task it helps to break the larger activity into smaller units or stages. After all, no task is overwhelming if it is approached in small steps.

A large number of visual organizers are available which may be adjusted to almost any purpose. In this section, four types of organizers will be presented which include organizers for classification and categorization, comparison and analysis, sequencing, and stories. Suggestions for semantic organizers were presented in Chapter 4 in the vocabulary section. Figure 5.6, Different Types of Visual Organizers, identifies a few of the many types of organizers that may be created. The variety is limited only by the developer's creativity. Available software, such as *Kidspiration* or *Inspiration*, enables a student to create a visual organizer directly on the computer. An advantage of this software is the ready availability of colors, shapes, and clip art.

Organizers for Classification and Categorization

These organizers are used to classify, categorize and arrange information. Many different names are used, depending upon the graphic format. Some examples are mind maps, concept maps, webs, clusters, pictorial organizers, network trees, or fishbone maps. Figures 5.5 and 5.6 represent two examples of a basic mind map. The hierarchy map on page 129 shows the relationships among structures of the brain. Examples of other concepts that may be visually represented using one of these types of organizers are the human body, parts of a plant, causes of the Civil War, or components for a book review. In the early grades, students may create a pictorial organizer about themselves: a "Who Am I?" description. In high school, students may create a cluster map regarding matter, with branches for properties, matter states, history of matter, and changing matter.

Organizers for Comparison and Analysis

These maps are useful to help students analyze similarities and differences. They highlight specific attributes that need to be compared while also presenting the global view. The structure of a basic Venn diagram is demonstrated on page 130. The first Venn diagram relates the music of the Beatles to that of Mozart. The Comparison Boxes on page 131 also show the relationship between the Beatles and Mozart in a different format. Many other concepts may be compared using one of these structures, for example, a comparison between mammals and vertebrates or between Alice's country and the Queen's country (after reading a story such as "Through the Looking Glass"). The second Venn diagram on page 130 demonstrates how the format may be expanded to include three different topics.

Organizers for Sequential information

Information that follows a sequence or chain of events can be organized graphically to show the relevant progression. These types of organizers are valuable for explaining events such as the metamorphosis of a caterpillar into a butterfly, the steps for recycling glass, or the subtasks necessary for completing a complex assignment. A timeline is another example of a visual sequential organizer, and in the early grades, students may create a timeline of events in their own or the lives of their families. These organizers may also be combined with a culinary event, such as having students visually map the steps for making a peanut butter sandwich or "bug on a log" (raisins on cream cheese on celery). After creating the visual organizer, the students may actually create what they described and then eat their creations. A sequential organizer may be developed horizontally or vertically. Page 132 presents a vertical representation of the development of a frog.

Organizers for Stories

Information from stories can be organized in several different ways. These graphic representations can be used for stories about fictional or historical events. Specific target components may vary depending on the nature of the task and the age of the students; however, many of the key components are often similar: events, characters, setting, plot, and theme.

- ▲ Events
  - ✔ What were the key events?
  - ✔ Which event was primary?
  - ✔ When did the primary event take place?
  - ✔ Where did the event take place?

▲ Characters
  ✔ Who was involved?
  ✔ Which played major roles?
  ✔ Which played minor roles?

▲ Setting
  ✔ Where?
  ✔ When?
  ✔ Over what period of time?

▲ Plot
  ✔ The problem: What set the events in motion? What was the goal of the main characters?
  ✔ The progress: What are the key events that describe the progress of the situation?
  ✔ The resolution: How was the goal reached? How was the problem solved?

▲ Theme
  ✔ What is the overall or larger meaning of the situation or event?
  ✔ What have we learned from this?
  ✔ How can I (the student) relate the event to my (his) own life?

Four graphic organizer formats for stories are presented on pages 133-136.
  ▲ General story map format — page 133
  ▲ Plot diagram — page 134
  ▲ Story map (also applicable to a history lesson) (Jones, 2000-2001) — page 135
  ▲ Event or story pyramid (Jones, 2000-2001) — page 136

Where to Start?
Looking for suggestions on where to start with these new strategies? Here are some ideas.

Remember: It is always critical to take into account your students' developmental levels and learning styles. Where you choose to begin may differ from these suggestions based on the specific needs of your students.

  ▲ Suggestions for early-elementary students:
    ✔ Sequential organizers combined with a culinary experience
    ✔ "Who I am" mind map

  ▲ Suggestions for upper-elementary students:
    ✔ Comparison boxes for concepts in one of their units
    ✔ Timeline to correspond with their history units

  ▲ Suggestions for middle-school students:
    ✔ Story maps
    ✔ Sequential organizer to correspond with an event from their science unit

  ▲ Suggestions for high school students:
    ✔ Venn diagrams
    ✔ Timeline to correspond with a unit in science or history

Review

Activity 5.1: Reflection

This activity is similar to Journal Writing that you may ask your students to do after a class. Thinking about or reflecting on a task or concept is an effective strategy to encourage transfer of the information in a way that will help it consolidate into networks and patterns. A reflection can be a valuable vehicle to help students refine their thinking about a concept. It also provides you, as the teacher, with valuable feedback on their understanding of the concepts.

Briefly answer the following questions.

1. What is the primary message you learned about reading comprehension strategies? _____
_____

2. Compare this message to what you already knew about reading comprehension strategies. How do they connect? _____
_____
_____
_____

3. How can you use this information with your students? Will you make any changes/adjustments in how you present assignments? _____
_____
_____
_____
_____
_____

4. Select one visual organizer format that you haven't used before. Use that format to organize a unit, chapter, or lesson that you will be teaching soon. Use color for emphasis.

Sometimes It's the Little Things

> James, age sixteen, handed in a too-short report. Instead of criticizing and admonishing, the teacher wrote, "I found your report interesting, tight, and concise. However, when I finished it, I kept wishing there were more to read." James felt motivated to write longer reports.
>
> — (Ginott 1972, p. 252-253)

Number Prefixes

Number	Latin Prefix	Sample Word	Greek Prefix	Sample Word
1	uni-	uniform universe	mono-	monograph monogram
2	bi-	bicycle biceps	di-	digraph dioxide
3	tri-	triangle tricycle		
4	quar-	quarter quartet	tetra-	tetrameter tetrahedron
4	quadr-	quadrangle quadraphonic		
5	quint-	quintet quintuplet	pent-	pentagon pentathlon
6	sex-	sextet sextuplet	hex-	hexagon hexagram
7	sept-	September septagenarian	hept-	heptagon heptameter
8	octo-	October octopus		
9	nona-	nonagon nonagenarian		
10	nove-	November novena		
10			dec-	decade December
10			deca-	decathalon decagon
10			deci-	decimal decimeter
100	cent-	centigrade century centimeter	hect-	hectogram hectometer
1,000	milli-	milligram million millimeter	kilo-	kilogram kilowatt kiloliter
10,000			myria-	myriad myriameter
1,000,000 one million			mega-	megameter [mega- also means large size]
1,000,000,000 one billion			giga-	gigameter gigahertz

Common Suffixes

Nouns	Examples
-sion, -tion Words ending in these suffixes are nouns that refer to *things*.	• decision • abbreviation • progression • intention • admission • production
-er, -or, -cian, -ist Words ending in these suffixes are nouns that generally refer to *people*.	• teacher • beautician • baker • pharmacist • Hollander • creator • physician • clinician

Verbs	Examples
-ize, -ity, -ify Verbs can often be made by adding these suffixes to nouns. Sometimes the accented syllable will change and the unaccented vowel may then convert to a shwa, as in *acidify*. A shwa sound is defined as a nondistinct vowel sound in unstressed syllables in English. It is often close to the /uh/ sound.	• human humanize • anatomy anatomize • apology apologize • acid acidify • class classify • beauty beautify

Adverbs	Examples
-ly Most words ending in this suffix are adverbs and describe a verb.	• quickly • desperately • slowly • **Exceptions:** Some words like *heavenly, bodily,* and *costly* are adjectives. • **Exceptions:** Words like *holy* and *silly* end in –ly, but –ly is not a suffix in those words.

Adjectives	Examples
-ous, -ful, -ar, -ive Most words ending in these suffixes are adjectives and describe a noun.	• generous • successive • spectacular • grateful

Vocabulary Word Map

Write the word. _____

Write a definition of the word. _____

_____

_____

Write a synonym. _____

Write an antonym. _____

Write the word here, in color. _____

Use the word in a sentence that shows
its meaning.

_____

_____

_____

_____

Draw a picture of the word or draw
yourself doing something related to the
word. Use color.

Dog Picture #1

Dog Picture #2

Dog Picture #3

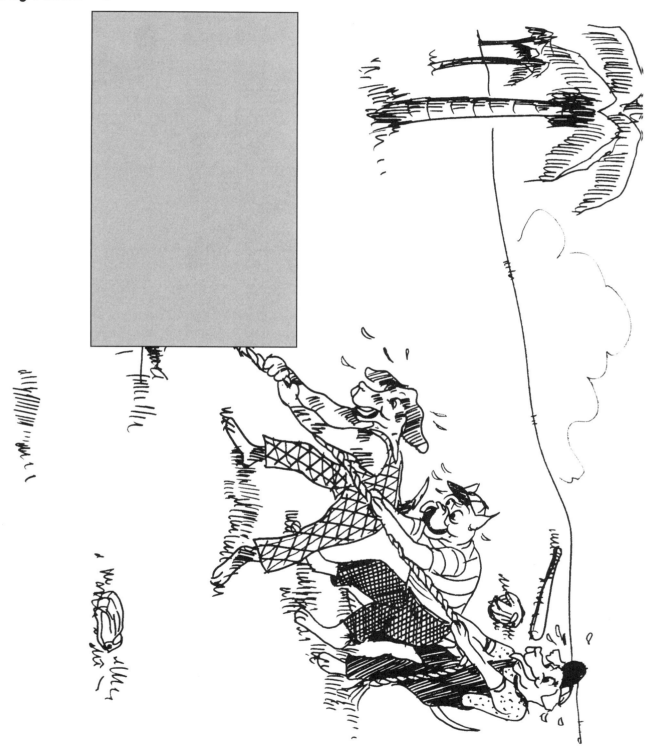

Dog Picture #1a

Dog Picture #2a

Dog Picture #3a

Rabbit Picture #1

Rabbit Picture #2

Rabbit Picture #3

Rabbit Picture #1a

Rabbit Picture #2a

Rabbit Picture #3a

Hierarchy Map

Structure of the Brain

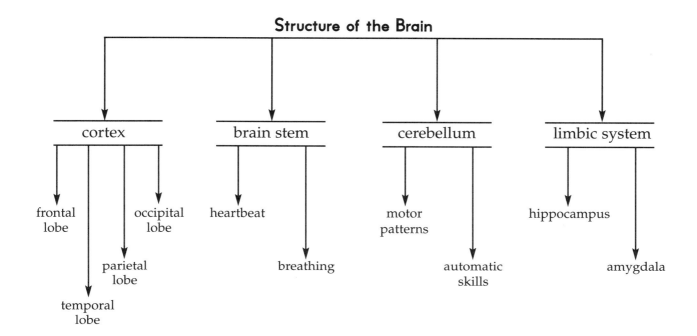

Venn Diagrams

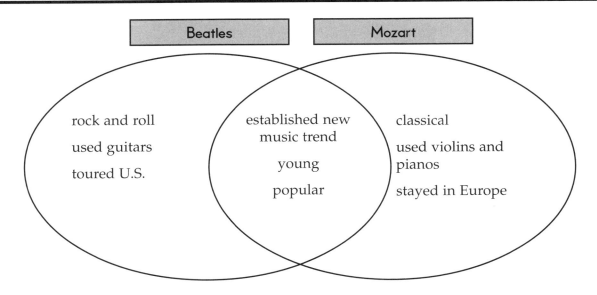

You can add an extra dimension to a Venn diagram by adding a third category. The Spelling Triangle in Figure 4.6 on page 71 can be represented by this format.

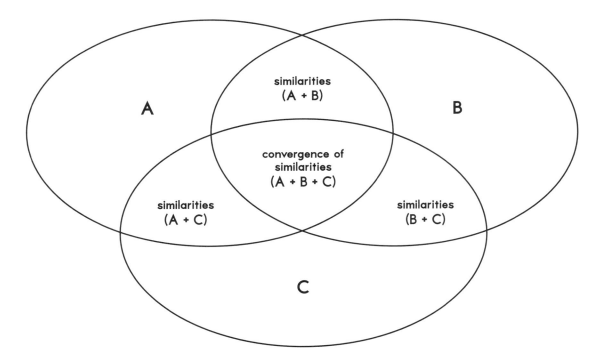

Comparison Boxes

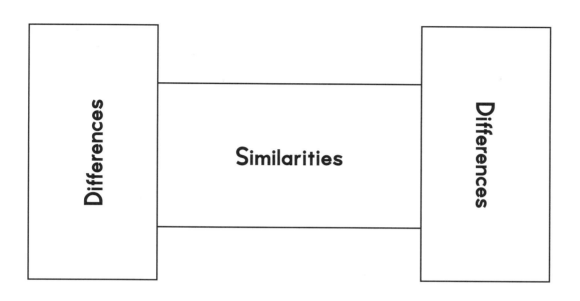

Differences | Similarities | Differences

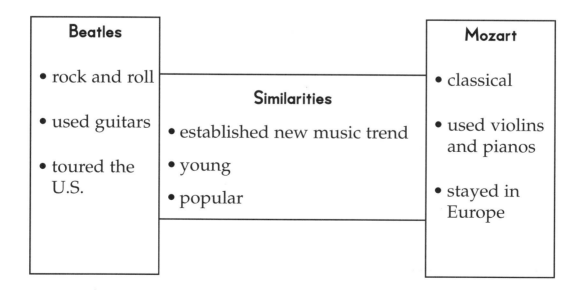

Beatles
- rock and roll
- used guitars
- toured the U.S.

Similarities
- established new music trend
- young
- popular

Mozart
- classical
- used violins and pianos
- stayed in Europe

Vertical Sequential Organizer

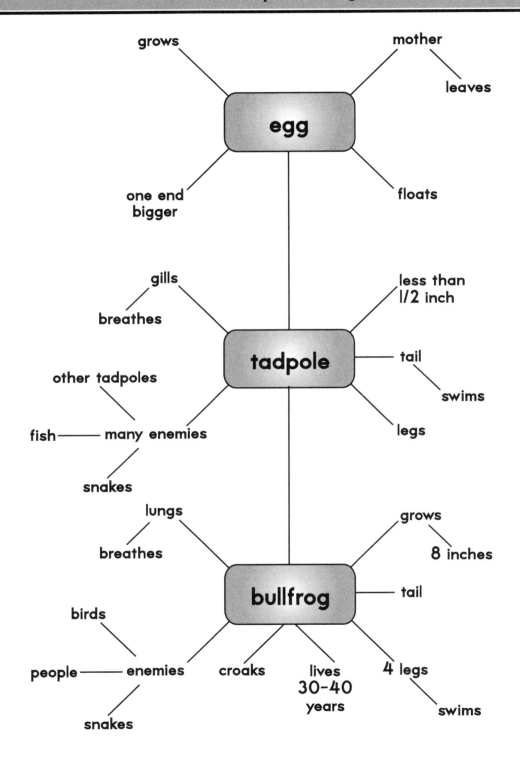

General Story Map

Title: _____

Author: _____

___ Setting ___   ___ Characters ___

___ Problem or Goal ___

___ Events ___

Themes:

A Personal Message

A Universal Truth

___ Resolution or Outcome ___

133

Plot Diagram

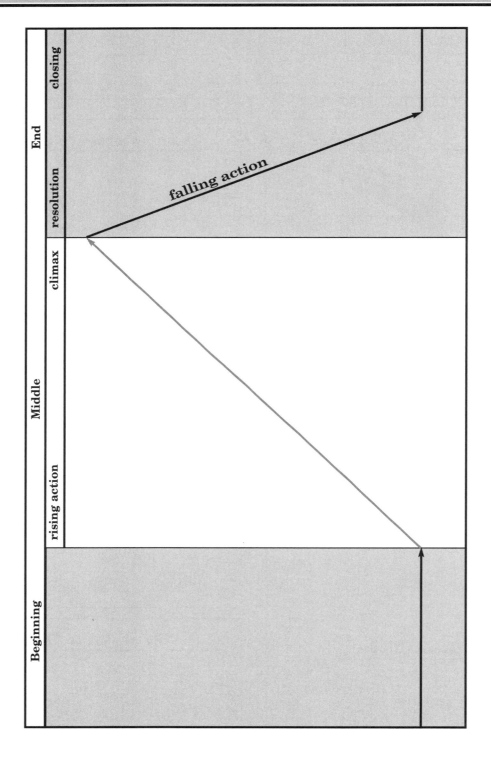

Story Map for Historical Event

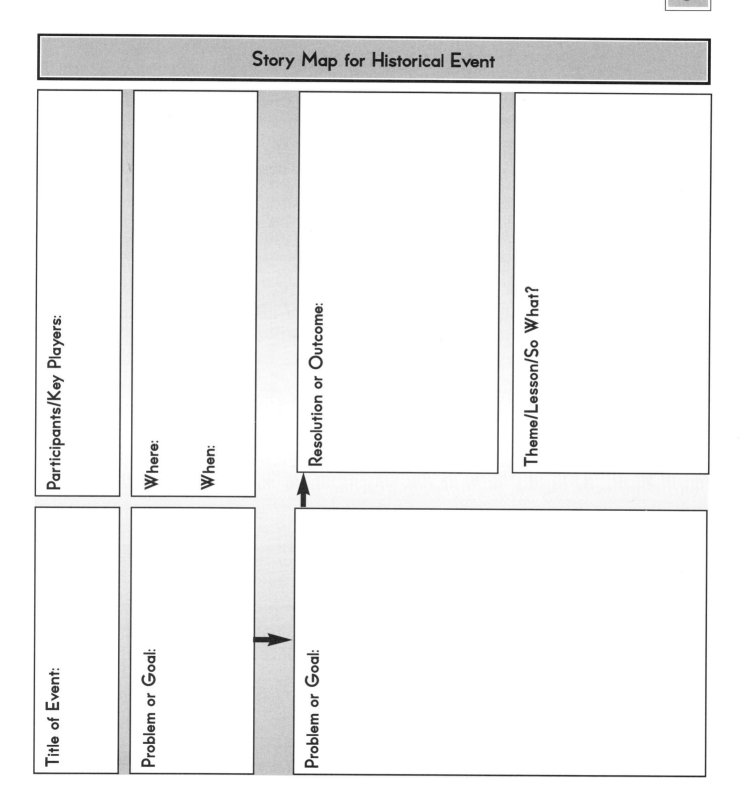

Participants/Key Players:

Where:

When:

Title of Event:

Problem or Goal:

Problem or Goal:

Resolution or Outcome:

Theme/Lesson/So What?

Event or Story Pyramid

_____
main character's name

_____ _____
two words describing this person

_____ _____ _____
three words describing the setting or place

_____ _____ _____ _____
four words describing an important event

_____ _____ _____ _____ _____
five words describing the main idea or importance of this event

Math Strategies

Chapter 6

Let's begin this chapter with an activity. You will find the answer to this problem on the bottom of the next page, but don't look at it until you have attempted the problem. Begin by selecting a 3-digit number, making sure that the first and third digits have a difference of more than 1. For example, 287 or 924 would be okay, but 283 or 928 would not be appropriate for this activity as the difference between the first and third digits is not more than 1. Do your calculations in the chart in Figure 6.1.

1. Write your number, in Step 1 in Figure 6.1.
2. Now reverse the digits to complete Step 2.
3. Subtract the smaller number from the larger in Step 3.
4. Reverse your answer in Step 4.
5. Add the reversed answer and the sum from Step 3 together in Step 5.
6. What is your answer?
7. Now look at the answer on the bottom of page 138. Are you surprised, or did you predict this outcome?

Figure 6.1: Math Problem

	Example	Your Problem
Step 1	287	
Step 2	782	
Step 3	782 −287 495	−_____
Step 4	594	
Step 5	594 +495	+_____
Answer	1089	

As we consider memory strategies to facilitate math development, we can think about the above activity.

▲ Was this a rote memorized task?

▲ Was it a magic trick?

▲ Is this a function of math patterns?

This math trick works because of the inherent patterns within numbers. Understanding this structure and being able to recognize patterns is a tremendous asset for students because this understanding greatly facilitates their abilities to recall math facts and procedures.

As we think about memory within the area of math, there are several cautions to consider.

▲ Allow a student to advance conceptually as she is ready, without holding her back until she "learns" her facts. This may necessitate the use of compensations and/or bypass strategies such as a number line, calculator, or multiplication grid.

▲ Frequently model strategies for step-wise problem solving and encourage students to ask themselves the important question, "What strategy do I need?"

▲ Vary your presentation mode to encourage priming and use of the Big 4 Memory Facilitators.

▲ Keep in mind the heavy cognitive burden that is imposed on a child when learning math. Three of the important considerations are as follows (Levine, 2002, p. 225):
- ✔ Mathematics is highly cumulative. The mastery of what has gone before is crucial for subsequent learning.
- ✔ Mathematics requires the integration of multiple developmental functions.
- ✔ Responses in mathematics usually need to be highly convergent, i.e., there is usually only one correct answer.

▲ Allow a student compensations if spatial organization is a problem. For example, if a student has difficulty lining up numbers in a problem, allow him to use large graph paper or loose leaf paper turned sideways. This provides guidelines to help in aligning columns.

▲ Remember the valuable teaching tip, "Too much too fast — it won't last."
- ✔ Students need to develop comfort with a given concept before moving on to the next.
- ✔ Spiraling (reviewing past concepts) is valuable for all students but especially critical for some.

Input Components

As students progress through the learning of math concepts, it is critical to attend to the efficiency of the input given to them as well as to the degree of their comprehension. If the words or concepts do not make sense, they will not stick. This can be observed when a student appears to understand a lesson on one day, but then on the next day is confused once again. The more complex the linguistic structures, the greater the chance for confusions.

Priming

An example of priming was suggested in Chapter 3 for teaching the concepts of circumference, diameter, and radius. It was suggested that you begin a lesson on those concepts by presenting the story, *Sir Cumference and the First Round Table* (Neuschwander, 1997). This story teaches the vocabulary words critical to the concept while also providing an attention-getting activity to prime, or prepare, the students for the concepts.

There are many ways that stories, magic tricks, and other activities can be used to introduce concepts that will be presented within a lesson. The following strategies can be used to add a component of fun and may be used as priming activities while also enhancing students' initial comprehension. They are input activities because they grab attention and increase comprehension while also providing a vehicle to rehearse and review the necessary information.

Answer to the math problem on page 137: **1089**

▲ Linguistic Strategies

It is critical that students understand the many linguistic components involved in math. Mathematics is its own form of communication. Wahl described it well in stating that math "represents an extremely concise portrayal of relationships among quantities" (Wahl 1997, p. 12). Some examples of strategies to help students explore and manipulate the language of math follow. Students can also be encouraged to use many of these suggestions in developing appropriate "self-talk" as an independent strategy to guide themselves through math problems.

When to Use These Strategies:
Use these strategies to prepare students for understanding, manipulating, and remembering the words associated with specific number concepts. Encourage students to participate in the activity as suggested and then expand upon the activity using a related concept.

Act Out a Number Concept

✔ Have students pretend to be the number 9 and pantomine how 9 feels compared to 10.

✔ This will help them focus on 10 as an important number in our number system.

Talk About Math

✔ Have students "teach" what they are learning to their parents as a homework assignment.

✔ Have students explain math concepts to younger students.

Student-Created Word Problems

✔ Creating their own word problems will facilitate students' ability to elaborate on and talk about computations and the language of word problems. When students create their own word problems, they also increase their understanding of how to manipulate language within such problems.
  • This activity is particularly valuable for students who struggle to understand word problems.

✔ Begin by creating a word problem template and having students follow it to create their own word problems.

✔ Progress to having the students create word problems without a template.

Explore Morphology

✔ Students explore the morphology (the word parts) of important conceptual terms.

✔ Following are some word parts that are relevant for mathematical terms:
  • multi-   • sub-   • equi-   • -lateral
  • poly-   • -gon   • tri-   • quad(r)-

✔ Students brainstorm words that include the above word parts. Encourage them to use words related to math.

✔ Students determine the meaning of each of the above word parts and discuss how the word part relates to the concept of the total word containing that word part.

✔ Examples:
- **multi-**: multiply, multiplication, multiple
  — The prefix **multi-** means "many."
  — *Multiply* means "to make a number many."
  — *Multiplication* means "the process of making a number many."
  — *Multiple* means "more than one or many."
- **sub-**: subtract, subacute, subcategory
  — The prefix **sub-** means "under" or "down."
  — *Subtract* means "to pull a number down or decrease."
  — *Subacute* means "less than acute" or "under acute."
  — *Subcategory* means "a division or part of the category" or "under a category."
- **-gon**: hexagon, heptagon, octagon, nonagon, decagon
  — The suffix **-gon** means "a figure having a certain number of angles."
  — A *hexagon* has six sides and six angles (hex- is 6).
  — A *heptagon* has seven sides and seven angles (hepta- is 7).
  — An *octagon* has 8 sides and 8 angles (octa- is 8).
  — A *nonagon* has nine sides and 9 angles (nona- is 9).
  — A *decagon* has 10 sides and 10 angles (deca- is 10).

✔ Additional strategies with number prefixes were discussed in Chapter 5 on page 90.

Explore Fractional Parts

✔ Use the three S's (structure, systematic, sensory) in presenting fractions in a meaningful manner, and have students explore the meaning of various fractional parts.
- Have students peel and section an orange and do the following:
  — Count the sections.
  — Discuss the fractional part of one section or two sections, etc. ("This is half an orange," These are two quarters of an orange," etc.)
- Perform similar activities with other items that can be eaten: pizza, a pie, a sandwich.
- Begin with larger fractional parts and progress to smaller units.

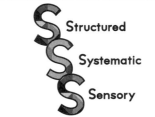

Structured

Systematic

Sensory

Step-by-Step Story Problems

The following five-step strategy helps students use staging and actively progress through a story problem in a step-by-step manner (adapted from Vail, 1999).

✔ **Step 1:** Identify the main problem or question within the story problem.
- The main problem is often presented as a question.
- Sometimes this problem is presented as a statement rather than a question.
- *Strategy:* Circle all of the questions or write each on a separate location.

✔ **Step 2:** Identify the background.
- The background is generally not necessary to solve the problem. For example, the problem may state that the activity takes place in a store or at a movie theater.
- *Strategy:* Identify the background information and cross it out.

✔ **Step 3:** Identify the facts.
- The facts are important and are the information that is necessary in order to solve the problem.
- The facts are often the longest phrases and may contain numbers.
- *Strategy:* Underline all of the facts.

✔ **Step 4:** Look for any extra information.
- Many word problems contain extra information that is not needed to solve the problem. Sometimes this extra information is a distraction to add confusion.
- The extra information must be identified and eliminated so that the facts (the most important part of the problem) can stand out.
- *Strategy:* Cross out all of the extra information that is not needed.

✔ **Step 5:** Review is critical.
- This step is necessary so the student makes sure he understands the word problem and what it is asking.
- The student carefully rereads the problem, saying it in his own words.
- *Strategy:* The student asks himself, "Does my answer make sense?"

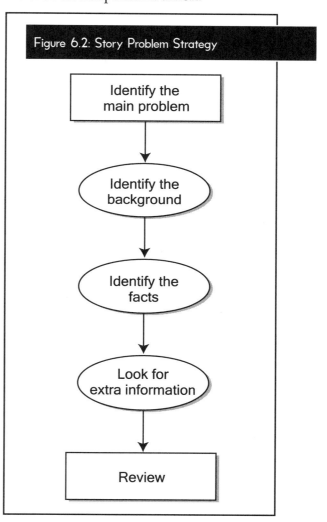

Figure 6.2: Story Problem Strategy

Identify the main problem

Identify the background

Identify the facts

Look for extra information

Review

Solidify and Clarify Directional Confusions: The Bleszinski Method

✔ Some students, after learning all four math operations, continue to experience directional confusions (they may subtract 2 from 5 in a problem such as 32-5).
  • These students often have difficulty with subtraction and long division.

✔ The Bleszinski Method provides a way to reteach the four basic math operations in a very concrete and consistent manner. The goal is for students to develop a dependable approach for all four operations using a consistent visual pattern and auditory cue (self-talk).
  • Once students develop understanding and accuracy using this method, they continue to practice until they reach a higher level of confidence and automaticity.
  • At this point they are taught the commutative properties of addition (A+B = B+A) and then multiplication (A x B = B x A).

✔ **Step 1:** Ensure that students understand the meaning of the words *top* and *bottom* by using a variety of manipulative techniques.

✔ **Step 2:** Present students with a four-part grid and explain that there are similarities in the patterns for adding, subtracting, multiplying, and dividing.

✔ **Step 3:** Present the addition section (box **a**) of the grid in Figure 6.3.
  • Pointing to the large **B**, explain that when adding, we will add the bottom number to the top number. Point to the large **T** as you say "top."
  • Have students repeat the cue phrase for addition: "Add bottom to top."
  • Practice with a variety of single digit addition problems using the cue phrase and making sure that the students consistently add the bottom number to the top number as they say, "add bottom to top."

✔ **Step 4:** Present the multiplication section (box **b**) of the grid.
  • Have students repeat the cue phrase for multiplication: "Multiply bottom times top."
  • Practice with a variety of single digit multiplication problems using the cue phrase and making sure that the students consistently multiply the bottom number times the top number as they say, "multiply bottom times top."

✔ **Review steps 3 and 4**, helping the students develop accuracy, consistency, and confidence.

✔ **Step 5:** Present the subtraction section (box **c**) of the grid.
  • Have students repeat the cue phrase for subtraction: "Subtract bottom from top."
  • Practice with a variety of single digit subtraction problems using the cue

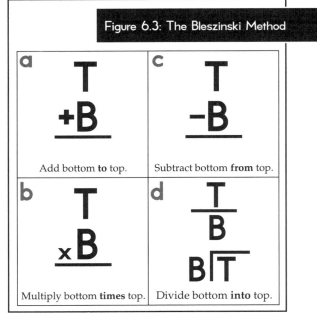

Figure 6.3: The Bleszinski Method

a	c
T +B	T -B
Add bottom **to** top.	Subtract bottom **from** top.
b	d
T xB	T B B‾T‾
Multiply bottom **times** top.	Divide bottom **into** top.

phrase and making sure that the students consistently subtract the bottom number from the top number as they say, "subtract bottom from top."

✔ **Step 6:** Present the division section (box **d**) in the grid and call your students' attention to the top figure in the square.
  • Have students repeat the cue phrase for division: "Divide bottom into top."
  • Practice with a variety of single digit division problems using the cue phrase and making sure that the students consistently divide the bottom number into the top number as they say, "divide bottom into top."

✔ **Review steps 3, 4, 5, and 6,** repeating until the students develop consistent accuracy and confidence.

✔ **Step 7:** Present the bottom figure in the division section (box **d**) of the grid, and explain to your students that this is another format for division.
  • Explain the relationship of this horizontal division format with the first vertical format.
  • Practice with a variety of single-digit division problems and the cue phrase, "Divide bottom into top."
  • Demonstrate how the two forms of division problems represent the relationship between long division and fractions.

✔ Monitor your students' developmental levels and their abilities to understand such concepts. Some students may be able to work simultaneously with more than one section of the grid and then proceed to practice for automatization.

▲ Visual Strategies

Visual organizers can be used to represent relationships among numbers and specific procedures. Presenting a concept using the visual mode provides an additional modality to reinforce the linguistic messages. Encouraging a student to have the flexibility to convert verbal messages into a visual format helps increase processing depth, which ultimately leads to greater recall. It is especially important for students who struggle with concept formation to visually map and organize the key concepts as well as talk about them. To further rehearse the information and enhance your students' understanding, they can also use their visual strategies and organizers to teach the concepts to younger students.

When to Use These Strategies:
Use visual strategies to help students understand the spatial components related to math and to develop visual patterns for the procedures.

Color-Coding Columns

✔ If a student has difficulty maintaining alignment of the ones' column and tens' column, it is useful to color-code each column.
  • Color-code the ones' column with a green marker (indicating that green means "go" or "start").
  • Use a different color marker for the tens' column.
  • As the student increases his understanding of the use of columns, omit the color for the tens' column and only use green for the ones' column.
  • To further decrease the cues, place only a green arrow above the ones' column to indicate "start."

Adding Using Two Rulers

✔ This strategy helps students who have difficulty learning and retaining addition math facts.

✔ Use two rulers. To add 3 + 4, do the following:
- Locate the 3 on the bottom ruler.
- Place the left edge of the top ruler directly over the number 3.
- Locate the 4 on the top ruler.
- The number on the bottom ruler directly below the 4 is the sum, as in Figure 6.4.
- To simplify the activity, create and use rulers that only show lines at the inch mark.

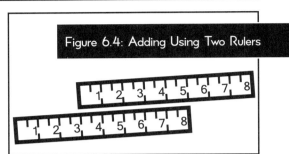

Figure 6.4: Adding Using Two Rulers

Visual Organizer for Addition and Multiplication

✔ This can be used as part of the initial introduction of multiplication along with related manipulative activities.

✔ Have students work in small groups. Provide some of the groups (groups A) with 50 manipulatives (pennies, peanuts, counters). Provide the other groups (groups B) with 50 of the same items, but arranged in groups of 10.
- Ask each group to count their items.
- Students in the A groups count their items one at a time: 1, 2, 3, 4, 5, . . . 50.
- Students in the B groups count their items by groups of 10: 10, 20, 30, 40, 50.
- Discuss why the B group students finished sooner than the A group students.
- Create a visual organizer to demonstrate the procedure that each group used, as in Figure 6.5.

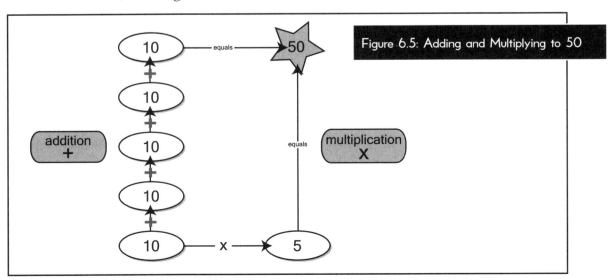

Figure 6.5: Adding and Multiplying to 50

Visual Organizer for a Multi-Step Math Procedure

✔ After students understand the meaning of fractions and the vocabulary for the basic components (numerator, denominator, LCD [lowest common denominator]), introduce the steps to use when adding fractions by creating a graphic organizer.

- Create the organizer with the students while simultaneously demonstrating the meaning of each step using manipulatives.
- Figure 6.6 presents the various steps and decisions that need to be made when adding fractions. The procedure starts with the box at the left.
- Figure 6.7 on the next page presents a more detailed format with examples for the same procedure. The procedure starts with the shaded diamond in the center.

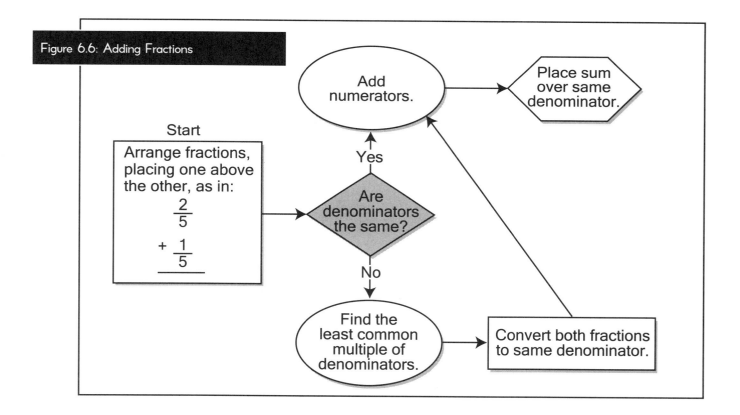

Figure 6.6: Adding Fractions

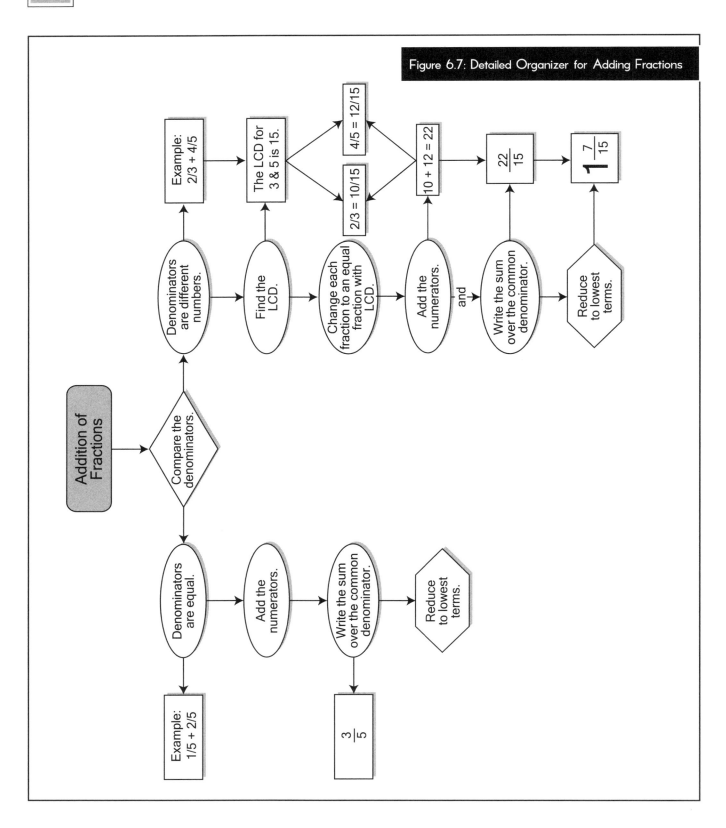

Figure 6.7: Detailed Organizer for Adding Fractions

Relate Circumference and the Right Triangle

✔ Use this activity after students have already been introduced to the concepts of *circumference* and *right triangle*. This activity is to expand their understanding of those concepts and demonstrate the relationships between them.
- Draw a large circle.
- Identify and draw the diameter by drawing a line through the center so that the circle is divided in half.
- Pick a spot on the circumference and draw a straight line to each end of the diameter, as in Figure 6.8.
- This triangle will have a right angle.
- Repeat activity using other spots on the circumference of the circle.
- Encourage students to creatively color their designs.

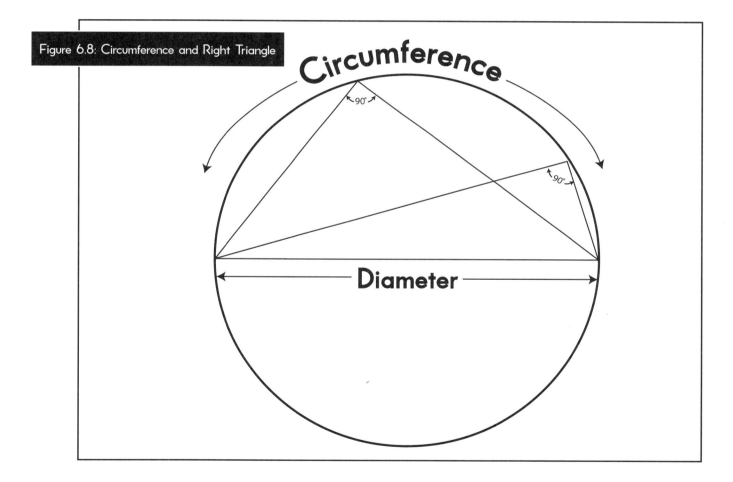

Figure 6.8: Circumference and Right Triangle

6

▲ *Kinesthetic Strategies*

Active learning involves being actively involved with the concept(s). Although not always necessary, activities may include moving one's body as part of the procedure, as movement adds a valuable dimension that aids memory. Sometimes the movements may be as simple as counting on one's fingers. Other times the activity may be more complex and include large motor movements. Following are some examples.

When to Use These Strategies:

These strategies may be used when students would benefit from a movement break or to provide an introduction for new vocabulary or concepts. They can also be used as rehearsal strategies to help consolidate the information.

Gestures to Represent the Meaning of Basic Procedures

✔ These activities are useful for young students or students who are confused about basic math operations.

✔ Associate *addition* with the word *smoosh*, encouraging students to develop a strong visual image.
  - When saying the word *smoosh*, hold your hands apart in front of your body and pretend you have a big lump of clay that you want to squeeze together into a smaller ball. While doing this say, "Adding is like smooshing."
  - Have students repeat the action with you. (To enhance the imagery value , use actual clay.)
  - Take two balls of clay and smoosh them together, explaining, "Now I smoosh two clay balls together and this makes a total. When we add, we take two (or more) numbers and create a total, which is the combination of the two numbers."

✔ Explain that subtraction is removing one part from another part and focusing on what is left.
  - Associate *subtraction* with a movement that can be labeled *take away* or *minus*.
  - Hold one hand in front of your body in an open position and with the other hand pretend to take something "away" from the inside of your first hand.
  - Label your movement while making the motion, using *take away* or *minus*.
  - Have students repeat the activity with you, being sure to associate the movement with the label.
  - Repeat the activity holding three balls of clay in your left hand and then take away one. Explain that what is left is the answer or the *difference*. Have students perform this and similar activities several times and then have students take turns explaining the procedure to others.
  - Repeat the activity with a larger number of counters (beads, pieces of cereal, etc.). For example, start with 18 counters and take away 11. The remainder is 7 counters, which the students identify as the answer.

Finger Calculation

✔ Counting on fingers for addition or subtraction:
  • Determine that students have appropriate finger discrimination so that they will count their fingers accurately.
  • Students may use a number line in coordination with finger counting.

✔ Finger multiplication:
  • Refer to pages 161-164 at the end of this chapter for details on finger multiplication.
  • To help reduce the active working memory demands, have the students place numbered stickers on each finger to encourage more efficient visualization.
  • The 9s are the easiest for many students to learn because the pattern is concrete and straightforward, as on page 161.
  • Multiplying a 2 digit number by 9 is relatively easy once students become automatic in finger calculation of a 1-digit number by 9, as on page 162.
  • The 6s through 9s may also be computed with fingers, but these facts require several steps to complete and students will need to be able to deal with the active working memory demands. These steps are described on pages 163-164.

Body Measurements

✔ Introduce a unit on measurement by presenting measurement terms in comparison with the students' own bodies.

✔ Introduce the concept of square vs. rectangle by having each student cut a piece of string that is as long as she is tall.
  • The student compares her height with her reach.
    – She holds her arms straight out to the side.
    – Using the string that equals her height, she stretches that length of string from hand to hand, keeping her arms straight out.
  • If the student's reach matches her height, she is a "square" (equal sides). If her length and reach are uneven, she is a "rectangle."

✔ A student compares the size of her thumb (from the length of the first knuckle to the tip of the thumbnail) to an inch on a ruler.

✔ A student compares the size of her foot on a ruler to her own foot.

✔ Have students develop other comparisons using their own body and discuss the results with their peers.

▲ *Patterns Strategies*
The brain learns and remembers by patterns, and therefore, it is important to help students to develop the habit of looking for patterns within new concepts. This is especially critical in the area of math because number patterns are so prominent in our environment. Manipulatives and body movements can be used with the following activities to reinforce the patterns.

When to Use These Strategies:
These strategies are valuable to use when introducing new patterns and new concepts, but they can also be used at any time throughout a lesson to reinforce a given concept.

Triangle Magic Trick

✔ Use 10 pennies to complete this activity.
✔ Arrange the pennies on a flat surface in the shape of the triangle, as in Figure 6.9.
✔ The goal is to change the triangle so that its flat side is on top and its point is down:

✔ The challenge is that you can only move three pennies.
✔ The answer is on page 165.
✔ Discuss the pattern involved and encourage students to try to discover why the "magic" trick works.

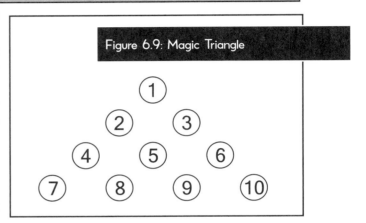

Figure 6.9: Magic Triangle

Multiplication Pattern of 10s

✔ The 10s tables provide an easy pattern: just add a 0 to the number being multiplied.
  • For example, 2 x 10 = 20; 7 x 10 = 70; 55 x 10 = 550.
✔ Discuss with the students why this works and have them use manipulatives to practice and explain the pattern.

Multiplication Pattern of 9s

✔ The 9s table is fairly easy because it has an obvious pattern due to the fact that it is so close to 10.
✔ Encourage students to observe the 9s table in Figure 6.10 and discuss what

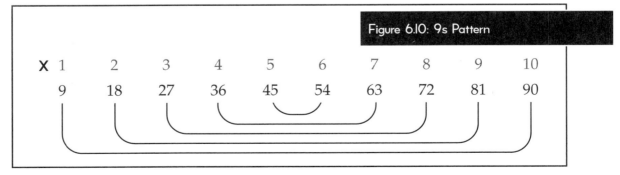

Figure 6.10: 9s Pattern

X	1	2	3	4	5	6	7	8	9	10
	9	18	27	36	45	54	63	72	81	90

patterns they may observe. Some patterns that students may notice about the facts of 9x1 through 9x10 are the following:

- Each answer has a reverse counterpart (18, 81; 27, 72; 36, 63; etc.).
- The sum of the digits in every answer is 9.
- The multiplier number minus 1 gives the first digit of the answer, e.g., the answer for 6 X 9 starts with 5 (one lower than 6) and 8 X 9 starts with 7 (one lower than 8).
  - When mentally computing 9s facts, the answer will always be one lower than the first digit.
  - Remind students that the combination (sum) of the first digit and the second digit will equal 9.

Multiplication Pattern of 11s

✔ When multiplying 11 by a single-digit number (11 x 1 through 11 x 9), double the digits being multiplied. Here are some examples:
  - 3 X 11 = 33
  - 9 X 11 = 99

✔ Use manipulatives to reinforce the pattern and have students double check their mental calculations.

✔ Discuss why the pattern works.
  - One reason the pattern works is because of 11s proximity to 10.

Multiplication Pattern of 11s with Two-Digit Numbers

✔ When students understand the pattern of the 11s as in the strategy above, they may be ready to multiply any two-digit number by 11.
  - Write the number to be multiplied, leaving space between the two digits.
    - For example, when multiplying 32 x 11, the 32 is written as 3 __ 2.
  - Add together the two digits from the original number (3, 2).
    - 3 + 2 = 5.
  - Insert the answer (sum = 5) in this space between the two digits
    - 3 __ 2 = 352
    - Note: if the sum of the two digits is greater than 9, it will be necessary to carry, as in 78 x 11
      7 ___ 8
      7 + 8 = 15
      7 15 8 = 858 (carry the 1 in 15 means add 1 to the 7)

✔ Multiply a two-digit number by 110.
  - To increase the complexity, provide more advanced students with this challenge: multiply a two-digit number by 110.
  - Example: 53 x 110
    - Temporarily ignore the 0 in 110 and first consider the problem as 53 x 11.
    - 5 __ 3 = 583
    - Reapply the 0 that was omitted to the end of the number.
    - The answer is 5830.

✔ Another challenge: encourage students to rapidly compute a two-digit number by 1.1.

Skip Counting

✔ Students practice skip counting in coordination with motor movements, saying one number with each movement.

✔ Skip counting (counting by 2s, 3s, 5s, 10s) is an important prerequisite for multiplication and children need to understand this relationship.

✔ Examples include:
  • jumping on a trampa, as in Figure 6.11
  • bouncing a ball
  • jumping or skipping

✔ To increase the complexity and challenge for the students, encourage them to skip count beginning with a number other than 0.
  • For example, skip count by 5s, beginning with 2: 2, 7, 12, 17, 22, 27, 32, 37, 42, 47 . . . .
  • Encourage them to look for a new pattern (in the above example, there is a repetition of the ones' digits, alternating between 2 and 7).

Figure 6.11: Jumping on a Trampa

Student is jumping on trampa to reinforce math facts. The active working memory demands were increased because he was also playing catch as he jumped and said the facts.

Music and Rhythm with Skip Counting

✔ Younger students may skip count to the tune of songs such as "Three Blind Mice."

✔ Older students may skip count or sing the multiplication tables using a rap, perhaps labeling it with a name such as "Tough *Times*."

Rapidly Square Any Number that Ends with 5

✔ The steps for this procedure are visually organized in Figure 6.12 on the next page.

✔ Example problem: $15^2 = 225$.

✔ Begin by multiplying the tens' digit by the next whole number.
  • The tens' digit is 1, so this is multiplied by the next whole number, which is 2:
    $1 \times 2 = 2$.

- Add the number 25 after that number.
  - The reason is that 5 X 5 (or 5^2) is 25.
- The answer is 225.

Short-Term Memory: Rehearsal Strategies That Also Help Enhance Active Working Memory Capacity

The strategies that help enhance short-term memory and enlarge active working memory capacity include many of the same strategies listed in the previous section. This is especially true for strategies that encourage students to re-verbalize the concepts, teach the concepts to someone else, visually describe the concepts, and use their body to demonstrate concepts. Students who experience weak cumulative memory (have difficulty hanging on to past learning), especially need spiraling: frequent review covering materials from weeks or months ago.

When to Use These Strategies:
Use strategies that encourage review and rehearsal for students who are struggling to retain facts or procedures. Strategies that stress the different steps in a procedure are helpful for those students who struggle to hold steps of a problem in memory while working on it. A valuable technique to help students enhance working memory is to have them write each step of a strategy and check off each step they complete as they work through the procedure.

Figure 6.13 represents the short-term memory component within the memory process. The tabletop is analogous to working memory space and the arrow on top of the table represents the recycling or review nature of rehearsal strategies.

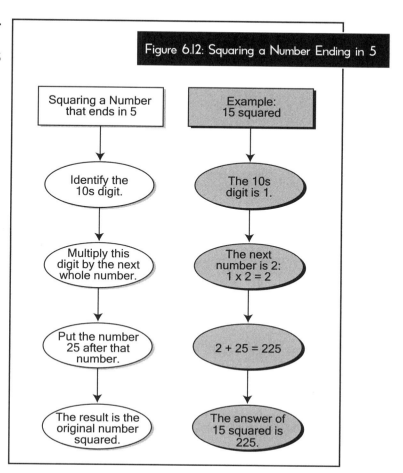

Figure 6.12: Squaring a Number Ending in 5

Squaring a Number that ends in 5 → Identify the 10s digit. → Multiply this digit by the next whole number. → Put the number 25 after that number. → The result is the original number squared.

Example: 15 squared → The 10s digit is 1. → The next number is 2: $1 \times 2 = 2$ → $2 + 25 = 225$ → The answer of 15 squared is 225.

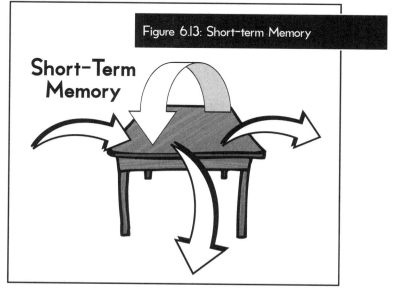

Figure 6.13: Short-term Memory

Short-Term Memory

Strategies for Rehearsing Math Facts

Math Variation of "Rock, Paper, Scissors"

✔ Each student works with a partner.
✔ Each student stands and faces a partner.
  • Each student puts his hands behind his back.
  • Each student selects a number from 0 to 10 and manipulates his hidden fingers to represent this number.
✔ A leader rings a bell (to provide an auditory cue) and at the sound of the bell, each student quickly displays his number.
  • The first person in each pair to compute the sum of both numbers wins a point.
✔ Continue the game until a predetermined number of points is reached.
✔ Challenge other math skills by using subtraction or multiplication equations.

Highlighting Difficult Math Facts

✔ Each student selects one stubborn math fact that gives her difficulty — for example, a multiplication fact, such as 7 x 8 = 56.
✔ Students select a review technique from a list of options.
  • The goal of this activity is for each student to review her chosen math fact in a way that makes it become more memorable.
✔ Some suggested options using the example of 7 x 8 = 56 are as following:
  • Write the math fact with chalk large on the sidewalk several times and then walk or jump on the numbers (tracing each number) while repeating "7 x 8 equals 56."
  • Write the math fact large on the floor using masking tape and then bounce a ball over the numbers, repeating "7 x 8 equals 56."
  • Use shaving cream to write the numbers 7 x 8 = 56 on a large wall.
    – Trace over the numbers several times while repeating them.
  • Write the numbers 7 x 8 = 56 large on a piece of cardboard and trace over them with Wikki Stiks (similar to colored sticky pipe cleaners).
    – Trace over the numbers several times while repeating them.

Artsy Flashcards

✔ Students select up to 6 troublesome facts.
✔ Students make flashcards for each of these facts, making each card visually interesting and different from every other card.
✔ Students write the full fact on one side, using various techniques to make it "artsy" and visually interesting.
  • Use different colors.
  • Outline the numbers.
  • Create borders or pictures around the numbers or within some numbers.
  • Enhance with Wikki Stiks or stickers.

✔ On the reverse side, students place the question without the answer, using a single color marker.

✔ Students practice with the plain side and check their answers by looking at the visually appealing side.

✔ To study a fact, students place the artsy side of the card about one or two feet in front of them, perhaps taping it on a wall.
  • Students study the card and then close their eyes and imagine the math fact and visual design, using the "chalkboard in their mind."
  • Students remove the card from its location and imagine it still being there with and repeat the fact.

Strategies for Procedures

✔ Dancing the steps for long division:
  • Teach students to perform "The Chicken Dance" ("Dance Little Birdie").
  • Once students are familiar with the dance, have them repeat it, changing the words to the procedure for computing long division.

Words	Movements
divide, divide, divide, divide	make hands move like little beaks chirping
multiply, multiply	flap wings (arms) four times
subtract, subtract, subtract, subtract	wiggle body down to a crouched position
bring down, bring down	clap hands four times

  • After students have performed the dance several times, review and discuss the steps of the long division process:
    – divide
    – multiply
    – subtract
    – bring down

✔ Acrostics to remember the sequence of steps for division:
  • Steps for long division: **d**ivide, **m**ultiply, **s**ubtract, **b**ring down
    – **D**ear **M**iss **S**ally **B**rown
    – **d**addy, **m**ommy, **s**ister, **b**rother
  • Steps for long division, including the process of "compare": **d**ivide, **m**ultiply, **s**ubtract, **c**ompare, **b**ring down
    – **D**oes **M**cDonald's **s**ell **c**heese**b**urgers?

✔ Using manipulatives to reinforce math facts and procedures:
  • Commercial manipulatives, such as Cuisenaire Blocks, Linking Cubes, Base-ten Blocks, and Pattern Blocks can be used to represent a variety of math facts and procedures.
  • Have students compare the written numerical problem with the procedures using the manipulatives to encourage greater transfer of the information and understanding.

155

✔ Diameter and circumference:
  • Have students work in pairs, and give each pair a large frozen mint patty, a piece of licorice (thin red licorice works well), and a plastic knife to cut the licorice.
  • Students measure the circumference of the mint patty, using the licorice and then they cut the licorice to the correct length.
  • Students use that piece of licorice to measure the diameter of the round mint patty.
  • Discuss the relationship between the diameter and the circumference of the mint.
  • Determine the radius using the licorice and compare the length of the radius to the diameter.
  • To enhance the complexity, determine pi with the same piece of licorice.
  • Use stories to introduce these terms, taking advantage of the process of priming to enhance memory. Suggestions include *Sir Cumference and the First Round Table* (Neuschwander, 1997) and *Sir Cumference and the Dragon of Pi* (Neuschwander, 1999).

Rehearsal Strategies for Terms

✔ Scavenger hunt:
  • Vary the criteria (objects required) to match the concepts and terms that need to be reviewed. Some suggestions follow:
    – Students look around the classroom or other specified area for objects containing specific geometric shapes.
    – Students use pieces of string and find objects for which they can use their string to measure the circumference or diameter of the object. Teams may compete to create the longest list.
    – Students look for objects that have fractional parts.
    – Students look for anything that contains numbers.

Figure 6.14: Pi puppet

✔ A puppet show with pi:
  • Students create a puppet named Pi using pipe cleaners and ribbon as in Figure 6.14.
  • Teams create a short puppet show, having Pi jump around and turn cartwheels while saying phrases such as:
    – "I'm a little bit larger than 3."
    – "I'm smaller than 4."
    – "I'm sometimes called 3.14, which is a decimal number."

Rhymes and Chants to Remember a Definition or Sequence

✔ Measurements:
- "A meter measures three foot three; it's longer than a yard, you see."
- "A liter of water is a pint and three-quarters."
- "Two and a quarter pounds of jam, weigh about a kilo-gram."

✔ Others:
- "The hypotenuse on a right triangle is as big as a hippopotamus — it's the biggest side."
  - Draw a triangle, placing a picture of a hippopotamus on the biggest side of the triangle, as in Figure 6.15.

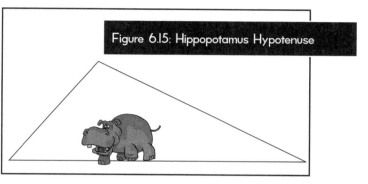

Figure 6.15: Hippopotamus Hypotenuse

- Dividing by fractions:
  - "The number you are dividing by, turn upside down and multiply."
  - "When the bottom grows, the fraction slows."
  - Use the rhyme to recall that a larger denominator makes a fraction smaller and incorporate with snapping fingers in rhythm or creating a rap.

✔ Temperature:
- Fahrenheit to Centigrade: "Take away 30 and halve it."
- Centigrade to Fahrenheit: "Double and add 30."
  - Note: these are often approximations. The technical method to translate Fahrenheit to Centigrade is to subtract 32, multiply by 5, and divide by 9.

Word Length Mnemonics

✔ Each word in a phrase or sentence is used to correspond to a digit in the number sequence to be remembered.
- Count the number of letters in each word and record each digit in the appropriate sequence. Recording the number provides a concrete method for remembering the number while counting additional letters, and is a strategy that is especially valuable for students who may struggle with working memory.
- In examples such as the square root and pi word-length mnemonics, a decimal is required in the answer. It is critical that students understand this concept and realize where they need to place the decimal.

✔ "The root of two? **I wish I knew.**"
- Count the number of letters in each word: I = 1; wish = 4; I = 1; knew = 4.
- The numbers are 1, 4, 1, and 4.
- The root of two is approximately 1.414.

✔ "The root of 3? **O, someone and me**."
  • The root of three is approximately 1.732.
✔ Using word-length mnemonics to remember decimal places in pi. Count the number of letters in each word to represent pi's decimal place numbers.
  • *Pi to six decimal places:* "**How I wish I could calculate pi**." How = 3; I = 1; wish = 4; I = 1; could = 5; calculate = 9; pi = 2. (3.141592)
  • *Pi to seven decimal places:* "**May I have a large container of acorns?**" (3.1415926)
  • *Pi to 14 decimal places:* "**How I like a fruit, raspberry of course, after the heavy lectures involving quantum mechanics?**" (3.14159265358979)

Retrieval Strategies

The keys for enhancing retrieval of information is to first ensure adequate comprehension of the concepts and procedures and then focus on rehearsal strategies as discussed above. Retrieval is dependent upon the student having the appropriate cues so that she may efficiently use her memory index to find the known information. Mnemonics, visual strategies, and movement activities are useful tools for developing these cues.

Where to Start?

Looking for suggestions on where to start with these new strategies? Here are some ideas.

Remember: It is always critical to take into account your students' developmental levels and learning styles. Always consider the specific needs of your students.

The content area of math is a very cumulative process. Therefore, rather than identifying starting points based on a student's age or grade, it is more important to select strategies based on each student's needs. When a student struggles, it is imperative to identify the breakdown point and determine what component of the task caused the struggle.

Mel Levine identifies several areas that could contribute to a breakdown point in math for students, and for each he provides some suggestions for tasks to strengthen that area (2002, p. 234). Figure 6.16 on the following page summarizes these breakdown points.

Other components that contribute to a breakdown pattern may be related to the format of the task and/or chunk size, as discussed in Chapter 3. It is important to maintain awareness of all these factors when working with students. While this is somewhat of a challenge in larger classes, perceptive teachers can learn to watch groups to determine when a given student may struggle. As a generalized strategy, teachers may also develop a habit of using a variety of techniques and formats, as this will facilitate a greater likelihood of meeting the needs of a variety of students.

Figure 6.16: Breakdown Points

The Breakdown Point	Description of Sample Tasks
Understanding the language of a word problem	• Students elaborate upon and talk about computations and word problems. • Students create word problems for different processes and situations.
Recalling facts and/or processes	• Students play games that drill on facts and are timed. • Students use educational software for practice and to develop more automatic recall.
Attention to detail	• Provide assignments that reward the students for detecting errors in given math problems. • Challenge students to detect their own careless errors.
Systematic problem solving	• Have students demonstrate and/or articulate a stepwise approach while working on a given problem. • Have students explain the stepwise approach to another student.
Mastering technical vocabulary	• Students compile a list of critical vocabulary words with definitions and examples as part of a personal mathematical dictionary.
Understanding concepts	• Students create paragraph descriptions or visual maps of specific concepts including examples of their practical uses.
Holding the parts or steps of a problem in memory while working on it	• Provide students with approaches that stress writing down all steps and calculations and require them to check off each stage or step after completing it.
Recognizing patterns in word problems or visual material	• Provide students with word problems, requiring them to study the problem, identify the process needed, and then circle the key word(s) that provide the clues.

An Example in Practice

Adeline came to me for educational therapy beginning in fourth grade because of significant difficulties in the area of math. Her greatest struggles surfaced as she attempted to memorize her multiplication tables. She did not really know her addition and subtraction facts automatically, but she was skilled in using her fingers for calculations. After helping her begin to understand some patterns that related to multiplication, she readily learned her 9s tables using finger calculations. Because she had fine motor difficulties, it was not efficient for her to learn other times tables on her fingers.

Adeline created artsy flashcards, focusing on only four facts at a time. She then used a trampa to rehearse these facts. The trampa was very successful in helping Adeline eventually memorize all of her multiplication facts. The critical contributing aspect was that she also began to understand the patterns among the numbers. She learned that it was only necessary to "memorize" 21 facts rather than all 100. By using a multiplication grid (10 x 10), she crossed off those multiplication tables she did not have to memorize. She crossed off the 1s, 2s, 5s, and 10s as well as those facts that were duplicates. For example, she left 6x4 but crossed off 4x6 because she understood the concept of reversibility (the commutative property). The 21 remaining facts are shown in Figure 6.17.

Figure 6.17: Multiplication Table										
X	1	2	3	4	5	6	7	8	9	10
1										
2										
3			9	12		18	21	24	27	
4				16		24	28	32	36	
5										
6						36	42	48	54	
7							49	56	63	
8								64	72	
9									81	
10										

Adeline successfully learned her multiplication facts because she was actively involved in the learning process. As she worked to discover the patterns, the concept of multiplication and the numerical relationships became more meaningful for her. As she developed her artsy flashcards and repeated a variety of trampa activities with the facts, she was also using substantial repetition and rehearsal. Because of the combination of these processing factors, her recall for many of these facts became fairly automatic. When she had difficulty retrieving a given fact, she was able to recall a nearby fact and then use her understanding of patterns to "get" the desired fact. For example, when struggling to recall 6x7, she remembered that 6x6 was 36 and then counted up 6 more.

The keys to Adeline's learning were:
▲ active involvement in the learning process
▲ discovery and understanding of the patterns
▲ integration of motor activities with visualization
▲ repetition and rehearsal

Epilogue

Adeline used similar memory techniques throughout all of her school career. She jumped on her trampa to memorize spelling words, vocabulary words, foreign language terms, science terms, and a variety of other rote memory tasks that she needed to develop on an automatic level. She was careful about also focusing on the patterns so that she would have enough retrieval cues to use at the appropriate time. School was not easy, but she worked hard, graduated, and was accepted to a four-year university. After the first semester, she requested a dorm room on the first floor because the noise caused by her frequent jumping on her trampa generated some complaints. She successfully graduated college in five years because she took a lighter load each semester to help achieve her success.

Finger Calculations – the 9s

When multiplying a single digit number by 9, students hold their hands in front of them with palms flat on the desk, or in the air. They label each finger from 1 to 10, beginning on the left. If students need assistance in visualizing the numbers, place a small labeled sticker on each finger as appropriate. The steps are as follows:

▲ Determine the number to be multiplied by 9.
  ✔ In this example, the number is 5.
▲ Identify the corresponding finger: the left thumb represents the 5.
▲ Fold in that finger, as in the diagram.

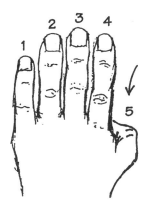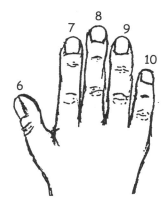

▲ Count the fingers to the left of the folded finger.
  ✔ This becomes the 10s digit in the answer.
  ✔ Some students may need to write down this number. Otherwise, have them visualize it.
▲ Count the fingers to the right of the folded finger.
▲ This becomes the 1st digit in the answer.
  ✔ The product (answer to 9x5) is represented by these two groups of fingers, as in the diagram.

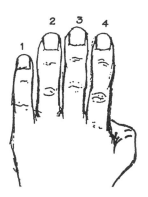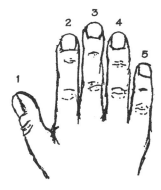

Finger Calculations – 2-digit 9s

▲ Example problem: 9 x 36

Step 1:
Multiply 9 times the ones' digit:
9 x 6.

Put down the finger (right thumb) that represents the 6.

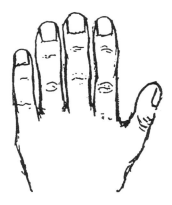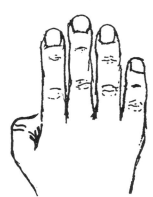

Step 2:
Separate out the tens' digit from the group, starting at the left.

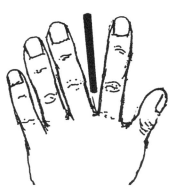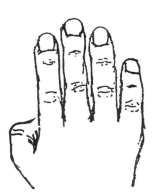

Step 3:
Write (or visualize) the digits represented by each group of fingers: 3 2 4.

The answer — these 3 digits represent the answer, beginning with the number in the hundreds' place: 324.

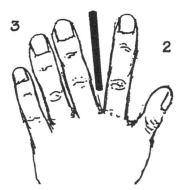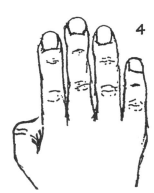

Finger Calculations – 6s to 9s

Students need to be able to hold several steps in mind to perform these calculations. They can be assisted as necessary by providing concrete assistance: number their fingers using labeled stickers; provide small cards, one with a multiplying sign (x) and another with a plus (+) sign; and have them write the numbers as they derive them.

This finger calculation technique can be used for single digits or the number 10 with the tables 6s, 7s, 8s, 9s, or 10s. The steps are as follows:

Step 1: Position hands with palms up.

Step 2: Label each finger the same on each hand, starting with the bottom:
- The pinkie represents 6.
- Label the remaining fingers 7, 8, 9, and 10.

Step 3: Use the example of 6 x 8.
- Touch the finger representing 6 on the left hand to the right hand finger representing the 8.

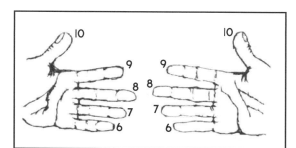

Step 4: Count the fingers on each hand above the fingers that are touching.
- On the left hand, there are 4 fingers. This number is 4.
- On the right hand, there are two fingers. This number is 2.

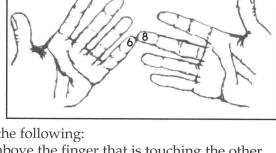

Step 4a: To help make the activity more concrete, do the following:
- Touch the left-hand thumb to the fingers above the finger that is touching the other hand; in this case, the thumb touches the first three fingers making an oval. This number is 4.
- Repeat with the right hand: in this case, the thumb touches only the first finger. This number is 2.

Step 5: Multiply the two numbers from step 4: 4 x 2 = 8.
- This number represents the 1s digit.

Step 6: Count the two fingers touching plus all fingers below.
- The total of 2 touching plus 2 other fingers is 4.
- This represents the 10s digit.

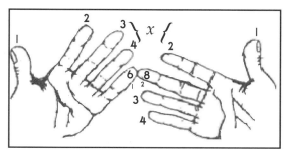

The answer (product) to the problem 6 x 8 is 48: 4 tens and 8 ones.

Finger Calculations – 6s to 9s, *continued*

There are two exceptions to the technique described on the previous page that could be confusing. These two exceptions will need to be taught separately, and only after students are familiar and fairly comfortable with using the above steps.

The two exceptions are 6 x 7 and 6 x 6. In both of these problems, multiplying the top fingers yields a two-digit number. Therefore, students will need to carry.

Step 1: To multiply 6 x 7, touch the finger representing 6 to the finger representing 7 on the other hand.

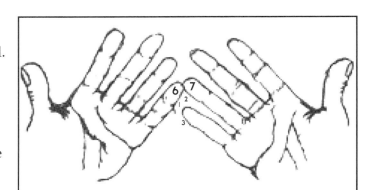

Step 2: To determine the 1s digit:
- Count 4 fingers above the touching fingers on the left hand.
- Count three fingers above the touching fingers on the right hand.
- Multiply 4 x 3 = 12.

Step 3: To determine the 10s digit:
- Count one finger touching or below on the left hand.
- Count two fingers touching or below on the right hand.
- Add 1 plus 2 = 3.

Step 4: Now combine the two numbers:

$$\begin{array}{r} 1\,2 \text{ ones} \\ +\,3 \text{ tens} \\ \hline 4\,2 \end{array}$$

Counters such as Cuisenaire Rods may be useful for students who are confused with the concepts of 1s and 10s.

Answer to Magic Triangle Puzzle

To reverse the 10 pennies in the triangle, you need to move pennies #7 and #10 up to the second row, and move penny #1 to the bottom.

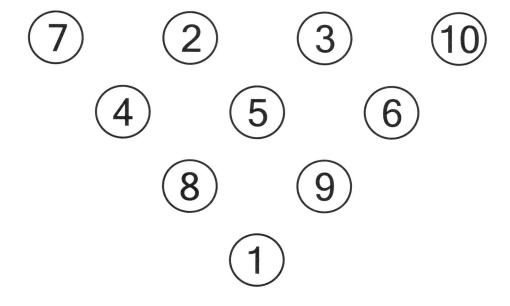

Memory Strategies for Learning Facts

Chapter
7

> Our chief want in life is somebody
> who will make us do what we can.
> — *Ralph Waldo Emerson*

Some students have difficulty easily retrieving information when desired, as for example, when they are taking a test. These students may be struggling because they have inefficiently filed information in their long-term memory system and/or it is not filed in a way that can be retrieved easily when desired. Information is not filed as a whole unit but rather, our filing system is organized into categories and subcategories. Such organization enhances the meaningfulness of the information and helps connect it to other, similar details. We use an indexing system to help locate the desired cues and connections.

The goal of these memory strategies is to help students develop an organizational system or framework that will allow facts to be organized and categorized appropriately. To do this, students need to be aware of how and when to use strategies. They need to be systematic in their use of memory by asking themselves, "How am I going to remember this?" Levine suggests that students should occasionally be required to submit learning plans or memory plans prior to taking a test on a subject. Examples of components that may be included are the following:

▲ a timeline for studying the material

▲ a description of the material that will be studied

▲ a plan for organizing the information into a format that will make it easier to remember

▲ methods for self-testing or review

To enhance the meaningfulness or relevance of the process, encourage students to compare the process of studying for a test with preparing for an important career event, such as meeting a major customer, going for a job interview, or making an important presentation to an audience. In any of these circumstances, the key is anticipating the relevant issues and preparing appropriately. Role-play relevant situations that require anticipation and preparation and, in doing so, encourage students to establish greater meaningful involvement with the concepts and relevancy of anticipating and preparing.

As teachers, we can help students learn how to learn by modeling the appropriate use of memory strategies and then encouraging students to create their own. The Big 4 Memory Facilitators (active learning, structure, systematic, sensory) can be used in many different ways, with all ages, and in all curriculum areas. Students who are encouraged to work with and interact with information, rather than just memorize it on a rote level, learn the facts and concepts with more depth. They are using active learning and, hopefully, will transfer the strategies to other relevant situations.

Ensure that students understand the following concepts (Levine, 2002, p. 119). Then post cues, perhaps as posters and/or diagrams, as reminders around the room.

- ▲ The best way to remember something is to change it.
  - ✔ Transform the information in some manner.
  - ✔ If it is visual, make it verbal.
  - ✔ If it is verbal, develop it into a diagram or picture.
- ▲ Associate information with what you already know.
  - ✔ Ask yourself, "What does this stuff remind me of?"

Teaching Memory Strategies

There is substantial value in helping students learn memory strategies. Strategies encourage students to slow down and think prior to taking action. Strategies also provide cues for retrieval. In several experimental research studies, students who received mnemonic instruction greatly outperformed controls that were taught by traditional techniques. Teachers using the mnemonic instruction reported that the strategies were especially valuable for children who often have difficulty learning (Mastropieri & Scruggs, 1991, p. 4). The authors laud the value of mnemonic instruction and conclude that the technique increases the initial learning and long-term retention of important information. Such instruction also presents effective strategies for learning and later retrieval of the information (1991, p. 3).

As teachers, we need to be comfortable with the strategies we use so that we may appropriately model them for our students. Students need to repeat our models and practice with structure. As they develop comfort with a strategy, they may then be able to independently use and develop similar techniques. The goal for students is to use a strategy appropriately so that they may complete the task in a way that facilitates their understanding and retention of the information. To use strategies in this way, they need to understand the key elements related to the process of the strategy as well as the information being studied.

Strategies Have Value

When teaching memory strategies, there are three key components to remember:

- ▲ **Modeling:** Clearly demonstrate and explain each step.
- ▲ **Staging:** Present the steps in small chunks.
- ▲ **Systematic:** Use systematic and logical explanations and encourage students to be systematic in their use of memory strategies.

Staging refers to the important process of chunking the information into manageable parts. This guideline is important for teachers as well as students. As teachers we need to remember the concept of "Too much too fast — it won't last" and realize that sometimes it may be best to cover less material but to do so with more depth, elaboration, and rehearsal. Students need to realize that they will store and be able to organize information more efficiently in smaller chunks. This requires pre-planning.

Students need to be systematic in their use of memory strategies. They are more efficient in learning the strategies when they have a basic understanding of the memory process and how it works.

Short-term memory can be compared to an entrance hallway in a house or the front office at school.

▲ In short-term memory, the information "waits" in the entranceway just long enough for our mind to organize it and give it structure.

▲ In an entrance hallway, the guests or visitors wait for a brief time while we say hello and guide them in.

We "guide in" our guests as a way of providing structure or organization to the situation: it is a critical step that provides a plan for our visitors. For example, we may take our guest's coat and lead them to a specific area. Similarly, we use strategies to "guide in" the information into our brain and develop a plan by converting the information to a structure that is more stable. Our isolated pieces of knowledge can acquire meaning only by being placed within a larger, more familiar framework. Once we have the framework, we are able to convert the knowledge to long-term memory and we will be able to remember it more efficiently.

Enhancing Working Memory

Some students efficiently memorize the facts within a lesson but then struggle to apply them. Because of difficulties with multi-tasking, their working memory system is reduced. Working memory is like the brain's scratch pad. It is where information is held temporarily when it is needed for a current task.

Students with reduced active working memory strain to hold information in mind while they are working with it. It is important to help students become aware of the concept of active working memory and specific strategies that will enable students to consciously activate working memory. The more that a student's working memory system is reduced, the more important it is to help her develop appropriate strategies to retain information.

There are several ways to help students learn to activate their working memory systems more efficiently. These include activities where they need to hold information in mind while continuing to work on that information. Example activities include active learning while also helping students to develop a greater understanding of working memory functioning. This is accomplished better if students understand the sequential development within such tasks and how such sequencing creates a greater need to hold on to information. The following activities will help your students activate their working memory systems:

Mental Math

✔ Verbally state a pair of numbers and have your students mentally add or multiply them.
✔ Continue to state numbers to be manipulated, one at a time, while creating a growing chain of numbers.

Simon Says

✔ A leader gives commands for the students to follow.
✔ When the leader says, "Simon says . . .," the students perform the activity.

✔ When the leader does not begin the command with the words "Simon says," the students do not perform the command.
✔ Any student who performs an activity that does not begin with "Simon says" is then "out" until the next round begins.
✔ Commands can relate to simple motor directions ("Point to your toes") or to content information ("Point to the south" or "Point to something in this room made of steel").

Round-Robin Stories

✔ Students take turns adding a component to a continuing story.
✔ A common example to start with is, "I took a trip with Grandmother, and on my trip I brought *a suitcase*."
✔ The next person repeats the previous statement and adds another item, such as, "I took a trip with Grandmother, and on my trip I brought a suitcase and *my shoes*."
✔ Students continue taking turns and adding items.

Humor

James Thurber once said that "Humor is our greatest national resource, which must be present at all costs" (Loomans & Kolberg 1993, p. 104). There are a variety of benefits to be derived by using humor in the classroom setting. Some of the benefits are physiological, such as an increase of oxygen and endorphins. Some benefits relate to classroom management as humor can be an effective discipline tool because of its ability to diffuse a potentially tense situation. Other benefits are educational.

Educational Benefits of Humor

Using humor can generate a variety of benefits that help increase educational efficiency and promote greater learning.

▲ Humor encourages attention.
  ✔ Students attend to novel and unusual presentations.
▲ Humor helps students relax.
  ✔ It can relieve tension in situations.
  ✔ It increases students' acceptance of making an error or giving a wrong response.
▲ Humor increases a feeling of safety in the room.
  ✔ It encourages more risk-taking.
  ✔ It provides safety for students to attempt new tasks.
▲ Humor increases retention.
  ✔ Novelty creates "hooks" or a framework for the facts.
  ✔ Humor creates meaningful associations.

> I like nonsense; it wakes up
> the brain cells.
> — *Dr. Seuss*

Humor can be incorporated into introductory activities to increase the students' priming or expectations for the facts and concepts that will be introduced. Similar activities can also be used as rehearsal strategies when reviewing content for a test. Some suggestions for using humor and novelty to set up a lesson follow.

Activities for Priming

Propping Up a Lesson

Use a prop to introduce a lesson.
✔ The relationship may be direct or somewhat subtle.
✔ The prop may be something that is worn or just something you hold as you provide the introduction.
✔ As a variation, inform one or more students about a topic that you will introduce on a subsequent day and encourage them to come to school that day with a related prop.
✔ Examples:
  • For a lesson about the revolutionary war, a silly prop might be a hat or a make-believe horse.
  • You might wear a large plastic nose to introduce a science lesson that includes a chemical with a strong odor.

A New Perspective

Vary where and how you stand within the classroom when you introduce a new lesson.
✔ Stand in a different location.
✔ Lie down on your desk.
✔ Stand at a 30 degree angle.

Eye Catchers

Prepare a humorous or thought-provoking notice for your bulletin board. Here are a couple examples:
✔ A grimace or a grin — how will your day begin?
✔ This will help set the stage for students' participation.

The Sound of Music

Sing introductions to classroom content.
✔ Introduce the main content about a lesson by putting the words to rap or a familiar song.
✔ Have the key words (or all of the lyrics) on the chalkboard, overhead, or a handout.
✔ The following example, sung to the tune of "Yankee Doodle," introduces a lesson on Emily Dickinson (Loomans & Kolberg, 1993, p. 95):

> Emily Dickinson was a poet
> Born in Massachusetts.
> She kept her poems in a trunk
> And hardly ever used them.

Emily Dickinson, keep it up,
Keep the poetry going.
One fine day, they all will see,
Your inner genius flowing.

Activities for Routines

Routines can be established that generate humor within the classroom. Loomans and Kolberg (1993, p. 36) offer a number of suggestions, among which are the following.

Go Bananas

Obtain a large, banana-shaped plastic nose (or any kind of funny nose).

✔ Periodically put on your banana nose as a cue for students to start thinking of unusual questions that relate to the subject matter being discussed.

✔ If students don't initially come up with questions, start asking bizarre questions to stir their imagination. For example, if students are studying the Revolutionary War, prompt them to consider questions such as the following:
  • How often did soldiers take baths? Where did they bathe?
  • Where did soldiers buy their food and everyday supplies?
  • How would the U.S. be different today if we had lost the Revolutionary War? Would we still be ruled by England? Would someone else have invaded us?

Listen to the Music

Set a positive tone within your classroom by using upbeat music.

✔ As students enter, play two or three minutes of fun upbeat music, such as "Can Can," the theme from *Chariots of Fire*, or the *1812 Overture*.

✔ Often students begin to mime lyrics or gesture dramatically to the beat.

✔ This lightens up the students' moods and begins class in a positive frame.

Activities for Reviews

Information and facts can be reviewed using humor. This technique helps students pay greater attention and also stimulates recall through meaningful associations. Some suggestions follow (Loomans & Kolberg 1993, pgs. 38 and 93).

Give It Back!

This is a valuable game for older students as it encourages movement and laughter while reviewing information.

✔ Students pair off, with one student (student A) facing the other student's back.

✔ The leader asks a series of 5 to 10 review questions.

✔ After each question, student A uses his index finger to "write" the answer on his partner's back.

✔ The second student writes the answer she felt on a sheet of paper.

✔ After completing all the questions, the pairs review the answers the second partners wrote.

✔ The leader provides the correct answers and each team checks those answers against its own responses.

Singing Reviews

The Sound of Music activity suggested on page 171 to introduce a lesson can be used to review facts, concepts, or other pertinent information from a lesson or unit.

✔ Either you or your students may develop a song (set to a familiar tune) that reviews key concepts in a particular curricular area.

✔ As a variation, students can work in small groups to create a song that provides the necessary information.

- Encourage them to use a song with a familiar traditional tune or a current popular song.
- After the group practices its song, have the group teach the song to the rest of the class.

> Humor is emotional chaos remembered in tranquility.
> — *James Thurber*

Peer Teaching

As a teacher, have you noticed that you develop greater understanding of a concept or procedure after teaching it? I certainly have had this experience. Our understanding of a concept is enhanced when we teach it because several important factors need to be in place in order to successfully teach a concept or procedure. Think about what these factors might be for your situation. Make a list of some of these factors as you have experienced them.

Here are some factors that must be considered before successfully teaching a concept or procedure:

▲ understand the concept

▲ chunk the components into smaller groups

▲ organize and sequence the subgroups of the concept

▲ determine the salient information

▲ decide upon a framework for presentation

In many classroom situations, it is typical to check for students' understanding by asking if they have any questions. This may be helpful for some students, but not for all. Often students may think they understand, but their understanding is inaccurate or superficial. Sometimes students are hesitant to admit they do not understand. Peer teaching is a valuable technique to help students check for understanding.

When students teach a concept, they are rehearsing the information and strengthening their neural connections. It also encourages them to develop an organizational system for the information.

Observing how the students explain the information further provides the teacher with valuable feedback on their understanding. The following activities are useful in peer teaching situations.

I'm From Mars

Students pretend that you or another student did not hear the lesson. You might pretend that you were out of the room, are a visitor from another state or country, or just landed from Mars. The students' task is to explain a given portion of the lesson in a clear, concise manner. Depending upon the age of the students, peer teaching options include having one student at a time teach, having the whole group teach each other simultaneously, or working in pairs or small groups. As a variation, related strategies may include having the students write or draw a short teaching plan before they present their activity.

Double Check

This activity is appropriate with older students, especially those in high school.

✔ Have students work in pairs or groups of three or four.
✔ Give students a specific time frame, (five minutes, for example) in which they are to perform two tasks:
  • *Task 1:* Each student silently reads a paragraph in the text.
  • *Task 2:* With the book closed, one student verbally summarizes the information while the partner (or the others in the group) checks the text for accuracy.
✔ The students then switch roles and perform the same two tasks with the next section of the material.

Generalizing Strategy Use

Because our brain is a pattern-seeking device, it is always searching for associations between information being received and what is already stored. This is why mnemonic strategies are so successful: they create valuable associations that provide the brain with an organizational framework. Mnemonics create hooks, like Velcro, for the new information. There are basically three steps in creating these hooks or an organizational framework.

▲ The hooks and the framework are presented to the students.
▲ New information is associated with the framework.
▲ The framework is used to assist the index mechanism in retrieving the new information.

The initial framework might be a plan or a system given to the students in a previous lesson, or it may be presented as part of the current lesson. The mnemonic hooks may be part of the initial framework or may be presented afterward. As the students become more familiar with their use of mnemonic strategies, they should be encouraged to generate their own frameworks for new information. In creating a framework, components of memory strategies may be used in isolation or in combination. For example, movement, visualization, and an acrostic sentence might all be combined to provide a framework, as in the following set of activities that might be used to develop a framework for remembering the order of the planets.

Planetary Sentence

✔ Teach students about the nine planets: their names, sizes, and locations, from the sun outward.

✔ Have students build a model of the planets.
  • Students place paper circles of varying sizes (designed to represent the varying sizes of each planet) on a wire sticking out of a grapefruit (which represents the sun).
  • This helps them understand and visualize the size and position relationships among the planets.

✔ Students focus on the sequence of the planets and use an acrostic sentence as their retrieval cue.
  • The sentence is, "**My Very Eager Mother Just Served Us Nine Pizzas.**"
  • The first letter in each word cues the name of a planet: Mercury, Venus, Earth, Mars, Jupiter, Saturn, Uranus, Neptune, Pluto.

✔ To help recall the correct spelling of the word *planet*, have students associate the second syllable with the movie character, E.T., as in "**E.T.** comes from a different plan**et**."

Research indicates that developmentally, students begin to demonstrate more efficient use of memory strategies around fifth grade. Studies also suggest that higher achieving students of all ages are more likely to invent effective learning strategies on their own. Similarly, lower achieving students or students with learning disabilities are less likely to do so. However, all students can be taught to use efficient strategies through demonstration and opportunities for rehearsal. A basic example is the memory strategy of repeating information. Many students do not automatically use this as a strategy until they have observed it being used elsewhere. A more complex strategy, such as the acrostic sentence above, needs to be directly explained and taught.

> As teachers, our job is to help our students understand how their memories work, demonstrate various strategies, and provide prompts for them to know when to use the strategies (Wolfe, 2001, p. 184).

Students will require practice, insight, and effort in order to generalize and use strategies appropriately. Mastropieri and Scruggs (1991, p. 94) suggest three specific steps that are necessary to help students independently execute any cognitive routine. The students must…

1. Recognize that the strategy is necessary. (Called metacognition or executive functioning, this requires awareness of the learning process and awareness by the student of how he relates to specific situations.)
2. Remember and use the specific steps in the strategy.
3. Correctly execute the strategy.

Efficient strategy execution must be practiced frequently until mastered, as it is possible for a student to remember the steps but execute the steps incorrectly.

Recognize, remember, and *execute,* are the three critical steps for many aspects of learning beyond the learning of memory strategies.

Movement and/or Rhythm Strategies

General Techniques

The following techniques may be adapted for use in a wide range of activities. They are generalized strategies that provide kinesthetic rehearsal opportunities.

Using a Trampa

A trampa, similar to a mini trampoline, has been previously discussed in this book. This device can be used to help students develop a feel for rhythm and timing. The jumping may be combined with visual input by writing words or numbers to be learned on a large piece of paper, the chalkboard, or overhead projector for the student to read as she jumps. The jumping may also be combined with visualization techniques, as in the RSV activity (described on page 79).

Descriptions of activities that incorporate a trampa follow. Adjust any chosen activity to the needs of your students, considering chunk size, curriculum goals, and developmental levels. Select a jumping motion that is appropriate for your student and then select a cognitive task for the student to perform simultaneously while jumping. Perhaps these activity ideas will stimulate ideas of your own. Here are some general principles to keep in mind:

✔ Students begin by standing on the trampa to get the "feel of it."

✔ Students move slightly and then jump with both feet.

✔ When relaxed, students start swinging arms in large circles, moving from the inside out.
  • The movement aids relaxation and relieves stress.
  • The goal is to help students coordinate upper limbs with lower limbs.

✔ When using the trampa to review curricular concepts and information, begin with the student's strongest areas.
  • Do not attempt to review a cognitive area if the student is having difficulty with the motor movements and cannot jump correctly or smoothly, as confusion will result.

✔ Begin with simple jumping patterns and progress slowly to more complex movements.
  • Progress only with those students who are able to do so comfortably.

✔ The activities are listed in the chart in approximate order of difficulty. However, students' skill and developmental levels will vary considerably, and it is important to consider these aspects in selecting the activities.

Jumping Motion (Choose one)	Cognitive Task	Visual Pattern to use with Cognitive Task
Jump on both feet.	Say every letter of the alphabet aloud and in order.	Optional
Jump on alternating feet.	Spell first name or first and last name.	Optional
Hop with one foot in front of the other in a scissor movement.	Read the alphabet letters aloud, one at a time.	Optional
Perform a two-part task: Jump on one foot for a designated part of the task and on two feet for the other part of the task — i.e., jump on one foot for vowels and on two feet for consonants.	Count forward in sequence.	Optional or use at beginning and gradually fade out visual cues.
Jump and perform jumping jacks.	Count backwards in sequence.	Optional or use at beginning and gradually fade out visual cues.
Jump and toss beanbags.	Count aloud from 1 to 10. Stop. Then count from 10 to 1.	Optional or use at beginning and gradually fade out visual cues.
Jump and play catch with a partner.	Count aloud from 1 to 25. Stop. Then count from 25 to 1.	Optional or use at beginning and gradually fade out visual cues.
Jump and toss ball to self or juggle.	Count using skip counting by 2s, 5s, or 10s, beginning with 0.	Optional or use at beginning and gradually fade out visual cues.
Jump rope while jumping on trampa.	Jump on both feet for underlined letters and only on one foot for other letters.	Create a two-part task: Write a word on the chalkboard and underline certain letters.
Jump and keep time to a metronome or music.	Jump on both feet for underlined vowels and only on one foot for consonants.	Create a two-part task: Write a phrase on the chalkboard; optional — write vowels in a different color or underline vowels.
	Spell words from the weekly spelling list, either from memory or while reading them.	Write weekly spelling words: use visual cues at beginning and fade out visual cues.
	Spell your name forward and then backwards.	Optional or use at beginning and gradually fade out visual cues.
	Read the **b** and **d** letters in the sequence written.	Write a line (or more) of random **b**'s and **d**'s on the chalkboard.
	Read the **b** and **d** letters in the sequence written, making a fist with thumb up on left-hand for each **b** and a fist with the thumb up on right hand for each **d**.	Write a line (or more) of random **b**'s and **d**'s on the chalkboard.
	A partner calls out a number (or letter) and student says the number (or letter) directly before it in sequence, e.g., partner says **18** and student says **17**.	None

Palm Tracing

This activity involves writing with dominant pointer finger on the non-dominant palm. Students may use this technique as a memory aid to recall a specific word, someone's name, or a short phrase. Depending upon the age of the student and the needs of the situation, there are several variations to this kinesthetic activity.

✔ The student repeats the target word and traces the first letter of each syllable on her palm, using the pointer finger of her dominant hand.

✔ The student repeats the target word and traces the whole word on her palm.

✔ The student repeats the target phrase and traces the first letter of each word (or each syllable) on her palm.

✔ The student traces the relevant letter or word on her palm without repeating the target word aloud.

Dancing

Students stand as they perform the following movements. The movements may be taught by having students copy a leader and/or by reading each direction (from a large chart) as the movement is performed. Have students repeat this sequence several times, until it becomes quite familiar and automatic.

✔ Right hand turns palm down
✔ Left hand turns palm down
✔ Right hand turns palm up
✔ Left hand turns palm up
✔ Right hand touches left shoulder
✔ Left hand touches right shoulder
✔ Right hand to back of head on right side
✔ Left hand to back of head on left side
✔ Right hand crosses to left waist
✔ Left hand crosses to right waist
✔ Right hand touches right hip
✔ Left hand touches left hip
✔ Turn in a circle waving hands above head

Do you recognize this sequence? It is the "Macarena," a dance that was popular in the late 1990s. Notice that there are 12 steps in this sequence; therefore, this sequence and its subsequent rhythm may be used to review any sequence with 12 items. Some examples are listed on the following page.

▲ **The Months**

Say This . . .	Do This . . .
January	Right hand turns palm down
February	Left hand turns palm down
March	Right hand turns palm up
April	Left hand turns palm up
May	Right hand touches left shoulder
June	Left hand touches right shoulder
July	Right hand to back of head on right side
August	Left hand to back of head on left side
September	Right hand crosses to left waist
October	Left hand crosses to right waist
November	Right hand touches right hip
December	Left hand touches left hip
Hey — the months!	Turn in a circle waving hands above head

▲ **Times Facts**

Say This . . .	Do This . . .
2	Right hand turns palm down
4	Left hand turns palm down
6	Right hand turns palm up
8	Left hand turns palm up
10	Right hand touches left shoulder
12	Left hand touches right shoulder
14	Right hand to back of head on right side
16	Left hand to back of head on left side
18	Right hand crosses to left waist
20	Left hand crosses to right waist
22	Right hand touches right hip
24	Left hand touches left hip
Hey — the 2s!	Turn in a circle waving hands above head

Say This . . .	Do This . . .
3	Right hand turns palm down
6	Left hand turns palm down
9	Right hand turns palm up
12	Left hand turns palm up
15	Right hand touches left shoulder
18	Left hand touches right shoulder
21	Right hand to back of head on right side

24	Left hand to back of head on left side
27	Right hand crosses to left waist
30	Left hand crosses to right waist
33	Right hand touches right hip
36	Left hand touches left hip
Hey — the 3s!	Turn in a circle waving hands above head

▲ **Memory** (suggested by Jeff Haebig in *The Body-brain Boogie*, 2001)

Say This . . .	*Do This . . .*
Memory	Right hand turns palm down
down.	Left hand turns palm down
Boost it	Right hand turns palm up
way up.	Left hand turns palm up
Repeat	Right hand touches left shoulder
body acts.	Left hand touches right shoulder
Ring the	Right hand to back of head on right side
cerebellum.	Left hand to back of head on left side
Grab all	Right hand crosses to left waist
the facts.	Left hand crosses to right waist
Build im-	Right hand touches right hip
plicit tracks.	Left hand touches left hip
Hey — remember!	Turn in a circle waving hands above head

Specific Techniques

The following activities are useful for specific terms that need to be remembered. It is necessary to thoroughly teach and explore the concepts for each term and use the memory strategies as hooks. The movements described do not have to be performed exactly as indicated. You may decide to change a movement to one that is more meaningful for you or your students.

The Continents

Students use their own bodies as a reference to review the location of the continents: the body becomes a mental map to help hook the spatial relationships to something concrete. To facilitate students' understanding of the relationships between the following body movements and the continents, have a large globe or world map easily visible. As each movement is presented, point to the appropriate location on the map and encourage students to visualize the geographic location on the related part of their body. After practicing the sequence a few times, encourage students to discuss why each body part was chosen to represent its related location on the map.

Say This . . .	Wave or Touch This Part . . .
North America	left hand
Europe	nose
Asia	right hand
Africa	waist (Equator)
South America	left knee
Australia	right knee
Antarctica	feet
North Pole	touch head
South Pole	touch toes
Equator	hands around waist

Expand the activity by also presenting the terms, *latitude* and *longitude*, along with rhymes and related movements.

Say This . . .	Do This . . .
Latitude attitude	circle body around
Multitude of longitude	jump up and down

The Gallon Person

This activity provides a mnemonic for the measurement terms *gallon, quart,* and *pint.* Young students may enjoy taking turns being "the gallon person" by coming to the front of the room and having the teacher or another student tape pictures of a gallon, quart, or pint on the related body part. Older students may perform the activity using visualization and/or drawing. Some students may require greater time for consolidation of the terms and relationships. These students may benefit more by only presenting two terms and quantities — *gallon* and *quart* — on one day and the remaining term, *pint,* on the next.

Measurement Term . . .	Related body part . . .
Gallon	the body
Quart	right arm
	left arm
	right leg
	left leg
Pint	2 pictures on right ankle
	2 pictures on left ankle
	2 pictures on right wrist
	2 pictures on left wrist

Review:
One gallon = 4 quarts
One gallon = 8 pints
One quart = 2 pints

The Water Cycle

Say This . . .	Do This . . .
Evaporation,	Push both arms up.
Condensation	Push with both arms straight out.
Precipitation on my head.	Use fingers and pretend rain is falling on your head.
Accumulation,	Make a sweeping motion in front of body using arms.
Water cycle,	Arms rotate and wave (like a snake) in a circular pattern in front of body.
And we start all in again.	Turn around in place, in a circle.

Once students are comfortable with the terms and movements, sing the sequence to the tune of "Clementine." The terms may be further reinforced by having students draw a picture depicting the meaning of each term.

Parts of an Insect

The primary components of an insect are *head, thorax, abdomen, legs, wings,* and *exoskeleton*. Have students draw and label the parts on a picture of an insect. Then they can sing about these parts to the tune of "Head, Shoulders, Knees and Toes" as follows:

Head, thorax, ab-do-men, ab-do-men.

Head, thorax, ab-do-men, ab-do-men.

Six legs, two wings and exoskeleton.

Head, thorax, ab-do-men, ab-do-men.

Have students point to the appropriate part on a model of an insect or their drawing as they sing.

Apostrophes

Students demonstrate the function of apostrophes in contraction words by physically replacing the appropriate letter with an apostrophe.

✔ Give each of several students a large card containing a letter needed to form two words that can convert to a common contraction, such as "c – a – n – n – o – t" or "d – o – e – s – n – o – t." Arrange students so that they spell the word as they hold their cards up.

✔ Have the class read the created word(s): *cannot* or *does not*.

✔ Another student, holding a large card with an apostrophe, comes up and replaces the **o** in the word *not*, explaining his actions as he does so.

✔ Have the class read the new word: *can't* or *doesn't*.

Mnemonics for Specific Situations

Following are some examples that can be used directly within a lesson. These examples may also function as models for developing your own mnemonics that will apply more specifically to your needs.

Visual Patterns

These patterns rely on a visual representation to help form a meaningful framework.

Right and Left

▲ Students make the capital letter **L** using their left thumb and first finger, as in Figure 7.1.

▲ The pointer finger is pointing straight up and the thumb is horizontal.

▲ The L cues them to recall that "left" is that side.

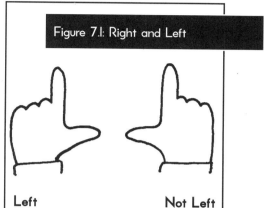

Figure 7.1: Right and Left

Left   Not Left

Days in the Month

✔ There are several ways to determine the number of days within each month. One way is the rhyme:
  * 30 days has September,
    April, June, and November.
    All the rest have 31, except February,
    Which has 28, except for Leap Year.

✔ Another way is to use the knuckles of your hands.
  * Make a fist with each hand and place them on a table with the knuckles facing up.
  * Recite the months of the year in order, touching either a knuckle or the space between knuckles for each month.
  * Touching a knuckle indicates that month has 31 days.
  * Touching a space indicates that month does not have 31 days.

The Y Axis

The y axis on a graph can be remembered by drawing a large letter Y as in Figure 7.2.

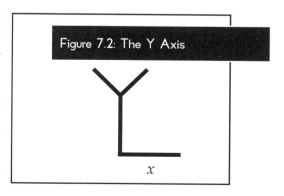

Figure 7.2: The Y Axis

x

Latitude and Longitude

✔ Latitude sounds like "ladder" and the rungs on a ladder relate to the horizontal lines of latitude.

✔ Longitude is "long" and runs the length of the globe vertically.

Chambers of the Heart

There are four chambers of the heart: the two on top are the atriums and the two bottom chambers are the ventricles.

✔ **A** comes before **V** in the alphabet.

✔ **A**trium comes before **V**entricle, alphabetically, and is on top on the heart as well.

The Earthworm

The earthworm lives in the earth, has many hearts, and has a segmented body. These characteristics can be combined into a drawing of a worm with segmented body parts and several hearts, as shown in Figure 7.3.

Iowa's Borders

To recall the borders of Iowa, look for a pattern:

✔ The state to the north has two **n**'s in the middle: *Minnesota*.

✔ The state to the south has two **s**'s in the middle: *Missouri*.

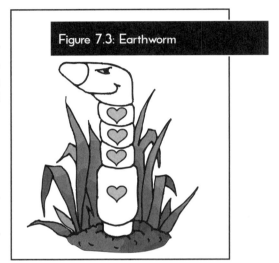

Figure 7.3: Earthworm

Acrostics and Acronyms

Both of these mnemonic strategies function as hooks to help recall information in a sequence. Following is a list of a variety of acronyms and acrostics that may be used to remember isolated facts or sequences. These suggestions may be incorporated into your lessons directly, or they may be used as a model to generate ideas for additional mnemonics.

General Mnemonics

✔ **Roy G. Biv**
  • The colors of the rainbow: **Red, Orange, Yellow, Green, Blue, Indigo, Violet**

✔ **FACE**
  • To recall the notes of the spaces on a musical staff: **F A C E**

✔ **Every Good Boy Does Fine**
  • To recall the notes of the lines on a musical staff: **E G B D F**

Definitions

• **Acronym:** a sequence of letters that may or may not form a word. Each letter represents one of the key words to be remembered.

• **Acrostic:** a short sentence with the initial letter of each word forming one of the words to recall in sequence.

✔ **The Great Lakes: HOMES**
   - The lakes around the state of Michigan are referred to as the Great Lakes. Each letter in the word **HOMES** provides a cue to recall one of the lakes: Lake **H**uron, Lake **O**ntario, Lake **M**ichigan, Lake **E**rie, Lake **S**uperior.

✔ **Directions on a compass or a map: Never Eat Shredded Wheat**
   - The four directions around a compass or map, beginning with north on the top are **N**orth, **E**ast, **S**outh, and **W**est. The acrostic phrase helps recall the directions in the correct sequence.

✔ **Alliance groups: TAG and FIRE**
   - As World War I was beginning in Europe in 1914, countries formed two major alliance groups.
   - The nations formed alliances to indicate that they would work together. The word *alliance* can be compared to *appliance,* which also works together with something else.
     — Students may be more familiar with the word *appliance* than the word *alliance.*
     — They can associate the words *alliance* and *appliance*: they both refer to working together.
   - The two major alliance groups may be remembered as TAG and FIRE.
     — TAG represents the countries in the Central Powers: **T**urkey, **A**ustria-Hungary, and **G**ermany.
     — FIRE represents the countries in the Allied Powers: **F**rance, **I**taly, **R**ussia, and **E**ngland.

✔ **Confusable words *affect* and *effect*: RAVEN**
   - **RAVEN** stands for: **R**emember, **A**ffect is a **V**erb, **E**ffect is a **n**oun.

Rhyming, Rhythm, and Song

The use of rhyming, rhythm, and song is a very powerful memory tool. Adding movement to the activity provides extra-sensory import and often results in increased learning and memory. Inviting students to create songs, raps, or chants that summarize, synthesize, or apply meanings from subjects they are studying moves the students to a higher plane of learning. Remember the important teaching tip: *Too much too fast — it won't last.* Use these suggestions periodically but do not overwhelm your students.

Examples of some common rhymes, chants, and songs for remembering information follow. Some suggestions are useful primarily for rote recall, whereas others may be used to summarize, synthesize, and apply meanings for expanded understanding. Rhyming and rhythmic chants can be used in almost any situation. Consider one of the most common reminders: righty tighty, lefty loosie. That rhyme reminds us to turn a knob or screw to the right to tighten it and to the left to loosen it.

Spelling and Writing

✔ **"I before e, except after c, or when rhyming with a, as in *neighbor* and *weigh*."**
  • Examples: *receive, piece, experience*

✔ **Punctuation Song**
  • This can be chanted with rhythm sticks or sung to the tune of "Row, Row, Row Your Boat."

> Stop, stop, stop the words
> With a little dot.
> Use a period at the end,
> So they'll know to stop.

History Facts

✔ **1492**

> In fourteen hundred and ninety-two,
> Columbus sailed the ocean blue.

✔ **1588**

> The Spanish Armada met its fate,
> in fifteen hundred and eighty-eight.

✔ **John Locke's concept of Natural Law:**
  • A two-part chant
  Half the class chants, "natural law, natural law, natural law . . ."
  The other half chants, "life, li-ber-ty, happ-i-ness, life, li-ber-ty, happ-i-ness . . ."

Songs About Specific Time Periods or Events in History

Listen to songs relating to a specific time period in our history and discuss the content of the songs in connection to the concepts being studied.

✔ **"The Ballad of Davy Crockett," lyrics by Tom Blackburn**
This is a song about the American Frontier in the 1800s and the Creek Indian Uprising. Davy is called the "king of the wild frontier," and the song describes how he fought against the Native Americans along with General Andrew Jackson. Eventually Davy became a congressman. The complete lyrics for this song can be found through a simple Internet search and can be used as a discussion for many issues including the settling of the Western frontier, our treatment of Native Americans, development of laws in Congress, the voting procedure that helped Davy become a congressman, and the Liberty Bell. For example, ask your students, "What is meant by the phrase, 'He patched up the crack in the Liberty Bell'?"

✔ **"The Battle of New Orleans," lyrics by Johnny Horton**
This song is about the battle led by Andrew Jackson that took place in New Orleans in 1814. Jackson scored a huge victory against the British and this helped increase his popularity so that he eventually became President. In this battle, 700

British were killed, 1400 were wounded, and the U.S. only lost eight soldiers. The irony is that the British had already surrendered the war, but because communication was so slow, Jackson did not know this had occurred prior to his battle.

The words to this song can be found through a simple Internet search and can be used to initiate study of this time period. Correlated activities may include role-playing the events, discussing this battle's relationship to the whole war, the issue of communication in the early 1800s, and/or the geography of the area. For example, students can create a large map of the area and then walk through the same areas where Jackson fought, i.e., the Louisiana River and the Gulf of Mexico.

✔ **The Civil War**
  • Examples of some relevant songs for the Civil War are:
    — "When Johnny Comes Marching Home Again"
    — "The Battle Hymn of the Republic"
    — "The Night They Drove Old Dixie Down"

✔ **Civil Rights**
  • Examples of songs from the 20th century related to Civil Rights can be used to compare the similarities and differences between that previous time period and current events.
  • Students' learning of past events will be much stronger and more meaningful if they can relate it to current situations.
  • Examples of songs relevant to the Civil Rights struggles of the 1960s are:
    — "We Shall Overcome," the hymn of the civil rights marchers
    — "All Men are Brothers" and "Cruel War," by Peter, Paul, and Mary
    — "What Did You Learn in School Today" and "Where Have All the Flowers Gone?" by Pete Seeger

Review and Rehearsal Strategies

Learning does not take place in isolation. It is critical to connect new information to an existing framework and for students to frequently review new information to strengthen connections. The challenge is that for some students, a classroom review of material is often boring and unproductive. However, review is an essential component of learning that enhances consolidation of the information and helps the information move in an organized manner into long-term storage. When the teacher takes full responsibility for the review, she is the one doing the work, and consequently, she is the one growing the dendrites. In contrast, the more that students are involved in the review, the greater the effectiveness for the students. Let your students grow their dendrites! Involvement can also be motivating and fun for them.

The following list of suggestions for review strategies can be used and modified according to the needs and developmental levels of your students.

Musical Chairs Review

✔ Place chairs in a circle, using one chair less than the number of students.

✔ Select a leader to manage the music.

✔ The leader starts the music and students walk around the chairs.

✔ When the music stops, each student takes a seat.

✔ The person left standing then shares one thing he's learned related to the current lesson or topic.

✔ That person remains in the group and continues walking around the circle when the music starts.

✔ Students may share more than one time.

✔ Continue until several students have shared information and/or a pre-specified amount of time has passed.

Clapping or Snapping Review

✔ Place students in small circle groups.

✔ Play soft rhythmic music in the background.

✔ A leader in each group begins a rhythm by clapping or snapping fingers.

✔ The students take turns offering something they have learned from the lesson, in rhythm, progressing in order around the circle.

✔ The student who is sharing may maintain the rhythm or change it.

Ball Toss Review

✔ Students sit in a circle.

✔ One student tosses a beach ball to someone else.

✔ The student who catches the ball states something he has learned or names a fact, such as the capital of a given state.

✔ The ball toss continues.

Student Chooses a Unit

✔ This works particularly well in upper grades and high school.

✔ During the first few weeks of school the teacher reviews each unit as it is completed.

✔ Thereafter, each student selects a review date and is responsible for reviewing content on that date.

✔ The content may involve the material just completed or previous material that is valuable to review for future use.

✔ Encourage students to use materials and props to help explain the information, such as puppets, cartoons, mini-dramas, or other visual aids.

✔ Have the students complete a "review plan" for you to discuss and approve. The following information may be included:
  • The topic and objectives
  • The content they have chosen
  • The materials or props they will use to explain the concept

Reflection

Downtime is important as it helps the brain process new information, strengthen neural connections, and deepen consolidation. Research indicates that the use of reflection can facilitate these processes.

In a study of 88 fifth and sixth graders, Shafir and Eagle (1995) found that students who spent periods in self-reflection after learning were better learners and problem solvers. These students also developed better corrective strategies than the students who did not reflect. Furthermore, it has been found that adequate sleep, another example of downtime, is important for students. CREB is a protein in the brain that facilitates long-term memory in REM (rapid eye movement) sleep and plays a role in consolidating long-term learning during mental reflection (Hasselmo, 1999).

Reflections may be performed in various formats. Some were modeled throughout this book, specifically at the end of Chapter 5, on page 113. Here are some specific suggestions to allow your students time to reflect:
  ▲ doodling
  ▲ a brief break with soft music playing
  ▲ writing a response to a specific question
  ▲ writing thoughts about the topic
  ▲ sharing thoughts with a partner

Messages

Here are some important messages for use in the classroom:
  ▲ Rehearsing is critical: neurons that fire together, wire together.
  ▲ Reflection time is necessary.
  ▲ Material can be reviewed by students.
  ▲ Downtime is necessary for consolidation.

Where to Start?

Looking for suggestions on where to start with these new strategies? Don't be overwhelmed by the large number of suggestions for strategies, especially in this chapter. Proceed slowly, because *Too much too fast — it won't last.* Always remember to consider your students' developmental levels, value and accommodate your students' different learning styles, and decide on a content of focus and select your strategies to match.

Some basic starting suggestions follow. Your selected starting point may differ based on the specific needs of your students.

▲ Suggestions for early-elementary students:
  ✔ Use trampa with cognitive tasks
  ✔ Kinesthetic techniques: the continents or the gallon person

▲ Suggestions for upper-elementary students:
  ✔ Sing reviews
  ✔ Peer teaching

▲ Suggestions for middle-school students:
  ✔ Humor
  ✔ Priming activities: props or sing introductions

▲ Suggestions for high school students:
  ✔ Reviews: give it back to me
  ✔ Palm tracing

A Mnemonic Story About Learning the State Capitals

One day in fifth grade, my son Eli came home from school upset. He said he had to learn the state capitals. I was at first confused because he had been learning state capitals and other facts (i.e., state bird) for several years. Associative memory for some rote material was difficult for him, but with perseverance and substantial multisensory practice, he was usually successful — at least for the short term. He explained that this situation was different because he had to learn all 50 state capitals for a test at the end of the year.

To help him ease his panic, we first made a list of the various rehearsal strategies he could use. His list included the following strategies:

▲ **Chunking:** He would work on only one state capital at a time.

▲ **Spiraling:** Each time he finished with one state, he would review all of the states he had learned so far.

▲ **Downtime:** He would study in small chunks of time, allowing himself plenty of downtime between sessions.

▲ **Recognition Before Retrieval:**
  ✔ He typed the name of each state on a blue index card and he typed the name of each capital on a yellow index card.

✔ He also typed an alphabetical list of all the states with their capitals to use for reference.

✔ He studied each state and its capital in two ways:
- He looked at the blue card with the state's name and then selected from 3 or 4 choices the appropriate capital using the yellow index cards.
- He looked at the yellow card with the state's capital and then selected from three or four choices the appropriate state name using the blue index cards.

✔ He tested his knowledge of the match using traditional flash card methods:
- He looked at the state's name on a blue index card and then said the capital.
- He looked at the capital on a yellow index card and then said the state's name.

▲ **Mnemonics:** He would use picture mnemonics for each state capital, using the Bornstein method (Bornstein, 1983).

▲ **Movement Activities:** He would devise a number of activities that incorporated use of the trampa.

▲ **Goal Setting:** He determined, using a calendar, how much time he had before the month when the test would be given and set goals for:

✔ Knowing 10 capitals

✔ Knowing 20 capitals

✔ Knowing 30 capitals

✔ Knowing 40 capitals

✔ Knowing all 50 capitals

Having this list and action plan helped relieve Eli's sense of panic and his feeling of being overwhelmed. He began to feel more confident that with enough work, he could achieve his goal of being successful on this test. He was right. His plan was successful and he received an A+ on his test.

The ironic part of this story is that Eli's teacher was quite used to his poor spelling and accommodated this issue. However, I was aware that some of his "misspellings" on this test were actually confusions with the mnemonics used. For example, he studied a picture about a guy named Cal who had a sack of memos. This picture of the sack of memos was to remind him of "Sacramento" and Cal was a cue for the state's name. On his test, next to the word *California*, Eli wrote *Sakamemo*. Here are some questions to ask in regards to this misspelling:

▲ Was this an actual spelling error?

▲ Was it poor associative retrieval of the pair of words?

▲ Did Eli need additional practice on the actual words that the mnemonic was to cue?

Epilogue: As a young adult, Eli is very skilled at map reading and knows how to identify a state's capital when he needs that information. He also automatically knows state capitals for those places that have personal meaning to him.

Memory Strategies for Conceptual Learning

Memory strategies for conceptual learning are similar to many of the other strategies throughout this book. A difference is that the strategy may involve more conceptual development rather than direct recall. The strategies presented within this chapter may be used directly or as a guideline or suggestion to develop a similar strategy that is better adjusted to your own needs and curriculum.

Remember to constantly consider the developmental levels and readiness factors of your students. Make sure the levels match.

Teaching Tips to Enhance Memory Development:
▲ Too much too fast — it won't last:
  ✔ Sometimes less is more.
  ✔ Increased depth generates more solid consolidation.

▲ Neurons that fire together, wire together.
  ✔ Use repetition and rehearsal.

▲ Monitor chunk size of information and assignments:
  ✔ Present assignments in chunks rather than all at once.
  ✔ Use visual organizers and graphics.

▲ Vary instructional styles within lessons:
  ✔ Use at least two different styles per lesson.
  ✔ Encourage students to use varying formats.
  ✔ Provide your students with a variety of tools.

▲ Personalize lessons for your students:
  ✔ Incorporate personal meaning to help ensure that the learning will become alive for students.
  ✔ Personalize the material to enhance its consolidation into long-term memory.

Brain Tips for Reinforcement and to Encourage Strategy Use
▲ The hippocampus is a "broker" that binds memory until the cortex can take over.
  ✔ Provide cues that students can use as a hook for the many parts needed to develop the concept.

▲ Working memory is the brain's scratch pad.
  ✔ Information (retrieved from long-term memory or new input) is held temporarily so that we can work on it.
    • "It is the mental glue that links a thought through time from its beginning to end" (Goleman, 1995).
  ✔ Provide students with strategies and activities that will help them learn to better activate their working memory system.

▲ The frontal lobes are the brain's conductor:
  ✔ These lobes lead the brain, sending other parts into action, and/or coordinating the action similar to the way a conductor leads the musicians in an orchestra.
    • This area is directly interconnected with every distinct functional unit of the brain.
    • This unique conductivity makes the frontal lobes well-suited for coordinating and integrating the work of all the other brain structures (Goldberg, 2001, p. 37).
  ✔ Strategies trigger the frontal lobes into action.

▲ Novelty and familiarity are critical components essential for learning and concept development.
  ✔ Novelty and familiarity trigger the coordinating action of the frontal lobes.
    • Novelty is necessary to gather attention and increase motivation.
    • With repetition and organization, the novel merges into the familiar.

▲ Concept development is dependent upon appropriate retrieval.
  ✔ A variety of components is retrieved in response to internally generated decisions.
  ✔ Provide students with organization and structure to facilitate this decision-making process.

Human Learning

The brains of higher animals, including humans, are endowed with a powerful capacity for learning. Unlike instinctive behavior, learning, by definition, is change. The organism encounters a situation for which it has no ready-made effective response. With repeated exposures to similar situations, appropriate response strategies emerge over time. The length of time, or the number of exposures required for the emergence of effect of solutions, is vastly variable . . . Invariably, the transition is from an absence of effective behavior to the emergence of effective behavior. This process is called "learning" . . . At an early stage of every learning process the organism is faced with "novelty," and the end-stage of the learning process can be thought of as "routinization" or "familiarity." The transition from novelty to routinization is the universal cycle of our inner world (Goldberg, 2001, p. 44).

Priming has Multiple Benefits

Priming establishes expectations and sets the stage for the information to come. Among its many benefits is that it focuses attention on the critical aspects of the concept or lesson. Explaining why a concept is important before starting the lesson will encourage students to add meaning to what they are about to study or explore. Priming helps establish similarities between new information and previously established frameworks — a critical component, since the brain stores information by patterns and seeks similarities.

Priming needs to help establish the meaning of key vocabulary terms. Concepts are dependent upon accurate semantic understanding. Students may think they have understood the concept, but if their semantic interpretation is not accurate, then their interpretation of the concept will also be faulty. The importance of semantic interpretation is exemplified by the essay on the following page, written by an eight-year-old student.

Why We Can't Go to Grandma's House

We used to go to visit Grandma every weekend and get cookies but we can't do that anymore. Grandpa got retarded and they moved to Florida. Now they live in a place with a lot of retarded people. They sent us pictures. They all live in little tin boxes. They ride on big tricycles and they all wear name tags because they don't know who they are. They go to a big building called the wreck hall, but they must have gotten it fixed because it looks all right now. They play games and do exercises there, but they don't do them very good. There is a swimming pool there, but they stand in it with their hats on. I guess they don't know how swim.

As you go into the park, there is a dollhouse with a little man sitting in it. He watches all day so that they can't sneak out. My grandma says that grandpa worked all his life and earned his retardment. I wish they would move back here, but I guess the little man in the dollhouse won't let them out.

Besides establishing vocabulary meaning, priming can highlight an upcoming concept as important and help students relate more efficiently. For example, before beginning a unit on Shakespeare's *Romeo and Juliet,* students who watch segments of the movie *West Side Story* and discuss gangs and feuds will be better prepared to understand Shakespeare's plot.

As another example, priming can be used to begin a lesson on punctuation to help the students understand the importance of punctuation and its necessity for clarity of expression. These students will develop generalized patterns more easily than students who merely attempt to memorize the various rules. Following are two options for a priming activity that may be used to introduce a lesson on punctuation.

✔ Play a segment of a videotape of comedian Victor Borge as he reads a passage using vocal noises to represent each punctuation mark.

✔ Have students perform the following actions to represent punctuation marks as they silently read a passage:
  • Pause for a comma.
  • Stop (or clap) for a period.
  • Wrinkle their face for a question mark.
  • Jump up for an exclamation mark.

When thinking about the importance of priming, an adaptation of a familiar saying comes to mind:
  You can lead a horse to water, but you can't make him drink.
  It's our job as teachers to salt the hay.

Strategies for Conceptual Development

Students need to progress beyond superficial comprehension and apply more depth to their understanding of concepts. With superficial learning, students tend to rely extensively on rote memory. As their learning progresses with more depth, the students move into abstract analysis and application of concepts. This allows them greater opportunities for comprehension and retention of the information.

A key factor in helping students learn to process information in more depth involves helping them develop more efficient organizational strategies. The visual organizers presented in Chapter 5 are excellent visual organization models to use with your students. It is important, however, not to overwhelm them or confuse them by introducing too many kinds of organizers at one time.

The use of organizational strategies may require more time for a student and, therefore, it is important to convince the student that this extra time is worthwhile to the long-term goal of learning. One strategy to accomplish this involves giving them a choice. Using the example of the concept of digestion, the following two activities can be presented to the students.

Digestion Activity 1

✔ The teacher presents vocabulary words for the students to memorize.

✔ The teacher describes the process of digestion from the time food enters the mouth until the time waste leaves the body.

Digestion Activity 2

✔ Each student is given an unlabeled diagram of the parts of the digestive system.

✔ The teacher places a similar diagram on the overhead projector.

✔ The teacher begins a visual organizer that has two main components labeled "the route" and "the process."

✔ The teacher describes the route that food takes from the mouth to the stomach and then through the intestines while also labeling the relevant parts on the diagram.
  • Students help complete the part of the visual organizer labeled "the route."

✔ The teacher describes the process of digestion while discussing the components of enzymes, nutrition, and waste.
  • Students help complete the part of the visual organizer labeled "the process."

Discussion:
Students discuss which format made it easier to understand the process of digestion and which strategy produced a more efficient format for use in review and studying for a later test. The goal of this dual activity is to demonstrate to students how concepts are comprised of a variety of components and that the more effectively these components are sequenced, categorized, and organized, the easier it will be for them to develop hooks and a more successful retrieval system for the information.

A similar mind-set applies to independent activities when students are reading for information as they study to develop and understand a concept. Lead them to appreciate the importance of strategic reading and an understanding that concept development is dependent upon some key facts and/or salient information. When students are identifying key information, either by highlighting or marking with a Wikki Stick or Post-it Note, it is important that they are strategic and selective in their choices. The following types of demonstrations may be used as a metaphor for this idea:

✔ Place large and small stones in a colander and shake.
- The large stones (representing the main idea) stay in the colander.
- The small stones (representing supporting details) fall through the holes.

✔ Pour liquid through coffee grounds in a filter.
- The coffee grounds represent the main idea and remain.
- The liquid represents the other details and quickly moves through the filter.

Conceptual Levels

Levine (2001, p. 115) describes six levels of understanding with respect to concepts. These are listed in Figure 8.1. Initially, the student just memorizes information and is unable to identify critical features or provide examples of the concept. As the student increases the depth of his understanding, he is then able to identify some features, apply or use the concept, and eventually explain the concept and apply it in novel ways. The level of innovative application of the concept represents the greatest depth of conceptual understanding. Innovative application requires that the relevant components that once were novel and unfamiliar are now understood and have become familiar enough that the student is able to apply the concept in an innovative manner.

Figure 8.1: Levine's Levels of Conceptual Understanding

Conceptual Depth	Description of Student's Activity
None	Student is unable to identify any critical features of the concept or cite examples.
Tenuous	Student can name one or two critical features but is vague about how the concept differs from others.
Rote	Student can mimic the teacher's explanation but cannot use the concept or think of examples.
Imitative	Student can apply the concept but does not really understand what he is doing and cannot generalize its use.
Explanatory	Student can explain the concept in her own words, cite examples, and can compare and contrast it with other concepts.
Innovative	Student can apply the concept in ways never directly taught.

As we help students learn concepts, it is prudent to consider these levels. Encourage each student to practice and manipulate various examples within each level. This will help develop conceptual understanding with greater depth. Using and including the Big 4 Memory Facilitators (Active Learning, Structured, Systematic, Sensory) will also contribute to increasing students' depth of conceptual learning.

Visual Thinking

Visual graphics are powerful memory tools that also enhance conceptual learning, which is why the use of visual organizers is so valuable for many students. Many of our students are familiar with menus used in electronic media through computer games, the Internet, and software, such as encyclopedias or dictionaries. In these activities, the user chooses from a set of options, each of which opens up a further set of options. Because of students' familiarity with such menus, it is useful for them to think of visual organizers, especially tree diagrams, as similar in structure: each option opens up a further set of options. Encourage students to use visual organizers to navigate through the concept(s) being considered.

Figure 8.2: Visual Thinking

Visual thinking can be encouraged in other ways as well. For example, a simple diagram may be used to represent a concept, with or without an associated mnemonic cue. For example, it is valuable for students to keep in mind the First Amendment Rights of free speech, religion, the press, and the right of assembly as they discuss the related concepts. Since it is the *First* Amendment and *one* rhymes with *sun*, you might use a sun as a visual cue. Draw a happy faced sun with legs and arms. Show the sun singing, with the word *RAPS* in a talk bubble and musical notes all around. RAPS is a mnemonic to remember the freedoms of **r**eligion, **a**ssembly, **p**ress, and **s**peech, as shown in Figure 8.2.

Some concepts are extremely difficult, if not impossible, to understand without a drawing or diagram. Many scientific concepts fall into this category, such as the structure of an atom, anatomical parts of an animal, the operation of a machine, or the growth cycle of a seed or development of a butterfly. Some of society's most innovative thinkers were said to have been visual thinkers. Albert Einstein is one example, and it is reported that he said, "If I can't picture it, I can't understand it" (Bell 1991, p. 1). West described Einstein as follows:

> Einstein used the most sophisticated mathematics to develop his theories, but often his sums would not come out right. He was a daydreamer who played fancifully with images in his mind, but in the process he created an objective image of the universe that transformed forever our view of physical reality. Einstein had trouble learning and remembering facts, words, and texts, but he was teacher to the world. He was slow to speak, but, in time, the world listened (1997, p. 129).

Another example is Temple Grandin, a Professor of Animal Science at Colorado State University. She is autistic and explains in her autobiography that her only way of understanding abstract concepts is by picturing them. She used this visualization method to become a leading expert in designing facilities to handle livestock (Grandin, 1995).

In our classrooms we may find that some students have difficulty visualizing patterns. For example, in contrast to their classmates who increase their understanding of the relationship of the sun, earth, and moon by representing this relationship in a drawing or hands-on creation, these students do not benefit from such activities without simultaneously using a direct verbal cue. These are the same students that need to focus specifically on the prefix **penta-** as meaning "five" when studying the Pentagon, rather than just picturing a five-sided building. Encourage students to use self-talk as necessary to increase their understanding. The caution is to pay attention to the learning preferences of your students and keep in mind that our classrooms are not composed of "one-size-fits-all" students. Using a variety of strategies will help ensure that you meet the variety of needs within your classroom.

While allowing students their individual preferences, activities can also be presented to encourage them to develop greater visualization skills. An example of a fun activity using poetry follows.

✔ Read a descriptive poem from a book to your students, without showing them any of the accompanying illustrations. The students then draw the images generated by each verse in the poem. Poems by Jack Prelutsky lend themselves to wonderful descriptive drawings, especially the poem "The Frogs Wore Red Suspenders," which begins as follows (Prelutsky 2002, p. 8):

> The frogs wore red suspenders
> And the pigs wore purple vests,
> As they sang to all the chickens
> And the ducks upon their nests.

Nanci Bell's program, *Visualizing and Verbalizing for Language Comprehension and Thinking* focuses on visualization and imagery. She describes her premise as follows:

> Visualizing is an answer as to how we process language and thought. The brain "sees" in order to store and process information. Both thinking and language comprehension are founded in imagery. Individuals with good language comprehension visualize concepts and form imaged gestalts. Individuals with weak language comprehension do not visualize concepts and therefore don't easily connect to language. Visualization is directly related to language comprehension, language expression, and critical thinking. Imagery is a primary sensory connection in the brain (1991, p. 8).

There are many ways we can utilize the power of imagery when helping our students with conceptual development. Imagery increases depth of understanding, which then increases the students' abilities to recall the concept at a later time. Our own and our students' creativity is the only limit. While using any of the following strategies, encourage students to also visualize the concept. Ask them questions such as these:

✔ Can you see the relationship/image in your mind's eye?

✔ Can you picture this (component)?

✔ How does (this _____) look to you?

Metaphoric Teaching

We know it is easier to adjust to a new situation when it contains similarities to something familiar. Similarly, it is also easier to learn a new concept if it has components that are similar to something familiar. For example, when I obtained my new ergonomic angled computer keyboard it was strange at first. However, as I adjusted to the new shape, it became easier to use. Because I was familiar with typing on a regular horizontal keyboard and because the angled keyboard had similar components (the location of the letters), I was able to readily adapt my typing to the new angle.

Metaphoric teaching is a wonderful tool to facilitate transfer and connections between new information and familiar information. It is a tool that can also enhance comprehension of abstract information. Using metaphoric teaching applies a word or phrase to a concept in a way that suggests a comparison with another, more familiar, concept. It is making a connection between the two seemingly unlike objects or concepts. Williams describes the process of metaphoric thinking as using the "language" of both hemispheres. Teaching concepts with metaphors "places the concept within the round of the concrete world, forging a connection between the abstract concepts and the learner's experience. Metaphors are, for most people, more engaging and satisfying than any exacting, one-dimensional dictionary definition. They both clarify the concept and tease the mind to explore it further" (1983, p. 55).

There are many advantages to encouraging metaphorical thinking within the instructional process.

- ✔ The use of metaphors provides an explicit strategy for the learning process.
- ✔ Metaphorical teaching presents new information in a way that makes use of what students already know.
- ✔ Metaphors organize and connect information.
- ✔ Metaphorical teaching is holistic: it focuses on recognizing and understanding patterns and the general principles that give meaning to specific facts.
- ✔ Metaphors encourage a sense of integration and an emphasis on seeing relationships.
- ✔ Student-generated metaphors value the students' own experiences.
- ✔ The use of metaphors encourages students to be more specific in identifying what they do not understand.

There are many different ways that metaphors can be used to help students understand and transfer new information. Because of the fact that metaphors connect information to the familiar, Lederer states, "small wonder that we take most of our common metaphors from things that surround us in our daily lives and that we find a rich vein of descriptive phrases in the most familiar" (1990, p. 5). He includes 15 chapters on metaphors in his book, *The Play of Words*. Technically, there are different forms of metaphoric teaching; however, in this chapter we will use the term *metaphor* as a global representation for metaphoric teaching.

▲ **Metaphors** are comparisons that merge or compare two objects or ideas that are generally different from each other but turn out to be alike in some significant way. They are a way of explaining the abstract in terms of the concrete. Here are some appropriate metaphors about the frontal lobes:

✔ The frontal lobes are the brain's CEO.

✔ The frontal lobes take an aerial view of all the other functions of the brain and coordinate them.

✔ The frontal lobes are the brain's conductor, coordinating the thousand instruments in the brain's orchestra.

✔ The frontal lobes are the brain's leader, leading the person into novelty, innovations, and the adventures of life.

▲ **Idioms** compare objects or ideas that are essentially dissimilar, as in the expressions, "He's as transparent as we thought" or "It's raining cats and dogs." The first obviously does not mean that we can see right through the person, but rather that his ideas and motives are obvious. The second expression does not mean that cats and dogs are falling from the sky, but rather that it is raining quite heavily, as if large things were falling from the sky.

▲ An **analogy** compares partial similarity between two items, such as comparing a car engine and a human body. While these items are very different, in some ways the car's fuel pump functions like a heart. Understanding the similarities and differences between the fuel pump and a human heart will contribute to an understanding of both mechanisms.

▲ A **simile** uses the word *like* or *as* to compare two unlike items, as in, "She is like a thorn on a rose" or "She is as pretty as a picture."

Curriculum examples of metaphors may range from fairly concrete to quite abstract. Some ideas that can be compared and connected follow.

New Concept	Compared to Familiar Concept
the process of electricity	water flowing through pipes
the function of human kidneys	a coffee filter or the system of parking passes that allow only certain cars to park in a given lot
germination of seeds	an egg developing into a chicken
the human circulatory system	a system of freeways, roads, exit ramps, vehicles, and drivers
the movement of glaciers	pancake batter flowing onto a hot griddle
a clam	the feeling of fear and animals' fear reactions

West, Farmer, and Wolff (1991) suggest considering seven specific steps when using metaphoric teaching.

1. Select the metaphor and consider:
   ✔ how well the metaphor explains the concept or process
   ✔ the degree or richness of imagery
   ✔ the students' familiarity with the concept

2. Emphasize the metaphor.
   ✔ Emphasize the metaphor consistently throughout the lesson.
   ✔ Alert the students to interpret the metaphor figuratively and not literally.

3. Establish the context.
   ✔ Establish the context for using the metaphor.
   ✔ Avoid using the metaphor in isolation.
   ✔ Determine the students' familiarity with the comparison and supplement if necessary.

4. Provide instructions for imagery.
   ✔ Help students benefit from the rich imagery in the metaphor.
   ✔ Suggest that they "form a mental picture of _____."
   ✔ Supplement by encouraging students to make a drawing of their mental picture.

5. Emphasize similarities and differences by helping students to:
   ✔ Focus on the similarities between the two items or concepts.
   ✔ Focus on the differences between the two items or concepts.
   ✔ Use visual organizers, such as a Venn diagram, as appropriate.

6. Provide opportunities for rehearsal.
   ✔ Use rote and elaborate rehearsal strategies to help students recognize the similarities and differences.
   ✔ Help students enhance their depth of understanding and the types of associations they made.

7. Beware of mixed metaphors.
   ✔ Choose metaphors carefully.
   ✔ Mixed metaphors can lead to confusion rather than clarity.
   ✔ Maintain the focus by asking specific questions such as:
     • How is X like Y?
     • What does X do that's like what Y does?
     • What does X do? Does Y do anything like that?

Strategy Selection

Students benefit by learning strategies that are modeled and explicitly taught. The goal, however, is for them to be able to independently select and use strategies appropriate to the situation at hand. When this is achieved, students are given a great gift and a life-long skill of enormous value.

To develop these skills, students must learn to think strategically. Encourage them to consider all of their strategies as being within a big "bag of tricks." They need to first analyze a situation and then review the options in their bag of tricks. Encourage them to use self-talk as they sift through their options. At that point they will be ready to select which strategy would best facilitate the learning needed for the process involved. Within the classroom environment, encourage brainstorming activities related to the options that could be used to help increase the learning and memory of the given situation. Begin the brainstorming with a simple question such as, "What are some ways we can think about this information so we will remember it and be able to use it?" This process is especially valuable for older students.

As students work to gain independence in strategy selection, they will find that some strategies are more or less efficient for a particular task than others. This will lead to some "mistakes," or time spent on strategies that do not work too well. Encourage students to view all experiences as learning experiences, perhaps by frequently using a phrase such as, "a mistake is your best friend." Help students realize how they can learn from their mistakes and they will begin to understand how an error can be a friend. It is critical that students learn from their mistakes as well as their successes, especially in strategy use. When a particular approach does not work, encourage them to discuss and analyze other alternatives that might accomplish a goal differently. Encourage them to ask how they could better approach a similar learning situation next time. This type of questioning leads to more in-depth metacognitive awareness.

Consolidation

Memory patterns need to be consolidated, as this is the process by which memories are moved from temporary storage in the hippocampus to more permanent storage in the cortex. This process is enhanced by rehearsal and by hooking the new information into a familiar framework. There are many useful strategies for this process, especially those that also function as a review of the concepts. In Chapter 7, strategies were discussed that are particularly valuable for reviewing material that is fact-related. Following are a few examples of review strategies that facilitate rehearsal of conceptual information.

The Wordless Text

The wordless text technique is a review activity wherein students create a series of drawings to represent the concept. This process is similar to writing a comic strip without words. Encourage students to be specific in their drawings. They can draw an arrow from one drawing to the next to show the sequence.

For example, after a unit on the hatching of eggs into a chicken, the following sequence might be drawn by a student.
- ✔ a hen walking
- ✔ a hen sitting on a nest

✔ eggs underneath a hen in a nest and hen looking down at eggs

✔ hen sitting on the nest and covering the eggs

✔ hen off the nest and one egg beginning to crack

✔ egg with a crack larger than before

✔ the head of a chick popping out through the crack

✔ the body of a chick popping out through crack

✔ chick out of the egg, lying on the nest bottom

✔ chick standing up

After completing the series of drawings, the student can then write a caption for each picture. This can be done on another page if desired: student numbers each picture and then writes the caption next to the corresponding number.

Journal Writing

Journal writing is a powerful technique that aids understanding, consolidation and retention. It can be done at all grade levels and is particularly useful as a closure activity for a unit. Sometimes only three to five minutes of journal writing, three times a week is sufficient. When I present workshops, I stop periodically and allow the participants "reflection time," encouraging them to write (journal) their thoughts and feelings. I particularly encourage them to relate the information we've been discussing to a given student in his own classroom and think about how he may apply the information.

✔ *What is journal writing?*
Journal writing is the process of taking a few minutes to write (or draw) information in a way that will make connections to previous information and help organize the concepts into networks for storage.

✔ *Benefits of journal writing for students*
Journal writing encourages reflection and facilitates the transfer of information into a consolidated pattern. Teachers may spot-check the journals to obtain feedback on the students' grasp of the concepts. Journal writing may be used as a closure activity and a preview for an upcoming related lesson. As students become accustomed to the process of journaling, many will find that it helps them refine their thinking and that they will begin to make more solid connections.

✔ *Some questions for students*
Following are some suggestions that may be used to stimulate students' ideas for journal writing. Here are two general guidelines for journal writing sessions:

- Be selective: Have students respond to only two or three questions in a session. Younger students may only respond to a single question.
- Be specific: Insert the appropriate conceptual objective within the parentheses in the questions on the next page to encourage students to think about the meaning of the unit, rather than just the activities performed.

Begin a journal writing session by asking your students to respond to your choice of the selections that follow. The chick hatching from an egg is the example concept used in these questions. Similar questions are presented to provide options, as different age groups, learning levels, and curriculum content necessitate different questioning techniques.

- What did I learn today about (*how an egg hatches*)?
- What is one thing I'll remember about (*how an egg hatches*)?
- In what way is (*how an egg hatches*) similar to something I already know or am familiar with?
- How does what I learned about (*how an egg hatches*) relate to what I already know about (*how a plant seed grows*)?
- How can I use what we learned about (*how an egg hatches*) in the future?
- What is one thing I'm still confused about?
- What questions do I have about (*how an egg hatches*)?
- What new insight or discovery have I made as a result of learning (*how an egg hatches*)?

Classroom Application

A student's brain physically changes every day,
The way you teach can either enhance or impair it.
By understanding how the brain learns,
You can help your students make significant gains (Jensen, 2002).

In this book we have explored the basics of the memory process along with strategies for enhancing learning, retention, and retrieval in the classroom. In several of our examples, you've had a chance to apply the learning to your own situation. Now take a moment and reflect. Ask yourself the following questions and write your responses:

- ✔ What are some key thoughts and strategies that are relevant to my teaching situation?

- ✔ What new strategies and approaches can I implement, given my particular time constraints and circumstances?

- ✔ Create a list of the three most useful or valuable strategies that will help your students enhance their retention in a given curriculum area.

- ✔ Commit to just one change you are going to make in your class or one new strategy. What will you use as a definite reminder to help you carry out his change?

- ✔ Once you've implemented the change, what will be the next change you implement?

- ✔ How will you remind yourself to implement this new change?

Now, share your plans with a colleague.

Remember,
We do not teach the brain to think. Our task is to help our students organize content in a way that will facilitate more complex processing and increase retention of the information.

Above all . . .
Have fun and
Enjoy your students'
learning experiences!

Memo: To all teachers

From: Dad S.[1]

RE: Students who learn differently

You have a choice
You can make a difference
You can find the key to success
Or you can turn the student off
But you do have a choice.

The student is very bright
The student doesn't know this
The parents are confused
The teacher isn't sure
But the teacher can help.

The student was born that way...different
The student doesn't want to be different
The parents want to help but feel guilty
The teacher is very busy with too many students
Who will help; who will help? All this confusion.

Dyslexia, dysgraphia, dysnomic... just labels
The parents will learn, there's much to learn
The busy teacher will learn, there's much available
The student doesn't want to be a label
Who will unlock the learning potential?

How many Einsteins and Edisons have we lost
Because the parent didn't know where to turn
Because the teacher was too busy or uninformed
Because the students were convinced they were stupid?
Sometimes the key to learning is hard to find.

Find the key to learning
Every student can learn; the key is there
Parents can help; they really want to
Teachers can help; that's what they do
You have a choice; you really do
And every child who learns differently can succeed.

And the world will be a better place!

[1]Dyslexic Adult Doing Spectacularly

References

Armstrong, T. (1993). *7 kinds of smart*. New York, NY: Penguin Books.

Armstrong, T. (2000). *Multiple intelligences in the classroom* (2nd edition). Alexandria, VA: Associaiton for supervision and curriculum development.

Auel, J. M. (2002). *The shelters of stone*. New York, NY: Crown Publishers.

Begley, S. (2000, January). Rewiring your gray matter. *Newsweek*, 63-65.

Bell, N. (1991). *Visualizing and verbalizing for language comprehension and thinking*. Paso Robles, CA: Academy of Reading Publications.

Berninger, V., Abbott, R., Abbott, S., Graham, S., & Richards, T. Writing and reading: connections between language by hand and language by ear, *Journal Learning Disabilities*.

Berninger, V. (1998). *Process assessment of the learner: guides for intervention*. San Antonio TX: The Psychological Corporation.

Berninger, V. (2001). Processes underlying timing and fluency of reading: efficiency, automaticity, coordination, and morphological awareness in Wolf, 2001.

Bloom, B. (1956). *Taxonomy of educational objectives*. New York, NY: David McKay.

Borge, V. (1992). *Victor Borge then & now* [video]. Great Neck, NY: CMV Video.

Bornstein, A. (1983). *Bornstein state and capital Memorizer*. Los Angeles, CA: Bornstein School of Memory Training.

Crowley, K., & Siegler, R. (1999, March-April). Explanation and generalization in young children's strategy learning. *Child Development, 70*(2), 304-16.

Damasio, A. (1994). *Descartes' error: emotion, reason, and the human brain*. New York, NY: G. P. Putnam's Sons.

Douglas, S. & Willatts, P. (1994). Musical ability enhances reading skills. *Journal of Research In Reading 17*, 99-107.

Feifer, S. G. & DeFina, P. A. (2002). *The neuropsychology of written language disorders: diagnosis and intervention*. Middletown, MD: School Neuropsych Press.

Gazzaniga, M. S. (1998). *The mind's past*. Berkeley, CA: University of California Press.

Gillingham, A. & Stillman, B. (1968, revised 1998). *Remedial training for children with specific disability in reading, spelling, and penmanship*. Cambridge, MA: Educators Publishing Service, Inc.

Ginott, H. (1972). *Teacher & child: A book for parents & teachers*. New York, NY: McMillan Company, 1972

Goldberg, E. (2001). *The executive brain: frontal lobes and the civilized mind*. New York, NY: Oxford University Press.

Goleman, D. (1995). *Emotional intelligence: why it can matter more than I.Q.* New York, NY: Bantam Books.

Grandin, T. (1995). *Thinking in pictures and other reports from my life with autism.* New York, NY: Doubleday.

Haebig, J. (2001). *The body-brain boogie: explore the neuroscience of learning through movement.* Rochester, MN: Wellness Quest.

Hall, S. L. & Moats, L. C. (1999). *Straight talk about reading.* Chicago, IL: Contemporary Books.

Hasselmo, M. (1999, Sept.). Neuromodulation: Acetylcholine and memory consolidation. *Trends in Cognitive Science, 3*(9), 351-9.

Holmes, O. W., Sr. (1858). *The autocrat at the breakfast table.*

Ihnot, C. (1997). *The read naturally program.* St. Paul, MN: Truman Publishing.

Jensen, E. (2001). *How the Student Brain Learns* [CD-ROM]. San Diego, CA: The Brain Store.

Jensen, E. (2000). *Music with the brain in mind.* San Diego, CA: The Brain Store.

Jensen, E. (1995). *Super teaching* (3rd ed.). San Diego, CA: The Brain Store.

Jensen, E. (2000). *Learning with the body in mind: The scientific basis for energizers, movement, play, games, and physical education.* San Diego, CA: The Brain Store.

Jensen, E. (1998). *Teaching with the brain in mind.* Alexandria, VA: Association For Supervision And Curriculum Development.

Jones, R. C. (2000-2001). *Strategies for reading comprehension: Vocabulary word maps.* ReadingQuest.org: Making sense of social studies. Retrieved from http://curry.edschool.virginia.edu/go/readquest/strat/wordmap.html.

Kesslak, J. V., Patrick, J., Cotman, C., & Gomez-Pinilla, F. (1998, August). Learning upregulates brain-derived neurotropic factor messenger ribonucleic acid: a mechanism to facilitate encoding and circuit maintenance. *Behavioral Neuroscience, 112*(4), 1012-19.

Kinoshita, H. (1997). Run for your brain's life. *Brain-Work, 7*(1), 8.

Lazear, D. (1991). *Seven ways of knowing: Understanding multiple intelligences, a handbook of techniques for expanding intelligence* (2nd ed.). Palatine, IL: Skylight Publishing.

Lazear, D. (1991b). *Seven ways of teaching: The artistry of teaching with multiple intelligences.* Palatine, IL: Skylight Publishing.

Lederer, R. (1990). *The play of words: Fun & games for language lovers.* New York, NY: Pocket Books.

Lederer, R. (1996). *Pun and games.* Chicago, IL: Chicago Review Press.

LeDoux, J. (1996). *The emotional brain.* New York, NY: Simon & Schuster.

Levine, M. D. and Reed, M. (1998). *Developmental Variation and Learning Disorders,* 2nd Edition. Cambridge, MA: Educators Publishing Service Inc.

Levine, M. D. (2002). *Educational care: A system for understanding and helping children with learning differences at home and in school* (2nd ed.). Cambridge, MA: Educators Publishing Service Inc.

Levine, M. D. (2000). *The memory factory.* Cambridge, MA: Educators Publishing Service Inc.

Lindamood, P. & Lindamood, P. (1998). *The Lindamood phoneme sequencing program for reading, spelling and speech (LiPS)* (3rd edition). Austin, TX: Pro-Ed.

Logan, G. (1997). Automaticity and reading: Perspectives from the instance theory of automation. *Reading and Writing Quarterly* (13) in Edward J. Kame'enue, Deborah C. Simmons.

Loomans, D. & Kolberg, K. (1993). *Laughing classroom: Everyone's guide to teaching with humor and play.* Tiburon, CA: HJ Kramer, Inc.

Love, J. & Richards, R. G. (1996). TREAT students to better reading skills. *Parents' Brochures.* Riverside, CA: RET Center Press.

Mastropieri, M. A. & Scruggs, T. E. (1991). *Teaching students to remember: Strategies for learning mnemonically.* Cambridge, MA: Brookline Books.

Michaud, E. & Wild, R. (1991). *Boost your brainpower.* Emmaus, PA: Rodale Press.

Moats, L. & Reid, L. (1996). Wanted: Teachers with knowledge of language. *Topics in Language Disorders*, 16, 73-81.

Moats, L. (1999, April). Presentation to the Inland Empire Branch of the International Dyslexia Association. Ontario, CA.

Moats, L. (2000). *Speech to print: Language essentials for teachers.* Baltimore, MD: Paul H. Brookes.

Nakamura, S., Sadato, N., Oohashi, T., Nishina, E., Fuwamoto, Y. & Yonekura, Y. (1999, November 19). Analysis of music-brain interaction with simultaneous measurement of regional cerebral blood flow and electroencephalogram beta rhythm in human subjects. *Neuroscience Letters*, 275, 222-226.

Neuschwander, C. (1999). *Sir Cumference and the dragon of Pi.* Watertown, MA: Charlesbridge Publishing.

Neuschwander, C. (1997). *Sir Cumference and the first round table.* Watertown, MA: Charlesbridge Publishing.

Ornstein, R. (1997). *The right mind: Making sense of the hemispheres.* New York, NY: Harcourt Brace.

Parish, P. (1963, 1991). *Amelia Bedelia .* New York, NY: Harper Collins Publishers, Inc.

Prelutsky, J. (2002). *The frogs wore red suspenders.* New York, NY: Greenwillow Books, a division of Harper Collins.

Richards, R. (1997). *Memory foundations for reading: A visual mnemonic system for sound/symbol correspondence.* Riverside, CA: RET Center Press.

Richards, R. G. & Richards, E. (2000). *Eli – the boy who hated to write: Understanding dysgraphia.* Riverside, CA: RET Center Press.

Richards, R. G. (2001). *LEARN: Playful strategies for all students.* Riverside, CA: RET Center Press.

Richards, R. G. (1999). *The source for dyslexia and dysgraphia.* East Moline IL: LinguiSystems, Inc.

Robbins, P. (2002, January). *Leave no child behind: Teaching with the brain in mind.* Learning Brain Expo, San Diego, CA

Roland, H. & Harn, B. (2001). The use of fluency-based measures and early identification and evaluation of intervention efficacy in schools, in Wolf, M., *Fluency and the brain.*

Sapolsky, R. M. (1998). *Why zebras don't get ulcers: An updated guide To stress, stress-related diseases, and coping.* New York, NY: Freemen & Co.

Schacter, D. (2001). *The seven sins of memory: How the mind forgets and remembers.* New York, NY: Houghton Mifflin.

Schacter, D. (1996). *Searching for memory: The brain, the mind, and the past.* New York, NY: Basic Books.

Shafir, U. & Engle, M. (1995, Dec. 18). Response to failure, strategic flexibility, and learning. *International Journal of Behavioral Development, 4,* 677-700.

Sherman, G. S. (2002). Dr. Gordon Sherman speaks with Schwab Learning about structural Brain differences [webcast]. http://www.schwablearning.org.

Siegel, D. (2000, Jan.). *The developing mind.* Speech given at the Learning Brain Expo, San Diego, CA.

Slingerland, B. (1977). *A multisensory approach to language arts for specific language disability children: A guide for primary teachers.* Cambridge, MA: Educators Publishing Service.

Sousa, D. (2001). *How the brain learns* (2nd ed.). Thousand Oaks, CA: Corwin Press, Inc.

Squire, L. & Kandel, E. (2000). *Memory from mind to molecules.* New York, NY: Scientific American Library.

Squire, L. (2002, Jan.). *Memory systems of the brain.* Speech given at the Learning Brain Expo, San Diego, CA.

Stetkevich, A. (2002). *Multisensory strategies for the dyslexic learner.* Presentation at the Inland Empire Branch International Dyslexia Association, Riverside, CA.

Teele, S. (1999). *Rainbows of intelligence: Exploring how students learn.* Redlands, CA: Sue Teele and Associates.

Torgesen, J. & Mathes, P. (2000). *Basic Guide to understnaidng, assessing, and teaching phonological awareness.* Austin, TX: Pro-Ed.

Torgesen, J. (1996). A model of memory from an information processing perspective: The special case of phonological memory. In Lyon, G. & Krasnegor, N. (Eds), *Attention, memory and executive function.* (1996). Baltimore, MD: Paul H. Brookes.

Vail, P. (1999, Nov.). Presentation at the International Dyslexia Association Conference, Chicago, IL.

Wade, N., Ed. (1998). *The Science Times book of the brain: The best science reporting from the acclaimed weekly section of The New York Times.* New York, NY: Lyons Press, New York Times.

Wahl, M. (1997). *Math for humans: Teaching math through 7 intelligences.* Washington, D.C.: LivLern Press.

Wesson, K. (2002). Brain basics for the teaching professional: What are the most important questions that educators should ask About the human brain? [Part 3 — *What are Neurons?*]. The KGM Group, Science Master, internet series retrieved from www.sciencemaster.com/columns/wesson/.

Wesson, K. (2002). Brain basics for the teaching professional: What are the most important questions that educators should ask about the human brain? [Part 3 — *The Brain's Hemispheres*]. The KGM Group, Science Master, internet series retrieved from www.sciencemaster.com/columns/wesson/.

West, C., Farmer, J., & Wolff, P. (1991). *Instructional design: Implications from cognitive science.* Englewood Cliffs, NJ: Prentice-Hall.

West, T. (1997). *In the mind's eye: Visual thinkers, gifted people with dyslexia and other learning difficulties, computer images and the ironies of creativity.* Amherst NY: Prometheus Books.

Wiig, E. & Wilson, C. (2002). *The learning ladder: Assessing and teaching text comprehension.* Eau Claire, WI: Thinking Publications.

Williams, L. (1983). *A guide to right brain/left brain education: Teaching for the two-sided mind.* New York, NY: Simon & Schuster.

Wolf, M., Ed. (2001). *Dyslexia, fluency, and the brain.* Timonium, MD: York Press.

Wolfe, P. (2001). *Brain matters: Translating research into classroom practice.* Alexandria, VA: Association for Supervision and Curriculum Development.

Yopp H. (1992, May). Developing phonemic awareness in young children. *The Reading Teacher, 45*(9), 696-703.

Web Resources

Franklin Education Products (producers of Franklin spellers):
http://www.franklin.com/estore/platform/bookman/category.asp?category=10

Inspiration Software, Inc. (publishers of Inspiration 7.0):
http://www.inspiration.com

Spoonerisms, mnemonics, oxymora, tongue twisters and more:
www. fun-with-words.com